Dancing With Destiny

Dancing With Destiny

Memoir

URMILA JHAVERI

PARTRIDGE
A Penguin Random House Company

To order additional copies of this book, contact
Partridge India
000 800 10062 62
www.partridgepublishing.com/india
orders.india@partridgepublishing.com

Contents

Part I

Part II

Part III

Dedicated
To
The ever lasting memory of my husband
Kantilal L. Jhaveri
With love

Foreword

Over a decade ago I read the obituary of a senior Tanzanian army officer of South Asian/Indian origin. It was unusual in more than one way. It is rare to find Tanzanians of South Asian origin in the army. Col. Kasmiri served in the Tanzania army from independence until his retirement in 1974.

Many years ago in Dar-es-Salaam, I recall leafing through a catalogue in an office of one of the member companies of the Karimjee Group of Companies and reading of the origins of the founder who had arrived in Zanzibar aboard a dhow in 1812 from Southern India. From then, his family's business expanded to become one of the leading family businesses in Eastern Africa with interests in industry, commerce, and finance. For the greater part, the historical origins of these communities and their contribution to the history of both Tanganyika and Tanzania have remained a footnote that only a tiny and dwindling proportion of Tanzanians is aware of.

Earlier, in my late teens and on my first visit to England, I occasionally made the error of assuming that every dark skinned person I saw in London was a foreigner and I recall the embarrassment I experienced when asking individuals where they came from. The responses revealed to me a fact that had remained hitherto hidden: They were British, from England.

From these experiences I developed a keen curiosity and interest in finding out how those Tanzanians who may not fit the description of "Tanzanian" by the description of some of today's politicians, had contributed to the history of both Tanganyika and Tanzania. When I began to write an op-ed column in the Sunday News more than seven years ago, I made a note to write articles on some of these individuals from Tanzania's past who had participated in the independence struggle.

Before I wrote the articles a journalist from the Daily News contacted me to say that the author, who I had not known before then, had asked to meet me when I visited Dar es Salaam. He explained to me that Urmila Jhaveri was the wife of Kanti L. Jhaveri, one of the defence lawyers in Mwalimu Julius Nyerere's 1958 criminal libel case. Jhaveri was also a member of the pre-independence Asian Association, which allied itself with the nationalist party, the Tanganyika African National Union (TANU) during the independence struggle. Urmila, I soon found out, had been an active member of the TANU women's wing during Tanganyika's independence struggle and after independence.

I could not have asked for better subjects on whom to write an article on the contribution of the South Asian community to Tanganyika's struggle for independence.

On my subsequent visit to Dar es Salaam, when I got off the taxi in front of the four-unit apartment building in the Sea View area, a man who I assumed was their son had just stepped off a car and I told him: "I am here to visit your parents." He led me to the apartment and to a sitting room whose walls had a few framed pre-independence photographs of my father with various individuals who I assumed included Urmila and K.L. Jhaveri.

Initially the son called his father who engaged me in polite conversation while I eagerly waited for Urmila who I thought, for someone who earlier in a telephone conversation had indicated was extremely eager to meet me, was spending an unusually long time in the kitchen. Close to an hour later, it was the husband who through a few probing questions realized something was amiss told me: "I think you are in the wrong house. Mr. and Mrs. Jhaveri live in the apartment downstairs." For more than an hour I had enjoyed the hospitality and cordial conversation of Mr. M.M. Devani and his son. Mr. Devani was also a member of the Asian Association and was elected Mayor for Dar es Salaam in 1958.

Although I had misled myself to his apartment, I did not forget to note down that Mr. Devani could also have a few interesting reminiscences from the country's history for yet another article that I should write.

With her memoirs, the author has embarked on an important task that will enable readers to appreciate the contribution that members of the Tanzanian community have made to the history of our country, in general, but more specifically in this case, to the struggle for Tanganyika's independence. She has not only reduced my writing assignments by one article, but her book should also serve as an important reminder to the younger generation of Tanzanians of a history that is increasingly being forgotten.

It is true that for some members of the South Asian community, including Amir Jamal—whose father, Habib Jamal, was a founder member of the Asian Association—and Alnoor Kassam, their involvement with other nationalists in the struggle for Tanganyika's independence is well-documented, but for others little is known.

This book is the author's contribution towards filling some of those gaps of the untold events from the past.

G. Madaraka Nyerere
Coordinator
Butiama Cultural Tourism Enterprise (BCTE)
P.O. Box 620
Musoma, Tanzania.
Tel. +255782640033/ (0)755570795/ (0)714447727
http://blogkili.blogspot.com/ http://www.tanzaniaculturaltourism.com/mara.htm http://www.facebook.com/pages/Butiama-Cultural-Tourism-Enterprise-BCTE/299030663471476?ref=hl http://madarakanyerere.blogspot.com/ http://muhunda.blogspot.com/.

Acknowledgments

I would like first of all to thank Doctor Bimlesh Pandey, Doctor Sanjay Saxena, Doctor Ajay Agarwal and their team at the Fortis Hospital Noida: because of their professional care, I am here today in a position to finalise my book.

I am deeply thankful to Godfrey Madaraka Nyerere who in spite of his heavy load of work, kindly agreed to write the foreword for my book, Dr. Veena Sharma for her friendship and support all these years and Mwalimu Kersibhai Rustomji for his boundless encouragement, advice and help. Asante Sana, thank you very much my friends.

The senior staff from Nitan's office, East One have always been at our beck and call; Rachna Sinha helped me with organising my computer files and sorting out computer problems which are beyond my grasp. I thank them all. I sincerely thank our friend Dr.Ned Bertz for permitting me to quote him extensively in one of the chapters about the Colonial era in Tanganyika, and Gabby Mgaya for readily consenting to let me base my comments on his very informative report on Zanzibar Revolution.

I would also like to thank Smriti Vohra for going through the manuscript and giving her feedback and

Ann Minoza my guide at Patridge for firmly advising and patiently allowing me my space throughout the publishing process.

My loving thanks go to Roohi's friends Ratna Desai and Shreya Banerjee for painstakingly designing this beautiful book cover, and Roohi, for being my constant consultant and guide. Since I started writing this book, I have been constantly telling my little stories to all my family members - Abha, Nitan, Roohi, Rohaan, Ridhi, Meera, Ratna, Chandrika, Atool and Nitan's sister Rita Khattar. They have been extremely patient listeners and ever ready to solve problems for us. Especially Abha and Nitan being nearby help us day and night whenever the need arise. I thank them all from the bottom of my heart.

Without my husband's silent support and encouragement I would not have written this book. Jhaveriji is always there for me; but he never tried to proffer his advice or even commented on what I was writing. I am truly thankful to him for letting me write our story in my own way. I am also deeply grateful to my parents who by their example taught me to find wonder in nature and discipline in work.

As kids Ratna and Meera were fascinated to hear about our life in Dar-es-Salaam and always asked me to 'write it down in a notebook'. That encouraged me to write about our life times experiences in Dar-es-Salaam! Thank you both.

Writing my memoir has been fun but editing and proof reading it myself has been a challenging and intimidating task. And so when it came to publishing it, I started having doubts which still persist. Consequently I had almost decided not to pursue the matter further. But a miracle happened on the way. My sister Niru and her husband Dr. Navin Vibhaker graciously offered to have my memoirs published. Had it not been for their timely support this book would have been languishing as one of my computer files. I just thank them both with all my heart. Bless you all.

My book is based on facts drawn from history and my personal experiences, limited understanding and some impediments. I am afraid there may be some unintended discrepancies, unseen gaps and even language shortfall and hope that, these may please be ignored.

I find that from the beginning the loving hand of my destiny has been working silently behind my memoirs, in fact throughout my life prompting me onwards to reach this stage. I have done so in good faith with the hope that this small book will be of some use to researchers and those interested in the history of East Africa.

Urmila Jhaveri
22- October-2013

Preface

His name was Ram Prasad; a short young man, clean shaven and dark complexioned, he was wearing freshly washed cloths. Due to health problems, we had just moved to Delhi from Dar-es-Salaam in Tanzania East Africa on 31-July-2009, and were in the process of trying to find our feet, being acquainted with the driver, doctors, clinics, car and other services. So when one fine morning Ram Prasad arrived for an interview as our prospective driver, I went happily with him for a short ride and on the way back stopped to buy a papaya from a street vendor, who just glanced at me and quoted an exorbitant price. Ram Prasad hopped out of the car and started bargaining on my behalf. That was helpful, but the problem started when we could not get back into the vehicle. He had locked the keys inside.

"Don't worry," he said, "I will solve this problem in no time." He started calling up people on his mobile phone while I stood to the side. Soon a rough looking man summoned on the phone arrived with an iron bar and began helping Ram Prasad to lever the door open. They stopped when I warned them sternly.

I in turn called my daughter Abha. She was already in Noida busy organizing our move where I and my husband were to live. She promised to rush back to Delhi with the spare car key and promptly sent Shanti, her trusted and energetic housemaid to give me moral support. By this time Ram Prasad was getting nervous about my state, and managed somehow to borrow a chair for me to sit on. Shanti arrived on her bicycle. So here I was, perched on a chair under a tree next to a very, very busy major traffic artery, with Shanti holding on to her bicycle standing guard over me and the papaya. And the brand new car on the side of the road sitting like a brooding duck while Ram Prasad and the other man struggled with the door and hovered around the car suspiciously.

For me time stood still; I gazed around in this milieu and saw at least a couple of banks, beautiful Mata Ka Mandir-temple complex, a clinic, a hotel, a corner kiosk selling flowers, and a cluster of crowded apartment buildings. Some people on the road were staring at me and others were walking past indifferently, absorbed in their own thoughts. Suddenly, disconcertingly, I felt a peculiar estrangement and panic—like a bewildered, disconcerted, disoriented foreigner in India. How had I arrived from familiar Dar-es-Salaam to Delhi, this place where even a roadside papaya vendor could instantly tell that I was an outsider! Any way, at my age, what was I doing here, rootless, motionless, next to this chaotic major road? Why was I feeling so uneasy, so disturbed, so paralysed? How would I survive my displacement? Indian blood flows in my veins and my entire lifestyle has always been based on Indian culture, religion and philosophy. I speak my mother tongue Guajarati; my dress and food habits remain traditional. Yet I felt that I did not belong here, that I was some where between what I had left in Tanzania and where I now found myself.

*My story began, nearly a century ago in the late 1920,
before the days of air travel and steamers, my Gujarati parents
had arrived in Zanzibar from Jamnagar by dhow. I am an
African, born in 1931 in Pemba-Tanzania (earlier known as
Tanganyika and Zanzibar). Dar-es-Salaam is my home town
where I had grown up, raised a family, progressed, and spent
some eighty years of my life.*

*This sudden rupture of normalcy through being locked out
of the car and stranded on the road, this bizarre encounter with
my selfhood, uncanny, elusive yet clear and loud, continued
as I sat in that chair within the clamour of horns and traffic
grinding by. Long minutes passed; I calmed down and my
panic subsided as my thoughts returned to the beginning . . . I
was back to hard reality trying to sort out how to get out of this
predicament and reach home!*

Part 1

Chapter 1

Family Diary

My earliest significant memory of 'actual' India is of my first meeting with my grandmother Motiba in Jamnagar. I was about twelve years old. It was early 1943, the peak of World War II. We had just arrived in Gujarat from our home in Dar-es-Salaam, sailing for over a month in a dhow across the Indian Ocean from East Africa.

A tiny petite figure, Motiba was about four feet tall. She was in her fifties, but to my young eyes she looked ancient, maybe a hundred and more years old, with untold stories hidden under her pillow. Born in the 1880s, she was widowed at a young age with two sons and two daughters. She raised them single-handedly by doing whatever work came her way. Motiba was very good with her hands and made beautiful razais (quilts) with intricate designs. These were much in demand. She disliked any kind of wastage and used even old clothes to make these beautiful, warm pieces for her family through out her life. A person of few words

1

my grandmother was self-educated and enjoyed reading the newspapers every morning. She was supportive of all her children and advised them well during any crises in their lives.

Motiba's eldest daughter, Hemkuvar Faiba also was widowed at a very young age. I thought that Faiba looked very dignified even at her advanced age. She must have been very pretty in her youth. Once when we were talking about old times I asked Faiba why she did not marry again. She replied that it did not occur to her, as for widows to re-marry was unthinkable at the time. Talking about her late husband she said, "I do not even remember his face now. I am glad we did not have any children." When I persisted she narrated the story of the popular Gujarati saint Sage Narsinh Mehta. "When he was told that his wife had died, his response was, 'Bhalu thayu bhangi janjad, shukhe bhajashu Shree Gopal (Thank God, I am free, now I can worship Shree Krishna Gopala without a bother.)'" Then Faiba sang a Meerabai bhajan for me.

She remembered, being young she was spared the ritual of shaving her head, but her glass bangles were broken deliberately as was the custom then. After that she wore only white saris.

By all accounts widowhood, a social condition imbued with stigma and vulnerability and struggling with financial constraints at the same time must have been a terrifying experience for Faiba as well as for Motiba. Between them, thanks to strong willpower, they managed to survive the personal trauma and continued to lead a meaningful life, even managing to visit Tanganyika several times together. Fortunately, within a short time Bapuji (my father) and his elder brother whom we addressed as Motabapuji had established their medical shop in Dar-es-Salaam. And through hard work and thrift succeeded to earn, save, and had managed to build two beautiful adjoining houses in Jamnagar with shops on the ground floor that were given on rent. This provided the family with ample funds so that they could comfortably live on.

Hard work for survival was Motiba's mantra, and through her example all her children learnt to be diligent from a very young age. I have never ceased to be fascinated by Motiba, her resilience and her quiet nature.

In the early 1910s, Motiba's son Gulabrai Gandhi, her first-born, our Motabapuji sailed from BediBander-Jamnagar in a dhow to East Africa in search of better opportunities. His younger brother Tarachand Gandhi, my father, Bapuji did the same in the early 1920s. Both the brothers were poles apart in nature and looks. Motabapuji suffered from sever bouts of Asthma and was a chain smoker. He was strict with us, and yet he was kind in his own way! On the other hand Bapuji was a sportsman; he played cricket, tennis, bridge, and chopat, and was a champion swimmer and loved music and movies.

If he was alive to day Bapuji would have been 112 years old. Bapuji's British passport No.12152, issued in colonial Tanganyika Territory affirms that Tarachand Pragji Gandhi's date of birth was 4 April 1900. Place of birth: Jamnagar State, India. Place of residence: India and Tanganyika Territory. Height: 5 ft. 6 in. Colour of eyes: dark brown. Colour of hair: black. Profession: Druggist—(Pharmacist)

Likewise my mother, Ba would have scored a century. My mother's passport lists her as Mrs. Labhkuver Gandhi. Date of birth: 21 February 1910. Place of birth: Sardhar, India. Height: 4 ft. 9 in. Colour of eyes: black. Colour of hair: black. Profession: Housewife.

Our grandfather had died at a young age when my father was a teenager. He had heard many stories about Zanzibar and was keen to go to Africa to try and built a better future for the family. My grandmother and other elders of the family set a condition that Bapuji was to get married before sailing for Africa. They arranged a good match for him. Ba, my mother was ten years younger than him. However, due to lack of funds he was compelled to leave her at home with his mother—Motiba till he had earned enough to return to India and fetch her.

Whenever I asked Ba how old she was when she came from Sardhar, the small village in Saurastra where she grew up all the way to Zanzibar, she said she could not remember exactly. "Maybe twelve or thirteen," she recounted. "I was married when I was barely eleven years old; it was an arranged marriage where true to custom the elders of both families meet the girl and the boy and decide whether the prospective match can be made, and whatever else is to be done. So I did not meet your father at that time." With a chuckle she added, "But I had a glimpse of him when ever he visited Sardhar on one pretext or other. He was so tall and to me he looked like a prince! We were married in Sardhar. I wore my gharchoddu; traditional red wedding sari embroidered with gold and silver thread, and had to veil my face completely. He wore a suit and a jari safo (turban with gold and silver threads) as was the fashion in those days." The wedding sari was later stored wrapped up together with Ba's jewellery in the huge, beautifully carved wooden pataro, chest, which had a chor khanu, secret drawers. It came as her dowry all the way to Africa from Sardhar.

Bapuji had joined the colonial Customs service in Zanzibar. After gaining some experience there he was posted to Pemba, part of the archipelago of the Spice Islands consisting of Zanzibar, Pemba and Mafia, lying off the east coast of Africa. [Note-1]

My mother gave birth to a son, who unfortunately died within a few days. I was born in Wete, Pemba, on 12th July-1931. At that time Wete was just a small village and Chake Chake, now the capital of Pemba, was a small town nearby with a government clinic and a German doctor. I was born with a club foot, with my left heel bent slightly inwards. Ba said that the German doctor in Pemba put it right by making a plaster-of-Paris cast for my foot. And as the bones are tender and malleable at that age, my deformity was cured by the time I was three years old. I have a studio photograph of myself from that time, all dressed up and looking cute indeed. However, considering that in those days female children were often unwanted, neglected, rebuked and even quietly put to sleep, as a first born, I was a difficult and stressful experience for my parents.

In 1932 my mother was expecting and decided to travel to Sardhar for the delivery of the child. We went back to Sardhar, where my brother Mahendra was born on 22 January 1933. After a few weeks Ba was ready to travel as Bapuji's leave was over, and it was time for him to return to his government job in Pemba-Zanzibar.

After returning to Tanganyika, Bapuji was once again transferred to Bagamoyo as a customs officer. He was finding it difficult to move from place to place with a young family. Besides that he wanted to be independent and start his own business. He decided to leave government service and join his elder brother in running a medical shop in Dar-es-Salaam. My younger brother Anant and sister Niru were born in our flat in the Hindu Mandal locality of Dar-es-Salaam. Those days it was normal to deliver babies at home. Anant was born on 3 December 1934. Our family

Dai (midwife) was Hali Ma with her assistant Premibai. A devout Muslim, Hali Ma lived alone in a corrugated-iron hut opposite the government-run Indian Primary School, and Premibai lived nearby with her young family. Between them, they kept track of the progress of the unborn baby, and one or the other intuitively knew when the time of the birth was nearing and ensured that they were present. I don't remember much about Anant's birth other than a sense that something tremendous was about to happen. However, when Niru was born on 18 March 1941, I was ten years old and an active member of the birthing team, as it were—running errands for the midwife, helping to bring hot water, utensils and towels, and waiting outside the room until the baby's first cry, a thrilling event that I in my innocence could not comprehend but knew was pure and miraculous.

I remember vividly being called from school on that day, and then not attending school for another four weeks. Ba was not allowed to enter the kitchen for forty days. Bapuji and I managed to feed the family with simple food like khichdi, batetanu shak, etc. Our elderly house-help Saidi, who had been working for us for many years pitched in by keeping ingredients for the meals ready and the kitchen fire blazing or subdued, as required. Apart from his cleaning and washing up duties, if the need arose Saidi even helped in cooking simple meals. Bapuji adjusted his duties at the shop so that he could return home in time to make rotli-wheat flour chapattis and rotla-chapatis made from bajri flour, while it was my job to put the khichdi to boil and cook the vegetables. Being the youngest, my sister Niru grew up as the darling of the whole family.

During those days when family planning was a vague idea, compared to others our family was small. Through their example my parents had instilled in us the dignity of hard work and disciplined life. They lived in the present and strived for a better future happy in their own world. Ba and Bapuji's only connections with India were their respective families who were living in different towns in Gujarat. Bapuji kept in touch with them by post. I remember that as a child or an adult, it never occurred to me that my roots were in India or some where else. For us that Hindu Mandal flat in Dar-es Salaam was our home. In fact for those of us who made our home in Africa, this sense of belonging was our bedrock on which we built our lives.

My parents were not in the habit of visiting Jamnagar-India frequently especially after Motiba's death. And so after many years of continuous absenteeism, the tenants had simply appropriated both the houses and the shops.

Chapter 2

Home

One bright Sunday morning Bapuji suddenly told me to get ready "fatafat" (quickly) as we were going somewhere special. That was enough for me; 'getting ready' those days for us meant having a bath and wearing freshly washed and neatly folded clothes. I rushed to get ready and off we went quietly, Bapuji riding his trusted bicycle and carrying me as his passenger all the way to the other end of India Street. We reached this brand new two-storey building and climbed to the top floor. Bapuji took a key from his pocket and opened the door of a flat. I followed him in timidly. He stood there sombrely for a moment, looked around and said. "Look, we are coming to stay in this new house, it is nice, naa?"

Then he lighted a diya, a small oil lamp and side by side with bowed heads and closed eyes we prayed in silence for a while. I was about five years old and in my childish manner, filled with wonder, uncertainty and expectations prayed for a happy home.

I loved the place; it smelt of fresh paint and wood, the walls were painted white, and timber doors were newly varnished. There were two large rooms, a kitchen, store room, bathroom, toilet, a big osri (veranda facing the kitchen) and a second veranda facing the road, from where you could watch the world go by.

Within a few weeks we had moved to this new flat. The bigger room became our master bedroom. It accommodated a four-poster bed for Bapuji, a smaller one for Ba, a bunk-bed and an extra bed for us kids, and Ba's big wooden chest and the mirrored cupboard with the beautifully painted dancing peacock on its doors. The other room was our sitting-room with a small settee, a side table for the radio and newspapers, a chest of drawers, a built-in cupboard and a few odds and ends. The bathroom had a copper bumbo with a stand specially made for heating water every morning with a handful of coal; a round water container joined in the centre by a pipe and a screen at the bottom for charcoal was called a bumboo. Early in the morning we filled the container with about three buckets full of water and put a handful of charcoal with a rag soaked in kerosene in the screen at the bottom and lighted it with a matchstick. In less then half an hour, hot water for our bath and other household purposes would be ready. It was very neat and economical and was always kept shining.

The baraza, our enclosed veranda facing the road had an extra bed, a few chairs and a tulsi as well as few rose plants, some red and some pink. The old-fashioned and sturdy dining table and chairs in the osri-second veranda, served as Saidi's ironing board, Ba's workshop, our study desk and a social meeting-place all rolled into one. There was a ghanti-grinding stone near the door in one corner. This house, newly built by the Hindu Mandal near the Hindu

Mandal Hospital on India Street, was our home for the next twenty years.

As was the custom prevailing then, Ba made beautiful bead torans, coloured beads woven into various patterns, to hang across the top of the front door as a message of welcome. The kit for making the toran contained a wooden frame with a special type of string knotted through its tiny holes. The beads were then threaded to follow the design in the book. From time to time Ba changed the designs and the beads of these torans. I loved to help her sort out those shiny multi coloured small beads, put them in neat piles and watch her create beautiful birds and flowers, hanging on the strings. It was a fascinating art! As girls, we even made tiny little bead bracelets and rings to match with our bangles and wore them on special days.

Our next-door neighbours were Buch Kaka and Tara Masi. Buch Kaka had worked with the railways in different locations in the country. After he retired from government service he spent all his time in various social service projects. In Dar-es-Salaam he was connected with the Hindu Mandal Hospital and Hindu Mandal activities, the T.B. Sheth library, Shishukunj and so on. Other interesting neighbours in that building were Master Kaka, a teacher, and Boal Kaka, the owner-editor of the *Tanganyika Herald*, the local Gujarati newspaper. They shared the first-floor flat; their families were in India. The ground floor had two flats; one of these flats was occupied by Kashimasi, her husband and two daughters. And the second flat was occupied by the second Kashimasi who was a widow with two sons and two daughters my age. She was running her little 'duka-shop' in her verandah facing the road. She had a fiery temper and a sharp tongue. Some how I always felt intimidated by her and never played in the compound.

Most of the other houses in the neighbourhood were either German-built solid brick houses or flimsier dwellings with mabati (tin or corrugated-iron roofs). In one of these huts opposite our house lived a very old couple, Ada-Boghabapa-Grandpa and Maa. Ada used to roast jugubisi (peanuts and popcorn), chana (chickpeas) and dhani (tiny seeds of other cereals) every day. We could buy them for one Heller—two cents, sizzling hot and delicious. I think this couple arrived in Bukene in 1880s, where Ada and Maa started their small tin roofed duka, selling 10 cents worth of salt and sugar, rice and beans by kibaba and oil by ladle full. They had four daughters. All got married and settled in and around Mwanza. By this time Ada and Maa had moved to Dar. They were very simple souls. Ada used to read Ramayana, Bhagwat and other religious books regularly after lunch every day. I accompanied my mother when she went to listen to these discourses. Ada wept copiously whenever he read out descriptions of Ram-Sitaji vanvas, forest exile. And I, profoundly moved by both the story and his emotion, would shed tears along with him. Even now I get the jitters when ever I am watching any such movies.

At the age of six I joined the Government Primary School on the old Bagamoyo Road. The medium of instruction up to Standard Four was Gujarati. I remember our mathematics teacher Rathod Master who made sure that we memorized all the Desi hesab—number tables in Gujarati by heart.

The Indian Primary School, had classes up to Standard Four. Later on Gujarati was completely phased out and English was made the medium of instruction. After finishing primary education we graduated to the Government Indian Secondary School near Jangwani Creek. [1]

I myself enjoyed school and rarely got into trouble, though I recall an English class when I was nine or ten years old, in which the teacher asked us to write an essay on 'Dogs'. I recalled a Gujarati proverb stating that a dog's tail always remains bent, it cannot be straightened however hard you try. I wrote something around this, and for some reason it upset the teacher enormously. He berated me in fury, made me stand up, and then read it aloud in class himself, stopping only to rebuke me further. I didn't understand what was so problematic about the proverb, and I still don't! But I did feel intensely humiliated. After Tanganyika attained Independence the government schools became Swahili-medium schools while a few select ones were allowed to retain English as the medium of instruction. Swahili was made a compulsory subject in all schools, and it was a matter of pride for me to see our children writing essays, doing projects and easily passing their Senior Cambridge exams which included Swahili language.

A couple of my best friends lived down the street in tin-roofed houses. Shushila was dark skinned but had a heart of gold. Her father, a quiet man with two daughters worked as a clerk in government service. Where by my other friend Daahi meaning 'wise', in Gujarati, was the eldest of six sisters; her father worked in a government camp as a mason, carpenter, electrician and supervisor all rolled into one, on a road-building project on the outskirts of Dar-es-Salaam. It was rough terrain in those days, with lions prowling right up to the edge of human habitation. Daahi's father would leave home early in the morning carrying his bajrano rotlo, millet bread, and chilli achar, pickle for lunch, and come back late in the evening a very hungry and angry human being. The whole family had to be quiet and remain virtually out of his sight till he had eaten his dinner and returned to being a calm and caring though strict father. Daahi was very clever with her hands. She could paint and make lovely toys from scrap, though she was always kept busy cooking and cleaning and doing household chores. When she was about eleven years old the family left for India so that a match could be arranged for her. Shushila's parents also planned to have their daughters married off in India. Both my friends were completely terrified at the prospect of getting married, but had no choice whatsoever.

Up to now, hand in hand we had skipped the rope together and shared our dreams. They had heard some harrowing tales about marriages and mothers-in-law in their villages in India. We were just kids, and the more we talked about it in secrete the more of a nightmare it became. They were scarred about their future in their villages and I was worried about my friends.

In secondary school our classes started at 8 a.m. and finished at 1 p.m. The distance from our Hindu Mandal flat to Jangwani creek was over two miles. We enjoyed walking to school early in the morning after a hearty breakfast; usually the previous night's leftovers with a huge bowl of hot milk. We were always encouraged to drink lots of milk. At times Ba would give us a Heller, which would buy a plate full of delicious chana-bateta (a chickpea-potato mixture) from Bachu Bapa's handcart. And occasionally if Ba felt rich enough she would give us five cents each, which enabled us to slurp down raw mango with chilli and salt and an ice lolly along with chana-bateta. Like all the girls at that age I kept moddakat, a five-day 'fast' during which we were allowed to eat Indian sweetmeats made from milk like barfi and pendas—sweet fudge, ice cream and fruit at any time of the day, and at lunch time even second meals if we managed to sit in one position. It was a funfest. We planted wheat in a special container, decorate it with a mala made from cotton wool and do a puja, ritual during those five days. It was considered lucky if the young shoots were growing well and meant that we would have happy and bountiful family life. The fifth night was a jagran 'keep-awake' when we girls and our mothers would be up all night playing games, singing, dancing or just enjoying the general company.

At home, I liked to help my mother in whatever she was doing. Sundays were reserved for washing and oiling hair, and as the eldest daughter it was my duty to sort out all the clothes, clean up the cupboards and medicine chest, organize our school books and so on. During those days buying storybooks or toys for kids was unheard of, and sons and daughters and even siblings had their roles fixed according to their respective ages. So we invented many games and learnt to make our own toys from discarded items. For us Sunday evening was best time of the week spent on the beach, having picnics or just relaxing with the family. Bapuji had very good memory. We had learnt from him to recite the names of our great grandfathers' unto eight generations just while playing games with him. Surprisingly I can remember the list even now. But the thoughts of India or any nostalgia was never a part of our day to day life. Even as kids whatever history or geography we learnt about India or Africa was entirely based on British view of those countries. The lessons were thoroughly censured and propagated. I remember an incidence in Shree Devkuvar Arya Kanya Shala, D.A. Girl's school, in Dar-es-Salaam [Present day Kisutu Girl's School]. The school was established through fund raising by the Arya Samaj. Later on the Government gave a part-grant. But the school needed to raise funds for its various activities. I do not recall the year but we were having Annual fund raising program where the children had outlined a map of India in one of their dances. By chance they had included Ceylon in this depiction. Some British administrator who was an invited guest with his family noticed this and objected strongly to Ceylon being included in the map of India. Those were Quite India movement days. The aftermath of this episode was that not only the teachers concerned but even the Headmaster of the school was reprimanded there and then and the fund raising committee Elders had to pacify the junior officer with an apology. This incident was hushed up and the school continued as usual.

Chapter 3

Happy Days

Just living is not enough,
One must have sunshine, freedom and a
little flower.

Hans C Andersen.

Uttho uttho, modu thai che—wake up wake up, it is getting late.

That was our kasuku, African gray parrot calling us the moment he woke up early in the morning. He could imitate us, call us out by name and even managed to bite once in a while if any of us pestered him too much. He loved red hot chillies, red papaya, peanuts and khungu—ripe almonds fruits from Africa but abhorred having his fortnightly bath. Every evening when Ba put a mosquito net over his cage, he said Ram Ram to her. They talked in their language for a while before Ba covered him with his mosquito net. We were not allowed to disturb him when he was resting. When

Bapuji was at home kasuku liked to perch on his shoulders and talk—talk while following him around. He was our playmate and died of old age in his cage. After that we never kept a pet.

The doors of our house were always open and neighbours and friends walked in all the time. One of the earliest visitors I remember was Dr. Divan Singh who was in charge of Hindu Mandal hospital next door. He visited us often on his daily rounds and spoke Gujarati just like any of us; he became our family friend and 'Doctor Kaka' Uncle, to all the kids in the neighbourhood.

The Hindu Mandal hospital at that time was situated in a friendly and fairly big brick-roofed house. Originally it was built as a spacious bungalow for one of the Government officers during the time when Germany occupied Tanganyika. Later on this building was demolished and in its place a five-storey state-of-the-art hospital was established. The dharamshala, free guest house reserved for upcountry patients, was converted into a maternity wing. And the block of six flats including the one on the top floor on India Street where my younger siblings Anant and Niru were born was converted into residential flats for the medical staff. The hospital and the Hindu Mandal continue expanding and providing community services along with medical care.

Bapuji was a keen sportsman, and believed in the adage that work while you work, do your best and the results will follow. And play while you play with all your heart in it and be happy! He used to tell me that even when I was doing fagiyo sweeping the floor, I must do it well. That is the secret of success! Every day including weekends he was at the shop before 8 a.m. Sunday was a half-day, the only concession. His breakfast was a glass of milk. After lunch he took a short break and then returned to the shop. At 4 p.m. he cycled off to play tennis; after a game and a shower he would be back at the shop, where he remained till closing time at 8 p.m. or often later. It became a ritual for all of us with Ba leading to go and fetch him from the shop at night. Mahen and Anant would be feeling sleepy by this time and had a bicycle ride coming back home. Bapuji's dinner was a glass of water. Apart from his daily tennis game, he played chopat (a game similar to chess but in a bigger format) on Saturday nights, and Sundays were reserved for cricket, a picnic on the seafront and a movie. Later on when he bought a car he stopped playing cricket and tennis and started swimming across the Hela Tatu Ferry every morning.

All of Dear-es-Salaam is developed along the coast. My parents loved outdoors activities and as such we children grew up on the seafront. Daily visits to the beach, swimming, moonlight picnics and weekend frolics in the sand were intrinsic to our lives. In those days the beach opposite the Governor's residence was a favourite place for everybody to relax and enjoy the sea breeze, and meet practically the whole town on a Sunday evening. At these gatherings people sat in groups with their own families and friends. And the children of all ages, Asian as well as African, used to have a field day eating roasted mihogo—cassawa, peanuts, icecream, drinking madafu—green coconut water and raw and ripe mangoes when in season. It meant roaring business for young and cheerful African vendors. Sunday lunch was also a feast day for us; Ba used to prepare laddoos, dhudhpak, shrikhand, mohanthal and various other kinds of sweets and savouries. This habit of treating us children on the weekend had started with Ba and Bapuji taking us to Koya's ice cream parlour each Sunday.

Cocooned thus within the family I was growing up unaware that it was indeed very limited existence. To start with our schools were segregated. The Asian, African and European children did not share lessons, play together in school or even on the sea-side. Our houses were separated, and even though Asians and Africans lived amicably there was little if any social interaction between them. People lived within the frame work of their own different communities.

Even within the communities there were cultural differences, boundaries and divisions rigidly enforced by each community. I remember one of my friends came from a Brahmin family. At their home some times I was offered a snack, but I had to partake it sitting away from my friend out side the kitchen. Our friendship did not last long.

Bapuji had a very rich voice and would sing old classical bhajans and songs in Gujarati on a beautiful harmonium that was his prize possession. I loved it so much that I too began to play the harminium and tried to sing. This upset my mother, who said to Bapuji, "This ruckus of songs will do us no good, and look, our daughter is imitating you, just think, what the neighbours will say . . . !" Those were the days when Ba also believed that daughters from 'good families' were not supposed to indulge in music and neither should they participate in any sports, for that matter. Consequently Bapuji's harmonium went out quietly, and my music lessons stopped for the time being.

Gandhi Medical Hall, my father's business was established in Dar es-Salaam in 1925; it flourished and became popular. The shop was opposite the clock tower on Acacia Avenue, near the railway station end. This road was so named due to being lined with acacia trees; at the time of Independence it was renamed Independence Avenue. Gandhi Medical Hall was the first such business to function as an optician, albeit with rudimentary equipment. Bapuji's elder brother Gulabrai Gandhi, Motabapuji to us, had experience working as a 'compounder' in a clinic in Jamnagar. This experience with medicines and minor illnesses was very useful and appreciated by everyone who came to him for help, knocking at all hours on the door of the shop. Similarly Bapuji had learnt the intricacies of his trade through experience and later on when Motabapuji was in Jamnagar he was also ever ready to provide service any time of day or night. Motabapuji was very strict and had volatile temper that could flare up without warning. All of us children were scared of him and scattered like a pack of mice in his presence. Kakiba made up for all that. She always welcomed us with a loving word or a treat to savour. Apart from giving birth to eight children, Kakiba had gone through a few miscarriages as well. The incessant pregnancies took their toll and she died in Dar-es-Salaam at a young age. Following that Motabapuji went back to Jamnagar with all his children, who were raised there by Motiba and Faiba.

Before we moved to Hindu Mandal flat, we lived as a joint family in the spacious quarters above the shop. The building itself, constructed during the German time, was huge. The shop had several extra big store rooms, a garage and the ample open central courtyard on the ground floor. We children had more than enough space to play, climb over walls and to get lost during games of hide and seek. At one time when I was four or five years old Motabapuji and his family left to stay in Jamnagar for a while, and the huge house became an arena for just for our small family. My mother used to light a divo, small clay lamp, and say her prayers every day. One fine morning when she had finished her morning prayers and was busy with her cooking I hid the divo under my frock and set off for the lower store room—to play or to pray, I am unable to guess even now! My clothes ignited and I became a struggling ball of flame. Fortunately my parents heard my cries and somehow managed to extinguish the fire and bring me out of the store room alive. We were lucky, for spare tins of kerosene and petrol were stored there too. I had already fainted in pure agony. I remained unconscious for almost a fortnight, and even after that continued to be delirious for a long time. In fact, my parents were surprised and said that I had cheated death and walked back. Ba nursed me back to normal with difficulty. I was really badly burnt, and it is a miracle that most of the savage scars have disappeared, save a speck here and there to remind me of my childhood misadventure.

By and by Motabapuji returned with his family and the house filled up again. Our two families shared everything, and the house rules applied to all the members, equally including Kakiba and Ba. We girls learned how to roll out puris, theplas and parathas and help with household chores. It was customary for the daughter-in-law to cover her face, a practice known as laj kadho, in the presence of elders from her husband's family. Even distant older cousins and husband's friends were to be accorded this partial veiling as a gesture of respect. If Motabapuji was around the kitchen at lunchtime when Ba prepared rotlis on the charcoal chulo, she still managed to make perfect items with her face completely shrouded by her sari pallu, enduring the blaze of the stove in total silence. Ba was also an expert at making sagdis, small portable charcoal braziers out of empty kerosene tins. This informal but demanding domestic art required exact measurements of cement combined with sticky mitti, clay brought from the kumbharwada, potters' locality and the tins and iron bars had to be cut out proportionately. Our house servant Saidi was Ba's chief assistant. I liked to help with mixing the cement and mitti, some times Mahen joined and Ba encouraged us all to join in the fun. Apart from fulfilling all her household duties, Ba managed a side business; Bapuji had arranged for the delivery of lorry loads of bags of charcoal which she stored in the garage and sold at retail price. As charcoal was the main fuel for domestic stoves, these supplies sold out almost immediately.

In Tanzania in fact the whole of Africa in villages and towns coal and wood is still being used as fuel for sagdis and chulos. A sagdi—jiko could be moved around, whereas a chulho is fixed to the ground or kitchen floor. Many women also cook expertly over simple jiko, a 'stove' improvised from three big stones or bricks strategically placed in a triangle on the ground, under which dry branches are lit. The woman would be carrying a bale of dry branches on her head which she had picked up on her way back from her shambha, farm, or from any other errands and use that for cooking the meal for the family outdoors, over this simple jiko.

At home in her kitchen Ba sat on a patlo, wooden board and ignited the pile of coal in the middle chamber of the sagdi. There was a little flap at the base that could be closed or opened as needed to regulate the amount of heat. We loved Ba's sakaria sweet potatoes, potatoes, makai corn on the cob and mihogo cassava, roasted on the sagdi. Ever practical, Ba roasted the baigans, aubergines for bharta over the smouldering embers in the base of the sagdi even while the khichdi for our meal was simmering in a pot on top. And she had developed an ingenious method of using the sagdi as an oven to make delicious biscuits. When the cooking was finished, a frond of coconut fibre was coated with the ash tipped out of the sagdi and used to scrub the grease from pots and pans. Reassuringly simple, in Ba's hands the humble sagdi turned into a most effective technology. There was absolutely no wastage of any kind.

On Sitla Satam day in the month of Shravan, no cooking was done. Instead, early in the morning Ba cleaned the kitchen whitewashed and decorated the chulo and the sagdi, perform puja-ritual prayers and offer specially prepared prasad to the Agni devta (fire God). Then we went to the Laxmi Narayan temple where Ba would join her friends, all wearing their best saris, and perform a different set of rituals to goddess Sitla Ma, praying for the welfare and safety of their children, especially for protection from small pox and all pox! Back at home we would picnic on goodies Ba had prepared a day earlier. I accompanied my mother to the temple almost daily. Even now I faintly remember holding on to her hand and attending all the ceremonies, including the consecration and the installation of the original Laxmi Narayan idols in the newly built temple, the first ever temple in Dar-es-Salaam. As time went more temples were added and at the last count there were ten temples on that street, now named Swami Narayan Street. And the number is growing. The special ambience of the temple, with the bells ringing and drums thumping, still remains with me. At home Ba had her own tiny idol of Thakorji, child Krishna. Each morning after her bath she would dress up and offer Him sweets. She had a fine collection of mini-costumes with matching jewellery, a box of wooden and silver toys and a ceremonial swing that fitted in my palm. Krishna was very much a part of our lives. I took it all for granted and sometimes even joked about Ba's practices, but later in life I often wished I had her simple faith.

We observed many religious festivals which not only reinforced the sense of community but also taught us to revere nature; the sun, moon, stars, sea, fire, rivers, trees, plants and animals. These rituals and celebrations took place over the whole year in accordance with the seasonal cycle and Hindu calendar which is based on a particular cosmology. The whole community participated in these festivities. When the celebrations and prayers were over, life rolled back on track towards the next destination with added enthusiasm.

At that time the Quit India movement was in full swing. My cousin brother Pramod, Nanabhai, took part in all the activities of the Hanuman Vyayamshala, a youth Gymkhana where the boys were coached in martial arts and played volleyball, football kho kho and hututu. He attended political meetings at the Vyayamshala wearing his Gandhi topi and white kurta-pyjama to express solidarity with the freedom struggle in India. This earned him the disapproval of his teacher and his father Motabapuji, and the tension affected their relationship. As a consequence Nanabhai became the focus of all Motabapuji's anger so much so that it sadly degenerated into cat and mouse game. Most of the time Nanabhai managed to keep out of his way. Nanabhai's volunteer activity at the Vyayamshala started early in the morning when the prabhat pheri, morning procession was held on weekends. People dressed in white would start the march with a salute to an imagined Indian flag, sing Vande Mataram with enthusiasm, and move around the town singing patriotic songs. It usually ended in an hour, with Gandhi's favourite bhajan Raghupati Raghav Raja Ram sung by everybody together, supplicating the Divine to bestow harmony and serenity upon us all. I found it very exciting to get up early, have a cold bath and join my friends in singing and marching along in step with the older activists. The Dar-es-Salaam prabhat pheris had started quietly, but were suddenly stopped within a short period after coming to the notice of the colonial administration, who warned the young organizers of dire consequences if this manner of anti-British political rallying continued.

Joint family life was wonderful for us children. Nanabhai taught me to ride his bicycle expertly; I particularly enjoyed riding it wearing his white kurta-pyjama, impressing my friends with both my skill and audacity.

Nanabhai was a keen sportsman and extremely good swimmer, from a young age easily fording the ferry creek. Tragically, during a picnic in Bagamoyo he dived into shallow water and broke his neck. Nobody could believe it and it was not even clear how or what had happened. Bapuji rushed to Bagamoyo, and Nanabhai was cremated there the same day. Sorrowful locals attended his funeral. We were in Dar-es-Salaam and I had no chance to say a final goodbye to my beloved cousin brother. I was shattered and felt utterly lost for a long time.

Way back in 1936-37, I remember one particular 'sari sale'. A family friend who had just arrived from India by steamer sent a word to Motabapuji that they had brought a baleful of beautiful cotton saris from Jamnagar. So next day Kakiba, Ba, and we girls went to their house all dressed up and excited about the sale. Kakiba and Ba both were to select about ten saris each. The ladies decided that they should choose in turn one sari each, so that nobody would have any advantage over the other. We all actively and thoroughly enjoyed this exercise in sharing. At the end of the day came back home, happily carrying two separate bundles of saris.

This was the mode of our childhood years. Now we are all scattered around in USA, Canada, UK, India and Mauritius following our own destinies. Thankfully, due to internet and mobile phones, our line of communications remains open. And the treasure chest of happy memory is always there to share and enjoy.

Watching the sun rise from the top of the hill,
Cycling down the street and enjoying the thrill.
Taking a long car ride simply to break free!
Like a bird flying from the top of the trees,
Flying, flying free with out any seams,
Life is all this and more to swim!

Chapter 4

Early Explorers and Slave Trade

The historical background of Tanganyika, Zanzibar and Pemba where I was born is very interesting, chequered and inter related since a very long time. It is worth to have a brief glance through its well documented history.

Scholars record that as far back as 1884, Karl Peters arrived in Zanzibar from Germany. He negotiated treaties with the African Chiefs on the mainland of Tanganyika within a period of five weeks. Looking back in time from the vantage point of today I can visualise the scenario. How the Chiefs would have been duped in putting their thumb prints to the paper which they could not even read, by a strange looking white man in his khaki uniform, topi, boots and a swagger stick, talking and going on in a strange language. Often shooting to terrorise people, and at times presenting with pomp a gift of shiny beads, marbles, mirrors, copper wire, salt, may be a knife and other metal ware knick knacks thrown in to impress the Chiefs. Thus in ignorance and unknowingly, the Chiefs signed away their lands to the Germans.

From then on the Germans ruled the African countries through the swish of their whips and the force of their guns and warships. And as they moved inland they quelled ruthlessly all rebellion and annexed the coast of Tanganyika and East Africa. So much so that by 1890 they had threatened the Sultan of Zanzibar brazenly by training their warships on his palace in readiness for bombardment any time. In the end the Sultan was constrained to give away the coastal stretch of Tanganyika to the Germans thus consolidating further their hold on the country. Perhaps their most cruel and vicious campaign in Tanganyika took place in 1905 during the rebellion of Maji Maji War when the Germans butchered the villagers en mass, burnt their granaries, huts and farms and continued with their scorched earth policy to cow down the inhabitants of the country. Their fortune changed only after the First World War when the British forced the vanquished Germans out of East Africa. In 1919 League of Nations decided to place Tanganyika under British rule through the Peace Treaty of 1919. This was changed again in 1946 when Tanganyika became UN Trust Territory under British administration.

Remarkably, before the Germans and the British arrived in East Africa, Portuguese and the Arabs had already established their presence in Tanganyika, Zanzibar and Kenya coast by taking over trade, again through use of force. But, even before that the seafarers from India had reached the shores of East Africa in search of trade and adventure. Many of these seasoned sailors originated from Gujarat and Kutch. From the beginning, the Sultan of Zanzibar and Oman had been actively encouraging the Indians to live and work in Zanzibar as customs officers, financiers, and financial advisers, salespersons, shopkeepers and teachers. As early as 1800 he had appointed merchant families of Tarya Toppan and Jairam Shivji, Kutchi Bhatiyas as Bankers to the Sultan and even the British administrators. In fact Jairam Shivji was officially given the job as collector of Customs & Charge duties in Zanzibar, Kilwa, Kisimayo, and Mogadishu for 5 years. He was also Head of the, 'Port in Zanzibar & State Bankers.' Alidina Vishram was another pioneer and a visionary who arrived in Zanzibar from Porbunder by dhow as a penny less lonely young boy. Through hard work and diligence he established himself as a leading businessman and was well known for his philanthropic activities.

Most of these pioneers started to bring their families and settled down in East Africa through Zanzibar since 1840s onwards. Way back in 1857, Sir Richard Burton-English voyager to Zanzibar has written a long treatise similar to a census. He describes in great detail his observations regarding the 'Banyans and Bhatia' and the Indian settlement in general in Zanzibar and elsewhere on the East African coast. He has even listed the origins of Hindus and Muslims, their divisions, customs, culture and religious beliefs, their numbers, arrival, trading practices and gaining prosperity in these countries. In his opinion, "the merchant par excellence of Zanzibar, are the enterprising Bhatia or Cutchi Banyas. Ladha Lamba farms the customs at Zanzibar; at Pemba Island his nephew has the charge: Mambasah is in the hands of Trikamdas and contains 20 Bhatias. Even the pauper Sa'adani has Ramji, an active and intelligent trader who presides at Bagamoyo . . . ." He goes on in the same vain and finally adds that, "The Bhatia at Zanzibar is a visitor, not a colonist.

Interestingly, it is further said that even to get to get Vasco da Gama and his marauding fleet of sailing ships away from his backyard, it was the Sultan of Zanzibar who lent Vasco da Gama, the famous explorer, services of his Indian Pilot Ibn Magid for his next leg of journey from Malindi to Calicut-India way back in late 15th century. According to Chitralekha dated First November 2010, this topic was discussed fully, at recently held three day maritime conference cum exhibition about 'Gujarat and the sea' in Mandvi where historians and scholars from research Institutes from UK, France Portugal, China, Singapore, Shree Lanka and India took part. They all confirmed the fact that it was indeed a Kutchi sailor Kanji Malaam who navigated Vasco da Gama to Calicut in India from Malindi on East African coast. Simultaneously, the ongoing exhibition compiled by Sarah Bancroft about the sailors and sailings from Gujarat, contained century's old rare maps, documents, articles, pictures paintings and hand written log books, recording those journeys by Indian pioneers to distant lands." Vasco da Gama died and is buried in Cochin in South India. Recently Roohi our grand daughter visited his grave while on a visit to Cochin.

Those sailors of the high seas sailed to Africa with dhows laden with silk, carpets, cloth, beads, sugar, rice, grains, pottery, copper, glass, ironware, dates, guns, gunpowder, and ammunition. They took back ivory, gold, slaves, minerals, copra, beeswax, hides, turtle shell, rhino horns, wood, mangrove poles, and ebony which were plentiful in Africa. It was a long journey, which took more than six months as on their way to Zanzibar, they plied their wares in and picked up commodities from the places like Persia, Oman, and even as far as Egypt before they reached the shores of East Africa.

On the East African coast, the trading route stretched from Zanzibar, Pemba, Mombasa, Malindi, Lamu, Bagamoyo, Tanga, Kilwa, up to Lindi and Mtwara on the Lake Ruvuma. We can stand on the shores of Lake Ruvuma, look across, and have a glimpse of Mozambique. I have watched this panorama while attending UWT, Umoja WA Wanawake—National Women's Organization meetings in Mtwara-Lindi, and travelled further down the trade route to Tabora, Kigoma on Lake Tanganyika, and Mwanza on the Lake Victoria.

This trade route stretches further across the lakes from Mwanza and Kigoma; thus making Zanzibar very important sea port and a gateway to whole of East Africa and beyond the coast for the adventurous sailors, as well as immigrants from Arabia, Persia, India, Germany and Britain.

This was also, perhaps the heyday of the slave trade in Africa during the Sultan's regime in Zanzibar. These slavers came from many backgrounds and colours. They considered it as a business like any other business fraught with danger notwithstanding the fact that theirs was a very cruel trade in human flesh. It is recorded time and again that they continued to capture slaves by any means with out any compassion for human lives. Often they would even supply the African Chiefs guns and ammunition in exchange for slaves. Notorious and much dreaded amongst these marauders was Tippu Tip from Oman. His full name was Hamid Bin Muhammad bin Jumna Al Marjeby. He died in 1905.

Their modus operandi was very cruel and spine chilling. The trader with his band of thugs armed with guns and hatchets would attack villages stealthily in the middle of the night, slit open the throats of babies and elders and terrorise the rest of the villagers into submission. The survivors were then forcefully captured and chained into fetters. Having thus looted and ravaged one community the slaver moved on to the next settlement.

On the way they hunted elephants for their tusks. Heavily chained and starving slaves, men and women even with babies on their backs carried those heavy tusks. After having collected enough of their loot, the slave caravan turned round towards Bagamoyo which at the time was a busy terminus from where slaves were transported onwards to Zanzibar and elsewhere. The name Bagamoyo means 'lay down your heart' because it was here that the slaves would finally abandon all hope of freedom.

It is surmised that for every slave who reached Zanzibar, eight to ten died on the route. The slave traders sold their human cargo at the major bazaars in Zanzibar, Bagamoyo, Kilwa Malindi, and Muscat, openly like cattle in a market.

In 1873 slavery was made illegal, but it was abolished completely only after the First World War. The constructive outcome of the slave trade is that, the people of African origin are settled down in all parts of the world.

Chapter 5

A Tale of Three Villages

We were lucky in being able to spend our school holidays in fascinating places such as Zanzibar, the island of spices and the kingdom of Omani Arabs, Bagamoyo, a former centre of the slave trade, and Pugu, the domain of farmers and explorers. My earliest memories of these places are of happy carefree days playing and running through swaying coconut trees lining the sea front and the mango groves that surrounded the villages. There were lots of butterflies and fireflies in the fields, waves rolling in the sea and the rainbows shining in the sky. I liked to chase the butterflies across the fields and the rainbow across the clouds. The butterflies flew away, the winds and the waves blew away and the rainbow stayed as far away as ever. But the exhilaration of the time remains, leaving a handful of memories for me to savour and share.

Pugu

Motabapuji had many German friends. One of them was sure that there were diamonds and rubies in some part of his sisal estate near Pugu, but due to the World War II inevitably looming, he was in a hurry to leave Tanganyika, and sold his farm to Motabapuji, also confiding this intuition about the possibility of the treasure. So apart from his duties at the shop in Dar-es-Salaam, Bapuji also ran the sisal farm and prospected for the gems, combining these duties from Monday to Saturday. On Saturday evening he paid the wapagazi—labourers working on his Pugu farm and drove back to Dar-es-Salaam, arriving late at night. Sunday was reserved for checking medical store accounts, ordering and documenting stock and finishing all the week's pending work at the shop. By late Sunday evening Bapuji was ready to drive back to Pugu. Monday mornings would see him out in the fields, wearing his khakis, heavy boots and topi, a pith helmet to shield him from the sun being a farmer out in the fields with his men and being a diamond explorer as well. By this time he had already started loosing his thick crop of hair and was getting bald!

As a result during this phase our family stayed in Pugu for long periods. At that time Pugu settlement was barely more than a one-track railway station. The farm itself was right in the jungle. We had a two-room brick house with the kitchen in the open veranda and toilet outside in the garden. In the dark of the night, sharing my mother's bed safely tucked under a blanket and with a mosquito net overhead, we would often hear elephants trumpeting, lions roaring and huge monkeys and their young ones shrieking nearby. We children found it exciting but it must have been a nightmare for my mother.

Formerly sisal was one of the main cash crops in Tanganyika. And it was much in demand during the war. Most of it was exported by the colonial government and fetched good prices. Sisal plants need a lot of sun, water and require careful handling. The plant has a 7-10 year lifespan. Each leaf contains about 1000 fibres. This fibre is threshed by specially designed machines and is washed thoroughly with running water. It is then dried, brushed and baled for export. The country's Tanga region was well known for its sisal; here Karimjee family had huge sisal estates and was one of the major exporters. On the Dar-es-Salaam coast the Mathuradas Mehta family owned big sisal farms. The Mehta family had built a beautiful bungalow with fountains and an exotic garden on a cliff over looking the sea in Oyster Bay in Dar-es-Salaam and named it romantically as Chandra Villa, Abode of the Moon. This building has been serving as the Police Officer's Mess in Dar-es-Salaam since a long time. Compared to these holdings Bapuji's farm was small. And apart from the fact that we learned some thing about sisal farming, Bapuji with his rudimentary equipment and mining knowledge never found any of the supposed treasure during his tilling of the land. Ultimately he sold the farm. Since then rich veins of minerals are found in that region.

Zanzibar

Occasionally, I spent my annual school holidays in Jungbar—Zanzibar. It was a quaint little town with a maze of narrow streets where cars could not pass. Usually we travelled by ships such as Amra or Kampala but sometimes we sailed even by small vessels which were plying up and down the East African coast.

Our adventure started the moment we boarded small boats or dhows from the old Customs House jetty and reached the ships anchored at a distance beckoning from far away. And there, up we climbed a dangerously dangling rope ladder to the main deck and peeped and dumped our bags in the cabins. Portholes in our cabins gave a glimpse of the sea, but it was more fun to spend the whole day on deck out in the open. It took five to six hours of pleasant sailing to reach Zanzibar. The sea winds blew the fragrance of cloves and other spices for which Zanzibar was famous from far away even before the ship entered the harbour. By evening we would be with our hosts, Mohan Kaka and Mukta Kaki, my father's close friends who were like our second family. My mother used to veil her face with her sari when Mohan Kaka was around, according him the traditional gesture of respect given to a husband's elder brother. Later, with great difficulty and deft use of his delightful sense of humour, he convinced her that this was unnecessary.

Mohan Kaka's family lived a two-storey Arab-style building on one of those very narrow streets. The other residents of the house were his friends Hira Kaka and Shanta Masi, and Rathore Master and Bajuba. There was a deep well in the central courtyard, with corridors and living quarters running around it on both the floors and a dark dingy basement down under. But even the cleaner refused to venture beyond its mysterious steps. Apparently Mohan Kaka, a customs officer, was living beyond his means. The open house he kept for one and all could not possibly be run on his salary. Often he wore patched trousers, hidden under his traditional long coat. If asked about this he would laugh at himself. He liked to joke about things and make others laugh with him. For me the evenings were best part of the day, when Mohankaka was home. He was a fantastic storyteller and enthralled us with traditional Indian stories about Akbar and Birbal, Raja Vikramaditya and Vaitali, the laughing she-demon who rode on his back and demanded interesting tales from him; if he refused she would take his life. Mercifully the king had the option of trying again, carry the Gene back and tell another story. Such spine chilling stories they were! To add more fun Mohan kaka told us stories about Ali Baba and the forty thieves, Bakor Patel and his Patlani and other Indian fairy tales. We encountered a range of compelling characters, kings, queens, their ministers, bards, jesters, magicians, ogres, and ordinary folks with their entices. Later in life I loved reading these stories to my own children, from the time when they had not even started going to nursery school. As they grew up, BAL Ramayana, Children's Ramayana, Mahabharata, Krishna, Hanuman Lila and the riveting Panchatantra animal stories, as well as all the children's magazines and comics of the time were added and became our favourites.

Mohankaka was also a walking repository of detailed information about the region. According to him, it was Said bin Sultan, the Sultan of Oman who introduced cloves in the isles and used the slave labour to cultivate these crops.

His son Majid continued to consolidate the slave trade. After Majid's death his brother Sultan Baraghash became the Sultan of Zanzibar. He ruled Zanzibar from 1870-1888. He had brought mangoes and many other fruits and vegetables from India to his kingdom; the tall Ashoka trees lining the Zanzibar seafront also had come from India. Initially Baragash had tried to out manoeuvre his older brother in an attempt to become ruler of Zanzibar, and consequently was banished to India by the colonial administration, ostensibly to pursue higher education. Baragash lived in India for a while, becoming quite a colourful and flamboyant personality. An energetic innovator, he brought electricity to Zanzibar as early as 1870, and installed oil-fuelled streetlights in the Stone town, which was the largest town in the archipelago located in the middle of the west coast of Unguja-Zanzibar. This town is named Stone Town for the coral stone buildings that were built largely during the 19th century. Baragash even installed a small stretch of experimental railway track and built palaces with bathing pools for his harem. Insider accounts claim he had one wife and 99 concubines. [1]

Bagamoyo

Our holidays in Bagamoyo were spent swimming, searching for seashells or just frolicking on the beach while watching big and small dhows, and massive clouds being driven over the horizon by playful winds. This sunlit village is set at the edge of a calm blue-green expanse of sea that seemed to extend to the edge of the world. It looked as if here, Father Time was in no hurry to make a move! However, in the past this tranquil place had been a notorious and flourishing centre for African slave trade, from where dhows sailed the high seas from the mainland full of chained and traumatised human beings young and old, men, women and children, as a commodity for sale in Zanzibar and elsewhere.

Bapuji had bought a huge coconut farm in Bagamoyo, and I remember the excitement of our first visit there. Ba made a lot of food to take along so that we could be fed without any tensions. The journey required elaborate planning. Bapuji bought the tickets in advance, and we began our journey before 6 a.m. in order to reach Bagamoyo by sunset. We travelled in a converted lorry with makeshift seats, passengers crammed in with their bundles, bicycles, chickens, and even a nervous goat to hold on to. The ramshackle vehicle groaned and rattled along the rough track optimistically called the 'road', breaking down several times. So the safari which takes less then three hours presently took a whole sweltering day of bone-jolting bumping and lurching.

Exhausted and yet excited we finally reached Bagamoyo before nightfall. And what a surprise it was! Khambhini, our spacious new home spread out over two floors around a central courtyard. There were rows of small rooms on all sides, skirting the compound making it a compact structure with a huge, sturdy iron gate. The building was actually the former headquarters of the slave traders, and captives had been chained in those dingy rooms while waiting to be transported. The spacious central portion that we occupied was in fact a watch tower. This building has now been declared a national monument and is a tourist attraction.

At that time there was a well in the compound which was the only source of water. Anant and Niru were too young but Mahen, and I immediately mastered the trick of drawing water from the well, letting down a tin bucket tied with a thick sisal rope. This was our morning chore and one we enjoyed, later having baths in a huge tub. Another of our favourite occupation was to have a feast of luscious pineapples and Embe shindhano-mangos, any time of the day or night. Occasionally it rained bringing with it the scent of the dry earth soaking up the first drops of rain, mingled with salty air wafting the from the sea near by.

There was no electricity either. In the evenings Bapuji lit a Petromax which gave a very bright light. The compound gates were locked at nightfall for fear of lions entering and attacking goats and people. The coconut farm surrounding the house had dozens of donkeys. They were used as pack animals to ferry the harvest. Morning and evening we heard the donkeys braying, and at night the lions roaring. And if a donkey was taken by a lion, the other donkeys rioted and brayed at full volume all night. As soon as the gate was unlocked early in the morning, we walked to the sea shore on tree lined lanes, through the still sleeping village; past its rows of small bungalows built during German occupation, past the Boma, government offices, the courthouse and the first-ever Church which was built in Tanganyika by the Germans. The Wharf had a huge customs house which was once used for slave trading. Now the building was decaying and locked up. We disliked its dreariness and never lingered there, moving further down the shore where we swam, played in the sand dunes, collected seashells by the pocket full, and relaxed in the coconut groves.

Apart from the Indian doctor who was in charge of the government hospital and the Indian husband-wife team serving as teachers, Bagamoyo had a group of Bhatia, Bohra and Ismaili shop owners. They dealt in construction material, farm implements, farm products and spices, rice, grain, blankets, mericani—a type of cotton cloth and khanga and vitenge 'sare' with colourful designs which the women wear. There was even one bar owned by a Parsi gentleman. Most of these Indians came from Gujarat and Kutch. My favourite were the little dukas (kiosks) which sold salt for 10 cents, sugar for sumuni (50 cents), oil and kerosene by the ladleful, strings of beads, coils of copper wire and safety pins which were coveted as ornaments for a shilling.

My best friends were Sakkar and Kulsa, Ismaili sisters who helped their mother to run their small shop selling khanga and other dress material. I spent as much time with them as possible and enjoyed watching their customers, mostly African women, bargaining with them in good humour. Every day at 6 p.m. sharp they would be ready to go to the Jamatkhana where the members of the Ismalia community meet for all their social as well as religious functions, all dressed up and excited, carrying a plate or two of specially made food as offering. Once I asked Kulsa if I could go with her. "No, you can't, it is not allowed," came her reply. She was even afraid of being scolded to be seen with me when once in a while I tried to walk with her on her way to the Jamatkhana. So we stopped venturing out together in the street and continued to spend time quietly as usual in their shop.

Bapuji kept busy with the farm whole day. In the evening he met his friends in the bazaar and shared the news of the day, while Ba was invited into various homes to meet the women of local families. We returned to Khambini to find Bwana Shambha the farm manager and other senior retainers, who lived in some of the renovated rooms, waiting to meet Bapuji. We all sat on cement bench in the compound where in former days baraza meetings had been held. Sitting on mikekas, mats made of dried coconut leaves the elders talked about the day's happenings; if there were problems and disputes, these were worked out amicably. Often the older people would reminisce about chiefs, Germans, slave history and the colonial system, and spontaneously start singing and dancing. Bapuji lighted the Petromax, while little kerosene lamps and korobois, lamps made out of milk tins, were lit. The women came back from their shambha farms carrying head loads of kuni firewood. They began cooking and joined the conversation when in the mood. The creaking Iron Gate was locked at night after Bapuji had checked that everyone was inside the compound. The talk was in Swahili language and occasionally it was in Arabic; a smattering of which Bapuji had picked up in Zanzibar and my birthplace Pemba. I enjoyed these evening sessions of sitting quietly and absorbing details about daily farm life and interacting with our neighbours who had become like family to us. After the coconut harvest it was time to relax and celebrate. Bapuji bought fresh milk from the farms, a few tins of condensed milk, and cardamom, nutmeg, saffron, almonds and pistachios from the shop of his Bohra friend. In the evening he got a huge fire roaring and made dudhpak, the special Indian milk pudding which we all loved. It was allowed to cool overnight and the next day we feasted on it, along with other delicacies that Ba had prepared. However, the big event anticipated by our family, farm workers and their kin, old and young, was Lele Mama's famous ngoma, a music-and-dance party that Bapuji organized and paid for. Ngoma is a popular coastal dance as well as a generic term for such festivities, and Lele Mama was a colourful and talented lady who headed a well-known troupe. The performers sang and swayed their hips singing Swahili and Tarab songs. They danced all night with the crowd dancing lustily along with them. There was a lot of food; chicken, mutton and other meats and pombe the local brew was allowed after we children had left the venue.

The drums and vigelagele, ululations, started early in the evening. At 8 p.m., after dinner, my mother, sister, brothers and I were escorted to the ground by several Askaris, guards, carrying lamps and burning branches to scare away any lurking wild animals. At the ground a huge bonfire was kept blazing all night and several Petromaxes were lighted to frighten off wild animals and ward off insects. All the women dressed in multicoloured khanga and vitenge warp, wore ornaments made of beads, cowries shells, copper wire and safety pins. They use lot of white powder on their faces and applied herbal scents. The elders who could afford it wore white khanju gowns, and the round embroidered caps, while the male dancers and drummers were clad in animal skins with leather bands decorated beautifully with shells and bead ornaments. They wore headbands and painted their faces, arms and bare chests for the occasion.

The ngoma itself started with a slow rhythm. By 11 p.m. with the drummers drumming excitedly and their leader whistling enthusiastically, the tempo would intensify. It was a signal for Lele Mama's group to start singing; they would begin to sway their hips and sing sweet melodies and Taraab songs. And that was the time for us children to be escorted back home with Ba. But before we left we were entertained by a great show; the men leapt high in the air, taking fantastic somersaults, the irons bells on their armbands and waistbands jingling fiercely and their eyes flashing in the firelight. We knew some of these men and could even identify them by name and so it was ever more exciting! The ngoma went on all night. And Bapuji would come home early in the morning, exhausted but satisfied that everything had gone well and that everybody had really enjoyed themselves. He himself was a teetotaller and strict vegetarian, a believer in Gandhian philosophy and self-discipline. He had never tasted tea, bread or cake and refused to eat them even when he was admitted in the hospital for his surgery

At night lying on my bed on the veranda I watched twinklers of tiny bright lights the fireflies glimmering outside my mosquito net. I counted the stars and watched the moon emerging from complete darkness as a fine small arc that over the nights slowly swelled into a radiant full moon. I would fall asleep and dream of the sunrise spilling its glory over the shimmering dancing waves of the Indian Ocean. I had no vocabulary to describe my encounter with nature's magnificence, and even now it seems indescribable. But the pleasant memory still lingers and entice! As Hellen Keller, deprived of sight, has so wisely remarked, "The best and most beautiful things in the world cannot be seen or even touched. They must be felt with the heart."

Recently our friends Padmaben and Pradipbhai Manek took me on a ride down the memory lane and made a special trip for me to Bagamoyo. From Dar-es-Salaam we reached Bagamoyo in less then three hours after a very pleasant drive. What was once a charming, haphazard one-lane African village is now an unfamiliar tourist town. The idyllic countryside has vanished; in its place the beach is cluttered with tourist hotels blocking the view of the ocean. Disappointed, we tried to compensate by visiting Kawe where slave trade relics are still preserved. It retains its old time charm. But as it was a Sunday the schools were closed and the village looked deserted and lost.

Chapter 6

Dar-es-Salaam

Founded in 1865-1866 by Sultan Majid bin Said of Zanzibar, Dar-es-Salaam was built on the site of Mzizima village on the coast line of Tanganyika, as a centre for coordinating and advancing his mercantile interests on the mainland. Originally the Sultan had named it from an Arabic phrase Bandar-a-Salaam meaning Harbour of Peace. By and by, it was changed to Dar-es-Salaam; Heaven of Peace. Charmed and happy with a close—knit community, it was Haven of Peace in all respects.

Dar-es-Salaam fell into decline after Majid's death. But in 1887 the Germans replaced the Sultan's power with their own rule. They built the railway station in Dar-es-Salaam and within three years made it the Capital of German East Africa.

All this was consigned to history books when I was born in 1931. By that time, even though the Sultan's flag was still fluttering in Zanzibar, Tanganyika was firmly under

British rule with Dar-es-Salaam as its Capital. The First World War was over and the only reminders of the War were two sunken German gunboats lying around right near the entrance of Dar-es-Salaam harbour. One of them was Koning, which I think was dismantled and sold as scrap. The second one was moved away from the harbour entrance, a mere skeleton in bits and pieces to be washed away with time and tide.

Dar-es-Salaam was a small but thriving growing town. The land beyond Salender Bridge was msitu, wilderness and jungle, where lions used to roam and roar at will, and Salender Bridge was just a small wooden bridge at the time and not many people ventured beyond that point. There was a Kumbharvado, a potter's compound, located some where near the present Central Library where several potters' families lived. They made clay water pots, flowerpots, tavdis, clay frying pans, and many other household items. The potters carried these by the sack full on their backs, and came peddling these in our neighborhood. Occasionally they even came with their donkeys loaded with all their heavy stuff. I loved the beautiful garbas clay lamps which were made especially for Navratri, the festival of Nine Nights. Whenever there was a wedding, the women of the family dressed up and went to the Kumbharwada, singing wedding songs carrying a divdo, a lit clay lamp on a specially made stand for lights. There puja was performed to herald the auspicious beginning of the wedding celebrations. I faintly remember potters wheel being part of this ritual.

Many of the original members of the Kumbharwada now have settled down in UK. Some of them belonged to extended Ladwa family of Dar-es-Salaam. The family had started from scratch and through hard work managed to establish themselves as major government contractors and hoteliers. While talking about those days in the potters' commune one of the younger members Chandubhai Ladwa explains, 'They had their own very reliable Banking system. At the end of every month, after retaining a little amount for their personal use, the men handed over all their earnings to the Patriarch of the group. Part of this money went to India to their individual families, and the rest was kept in reserve by the elder, for a rainy day for the members concerned. All this was done with complete trust.

In fact, those days all the businesses ran on mutual trust. Goods were delivered and payments to be made were agreed through words of mouth and a piece of paper, called chithi, a chit.

Another friend, Gulabbhai Shah's family is one of the leading industrialists in East Africa. They have an interesting story to tell. Three generations of Shah Family have run their flagship Sumaria Holdings Ltd since their start and a forth generation family member recently joined it to continue the tradition. Theirs is an amazing story of success, and human enterprise to build up a business empire from a scratch.

According to his biography, Gulabbhai Shah was born in 1932 in Jamnagar, India. They were a well-knit family of seven brothers and two sisters. Money was scarce and life was a challenge for the improvised family. He remembers that he got his first pair of shoes when he was ten years old. When the opportunity arose for his elder brother to migrate, his mother sold her gold chain so as to be able to send her first born Kantibhai Shah to Kenya where he started as a small trader and established well known Kanti & Company.

In 1957 Gulabbhai followed his brother and started their branch in Dar-es-Salaam dealing in enamel ware and sundry items, selling these all over the country. They transported the goods in trucks to Mwanza, Tabora, and

Tanga onwards through rough and tough road safaris. He also says that, all the transactions were based on complete trust and in spite of the low profits and there was never a worry of deceit. It was a normal practice to pay for the goods only after the goods were sold. Nor was there any need to lock front doors until 1978. Until then Dar-es-Salaam was very safe and secure place. Things changed after the 1978-1979 war with Idi Amin of Uganda.

One of the earlier institutes which I remember, the then Hindu Volunteers Corps together with the T.B. Sheth Library in Dar-es-Salaam were established on 10th March 1941. The Corps later became Indo Tanzania Cultural Centre. Initially this library was running from a ramshackle building where people used to dump their old books and magazines. The present magnificent building owes its inauguration to Mr. T. B. Seth who laid its foundation stone on 26-Jan-1947 and donated Shs. 25,000. At that time it was big money. Jivrajbhai Patel-Indiraben, Chandubhai Chohan-Dhirajben, Beniben-Mayurbhai Shukla, Buchkaka and Taramasi, Pranshakerbhai-Bhabhi, Randhir Thaker and his entire family and many others worked day and night putting their dreams into concrete shape. As work progressed other generous donations in cash and kind followed and gradually facilitated the additions of Shishukunj Hall, a special wing for children's library, an office block, a small flat, and servant's quarters and an open air kitchen as well. There is a life like statue of Mahatma Gandhi and several paintings right in the entrance of the library. The library and the Shishukunj were established through voluntary work and they are still being run on the same principles and high ideals.

Tapubhai Tank was one of the earliest volunteers at the library almost 75 years ago. The old timers say that his wife was mentally unstable and not keeping in good health either. Tapubhai was a darji, tailor, by profession who was also working for the PWD. A simple man he was brilliant artist. It was he who created the beautiful bust and the paintings of Mahatma Gandhi for the library. He also taught children handicraft at the Shishukunj-Sunday school.

Shishukunj in Dar-es-Salaam was established on 23 June 1955 by Indubhai Dave. His is a fascinating story of human Endeavour and determination. Indubhai was living in Karachi where in 1943 he organized story telling and playing Indian games sessions on regular basis in H.P. Karia High School and named the group Shishukunj. In 1947 due to partition and communal riots he migrated to Limbdi State of Gujarat and then went on to Dar-es-Salaam, Nairobi and finally reached UK. Shishukunj ceased to exist in Karachi but with persistence and hard work Indubhai Dave established Shishukunj in many villages in Gujarat, Dar-es-Salaam, Nairobi, London and even in USA. My kids Atool and Abha attended Shishukunj classes when Janardhanbhai Shukla, joined Shishukunj in 1956. Janardhanbhai remembers the children meeting in a jumba, a tin roofed hut. His wife had died and he used to carry his son Atool to these Sunday morning classes. When it was time for a nappy change the older kids used to tinga toddi the baby Atool dangling him like a kitten, took him to the water tap, splash water on him, flap him this way and that and hey presto, Atool was all clean and gurgling and there was merriment all round. Now all those kids are parents themselves and well settled in life in many parts of the world. The pleasant memories linger; Shishukunj is thriving and the T.B. Sheth library continues to be an oasis of tranquility and friendliness.

Another institution that comes to my mind is Shree Devkuver Arya Kanya Shalla, D.A. Girl's Primary and Secondary school where I had studied at different times.

Founded on 17-10-1929 the Primary School started with just 17 girls. Initially the classes were held in Arya Samaj Temple in Dar-es-Salaam, but as the number of girls increased within a short time, the founding members of the Arya Samaj, Shree Mathuradas Kalidas Mehta, Shree Govindji Purshotam Jani, Shree Arjun Kuverji Patel, Shree Madhavji Vishram and Shree Jamnadas Gordhandas decided to build a proper school in Dar-es-Salaam through fund raising and self reliance.

All these gentlemen had arrived in Tanganyika by dhow as young penny less teenagers in the late 1880s and perhaps earlier. They prospered in life by the sheer dint of their hard work. And in spite of the fact that they themselves had little formal education they were very enlightened men who aspired to build an educational institute for girls in Africa. Janiji, Narotambhai's father and Arjunbhai took over the task of supervising day and night, the actual building of the school. For years D.A. Girl's School was the only school to have sports, music and other cultural activities as a proper subject for girls. Lezim, an African wooden rattle with thin metal discs, and lathi, wooden staff drills were very much part of the student's daily routine. My most pleasant school time memories come from D.A. Girl's School, where I felt nurtured and gained all round confidence.

Incidentally in late 1960s I was appointed on its Board of Governors, when all the community schools were nationalized. At that time D. A. Girl's School was renamed Kisutu Girl's Primary School and Kisutu Girl's Secondary School. Those buildings still stand solid and continue to be the temples of education for girls.

Indian contractors and artisans mainly built Dar-es-Salaam the original Capital of Tanzania. Just to mention a few names whom we knew personally Jivrajbhai Patel and Gulabbhai Patel of G.A.K. Patel Ltd, Girdharbhai Chavda and his son Pravin Chavda of V. M. Chavda & Co., MECCO people, Tara Singh, Lashkar Singh, Kartar Singh and Hari Singh, Ladwa brothers, Tony Almeida the Architect are all major Architects, Builders, and Contractors. There were many others before them who were assisted by carpenters, masons, electricians, tailors, clerks, shoemakers, barbers and various artisans. Together they designed and built government offices, houses, bridges, railway lines, hospitals, libraries, courts, major roads and by-lanes. And in the process, they trained their African staff as they progressed. They built two and three story buildings with shops on the ground floor and they built Temples, Mosques, Gurdwaras and Churches.

As time went many of these buildings in Dar-as-Salaam with names like Mahals, Manjils, Nivas, Kunj and such have been demolished. Many stories about inspiring personalities of the past are gone with the wind of change and a very important part of our collective history is lost with that. But then change is inevitable and an ongoing process. Now Dar-es-Salaam is growing in leaps and bounds and is a bustling modern city with glass fronted office buildings, large glitzy malls, skyscrapers and beautiful bungalows with swimming pools and private car ports. I grew up in Dar, witnessed its ups and downs and saw it grow into present day mega city stretching for miles and miles along the coast of East Africa. Naturally many of its basic characteristics have changed along the way but, its friendliness and sunshine nature remains the same, as fresh ever.

Chapter 7

Migrations

It is refreshing to see that the history of migration in East Africa is not about slaves, robbers and coolies only. On the contrary it abounds with many riveting family histories of endurance, endeavours, struggles and success.

The families of most of our friends have been residing in Tanganyika for at least four or five generations. Often their forefathers from India had arrived in East Africa penniless; where they had established their businesses through hard work, using whatever resources were available to them. A case in point is the Manek family. I knew Maganlal Manek briefly during my schooldays. At that time girls and boys were not allowed to socialize; even a nod was frowned upon by conservative parents. Consequently I had very little direct contact with Maganlal, though I was destined to meet him indirectly through his son and daughter-in-law, Pradipbhai and Padmaben Manek. I met them for the first time in 1996-97 during study group meeting at the Chinmaya Mission in Dar-es-Salaam. They more or less adopted us, and since then they have been helping us all the way whenever we need them.

Pradipbhai enjoyed reminiscing about his family's history and remembers it with all the details. He describes, "My grandfather Kanji Jeraj Manek arrived in Dar-es-Salaam from Jamjodhpur in Gujarat by dhow in 1870. It was his dream to make Rs. 25 and return back in his village, a rich man. Our Kanjiada started his first job with Jiwan Hirji at a salary of 'khavu, pivu and suvu' food,—water and sleeping space and one set of new clothes on Diwali. He slept on gunny bags in the shop and got up early in the morning, swept the entrance, cleaned the place, opened the shop and also did errands such as buying vegetables for the family. One of his assigned tasks at the shop was to make ushanga malas, multicoloured bead chains and necklaces, late at night after finishing all the other chores. These bead ornaments were very popular items of adornment then and still are very popular items amongst the present day women as well as men all over Africa. After working there for few years, when Kanji Ada had saved enough money he started his own duka as by that time his malas were selling very well and his brother from Gujarat had joined him. They set up a wholesale business in the name of Kanji Jeraj & Company in Dar, and sent Maganlal, newly married to Chanuben, to open a branch in Lindi."

Maganlal prospered there, supplying all kinds of goods driving through rough tracks and inhospitable environment to upcountry centres. His sons Pradipbhai and Yogesh and his daughter Urmila were born in Lindi Ndanda Mission Hospital. Pradipbhai recalls that during his childhood, when he was five or six years old, their family was the first in Lindi to own a radio and a pressure cooker. "The townsfolk used to come to the house to listen to the news. Women came to see my mother demonstrate the preparation of dal in ten minutes using the pressure cooker rather than the traditional dabbo (oil tin) in which formerly she used to put some water, and put the pans containing dal, vegetables, and rice one on top of the other, close the lead and put it on the sagdi to cook. In about two hours time the dals, vegetables and rice would be ready and remain piping hot for a long time. The advantage of using the dabbo was that it used very little charcoal and left the lady of the house free to help her husband in their duka or shop and continue with any other work. But then the pressure cooker was amazing: the dals were being cooked in less than ten minutes!

My father loved cars and changed them frequently. He also donated freely to all the worthy causes. During that period he used to tell all donation seekers to come to him at the end of their fund-raising effort and without wasting his time, just mention how much more money they needed for that particular cause; he would then write out a cheque for that amount. We had the largest house in Lindi, with a fort surrounding it. After more then fifty years the fort is still there, but the house has vanished.

"Fortunes can change at any point, and by some quirk of fate my father suffered a huge financial loss. Our easy existence was transformed overnight, and he decided to move back to Dar. He said of our life in Lindi, 'I lived like a king in this place, now I cannot live here in changed circumstances.' We relocated to Dar and my father opened a small retail shop in Kariako, Dar-es-Salaam. Things were very, very tight for some time. We tried to improvise and worked very hard to earn our living. I remember the days when we used to sell a packet of pipi sweets for 5 cents, Bizari-termeric and coarse salt for 5 cents and 10 cents. We used to fill water in empty Coca Cola bottles, refrigerate it and sell the cold water for 5 cents . . ."

The Manek family has come a long way since those struggles of the earlier generations. Maganbhai's sons Pradipbhai and Yogesh have both become grandparents. Through lifelong diligence and hard work they have created a huge network of business enterprises. Today they are running successfully several industrial units and own the Exim Bank in Tanzania.

Those were the days when African and Indians, Hindus and Muslims, farmers and shop keepers lived side by side in harmony. Our friend N. S. Patel and his family initially had a small farm near Magole, in Morogoro Region. Though he himself was a practicing Lawyer and took keen interest in social services, his main interest lay in farming. His father Shankar Dada and younger brothers, farmed on this land and started experimenting with different crops especially sugarcane and making gor-brown sugar. They brought many vegetables and fruit seedlings like chiku, sitafal, several types of mangos including Hafus and vegetables like parval, valore, Amba haldar and so on from their farm in Gujarat and planted them on Magole farm. Latter on Patel family bought and developed, 100 acres Dizungu farm. Apart from fruits and vegetables they started sugar cane farming and produced gor as a full scale business undertaking on this farm. Their children and our children are the same age. During 1950s and 1960s we spent many a school holidays in Magole and Dizungu and visited surrounding farms in the beautiful, friendly countryside up to Lushoto. On every visit Sankar dada, used to measure and record all the children's length and weight on the front door of their main building. Now Shanker Dada, N.S. and Girishbhai are no more with us, the ever green farm with a running brook of crystal clear water has been sold and the door with etchings on it has vanished. But the lovely memory remains!

Our friend, Late Amirbhai Khatri is another farmer friend whom we remember fondly. He was born in Kamachuma district in Tanganyika where his father had a small shop. After completing his secondary school education, Amirbhai was engaged to Rahmatben, who was born in Kwimba District in 1949. He used to phone her often when they got engaged. Way back in 1960s and even 1970s few people had telephones. Fondly Rahmatben remembers Shanta masi whose family had this magic instrument, happily giving her a shout from across the fence, 'Remti, taro saglo bolawe che, Remti your boy friend is calling you, hurry up!' They were married in 1970 and settled down in Dar-es-Salaam. As time passed our families became close. When they went to Mecca for Haj pilgrimage, Rehmatben brought a bottle of Zam Zam holy water as blessings for us. It was a rare experience for us. She said that this water came from ever flowing sacred fount near the Kaaba. No body knows the source of the Zam Zam water spring and millions of devotees vouch for its sacred and magical properties.

An Accountant by profession and a farmer by choice, Amirbhai had a farm in the Coast Region and planted a variety of mangos. Chiku and several other fruit sidling brought from Kutch in India. When his son Arif joined him as a full fledged Chartered Accountant, Amirbhai spent more time on his farm. Like his father, apart from his work as a busy Chartered Account, Arif also continues expanding his farming activities, and grows fruits of best quality. We attended Arif's wedding to Taiba in Nairobi as elders of the family, it was wonderful.

One of my good friends in Dar-es-Salaam Hilda is more then six feet tall; she is a true blue blooded German lady with a hearty laugh and friendly nature. Some time back her husband, a Tanzanian Doctor died of kidney failure leaving her with two kids in their teens. Fortunately Hilda had a job and was able to educate her children. Her son finished his secondary school, converted to Islam and married the girl of his dreams from Zanzibar and started a dance club in Zanzibar, and the daughter settled down in Germany.

Hilda lived in Sea View near our house in a large flat, over looking the vast expanse of the Indian Ocean. In the evenings it was sheer bliss, just to sit on her balcony and watch the Sun set and gaze at the moon rise over the sea in the horizon. Hilda was interested in any and every thing Oriental. We used to meet often at her flat for meditation and many other group meetings. On one occasion in celebration of her mother's birthday, she had invited the famous Wasukuma group of snake dancers. These men dance in step with the drum beats carrying huge heavy pythons wrapped around their bodies. This time around they were cheerfully offering their play mates for photographs. I said no thank you as best as I could, but our hostess and her mother who was visiting from Germany, happily had their photographs taken with those pythons draped around their shoulders and arms, dancing in step with the drummers. At that time her mother was, 90 years old and the fat sleepy pythons were more then twenty feet long! Hilda's Mother loved story telling and even entertained Shishukunj children one bright Sunday morning.

Hilda used to travel often to India and spent her days mountaineering and trekking on the Himalayas, meeting holy men and visiting Ashrams. On one of these trips she met a Moni Baba near Rishikesh who was observing Maun

Vrat: keeping a vow of silence and leading solitary life for past twelve or thirteen years. The Baba was living in a small cave like hut on the Himalayas when he met Hilda, a friendly white woman. She spent all her spare time in his hut against many odds, cooking and sharing meals, or just sitting quietly. For her it was Himalayan retreat, but for him it was love and the beginning of a new life. He started writing to her, when Hilda returned to Dar. Said he was keen to follow her all the way to Africa. But what to do he did not know English and she could not understand a word of his written Hindi. Obviously those were the letters written by a lonely man who was rediscovering his lost ground; a Baba who had no contacts with mere mortals for a long time. We had hilarious time trying to decipher his letters!

While looking back seriously at another aspect of transmigration from Tanganyika, it must be noted that as an aftermath of Zanzibar Revolution in 1964, the people of Indian origin in the Isles, who wanted to return to India for good, were allowed by President Karume's Government to take a certain amount of cloves with them and leave. Many families who had spent their life time and some even several generations in Zanzibar took advantage of this offer and left for India.

Migration also took place in the other direction, i.e. from East Africa and Mozambique to the west coast of India, particularly Sindh and Gujarat. Africans arrived not only as slaves but also as soldiers and seafarers. In India they are known as Siddis, some of whom over time settled in Maharashtra, Andhra Pradesh and Karnataka, assimilating into local cultures, learning local languages and adapting social practices and religious rituals from the surrounding Hindu, Muslim and Christian communities. However,

Siddis still strongly retain aspects of their African heritage and culture, most strongly expressed through music, dance, storytelling and drama, using typically African musical instruments and rhythms in their performances. Many Siddis are closely linked with Sufi cult and venerate the Sufi saint Gori Pir, who came from Africa to Gujarat in the 15th century, accompanied by several of his brothers and sisters. It is said that Gori Pir was a saint and grants the desired boon if we pray sincerely to him and offer him a present with an open heart—a manaat. Gori Pir shrines in Gujarat and Maharashtra continue with this tradition and hold annual festivals with music and dance. And people of all denominations and cultures visit his shrines for the fulfilment of their manaats.[1]

A few years ago Siddi Goma group was formed as an auxiliary of the organisation TADIA (The African Diaspora in Asia). They regularly participate in the 'Dhow celebrations' in Zanzibar and other international events.

The cycle of time thus continues to race. All these enterprising family traders, not only did well for themselves, but their business activities also aided the economic growth of the country largely and placed it on industrial footing. A bygone era has passed, yet it is a crucial period in the development of Tanzania from uncharted land to a thriving third world country.

It is over ninety years since my parents migrated from British-ruled India to Zanzibar, the land of the Omani Arabs. They travelled by dhow, the standard sea transport of those days, to Pemba, then to Bagamoyo and ultimately settled down in Dar-es-Salaam. This long period of our family history has nurtured our four generations.

Chapter 8

World War II

Life changed suddenly for people in East Africa when Germany invaded Poland on 1 September 1939, and World War II began. Initially as the battlegrounds were in Europe they were remote to us mentally as well as literally, but as the war spread and engulfed more countries, we in East Africa also began to experience its repercussions. Overnight in Dar-es-Salaam, trenches were dug around schools and public places. Windows at home were shuttered and covered with black cloth or thick black paper. At night the blackout was total, and no one was allowed to go out or to switch on the lights. Only faint lanterns were allowed. People were advised to dig trenches around their homes, and we were subjected to drills; sirens and whistles would start blowing and we had to either dash indoors or sit quietly in the nearest trenches. Medicines were in short supply, and common items like quinine and glucose were almost unobtainable. Often people came knocking at our shop door in the middle of the night for the anti-malaria tablets that Bapuji had to ration. Sisal, food grains and other essential commodities were carted away to the war zones, resulting in general shortages all round, and taxes were increased. I remember groups of Askaris policemen, some times supervised by a white man, harassing men on the streets, catching and beating them with truncheons and packing them off in open police vans to do forced labour simply because they did not have the mandatory kipande—identity card, costing a few Shillings. It was horrible to watch and even as a child I saw the injustice and felt the pain when I spied the Askaris being so brutal to ordinary people on the street.

I also vividly remember Bapuji's German friends coming stealthily to our house at night with their valuable books, artwork, paintings, delicate porcelain tea-sets and coffee-sets, for safekeeping, or just to give away before they fled the country. In particular I recall a very heavy book of beautiful paintings, with double-spreads that folded to create envelope-like spaces. Bapuji thought it was most probably for people who wanted to carry their documents and money secretly and safely. He managed to keep the book out of our hands, but we children had already damaged many of the porcelain items through playing 'housey-housey' with them. The book's rightful owner eventually came to collect it, but Bapuji had to apologize for the broken crockery to the friend who was sad to find his prize collection ruined. In general only a few Germans returned to retrieve their belongings. Times were so unsettled that most of their possessions got destroyed or got lost.

Everyone had to tighten their belts, and there was a lot of troop movement; people were also moved by the Government away from the danger zones. While the soldiers from the King's African Rifles in Tanganyika were sent to join allied forces in Burma, and Ceylon, and fight in defence of Sudan, Madagascar, Egypt and Libya. [*1*]

Our only source of information during that period was All India Radio and BBC World Service which often relayed live broadcasts of Churchill. I didn't understand him but I did follow the elders of our house discussing the war. Hitler was on his demonic march to conquer the world and was destroying human lives ruthlessly in the process. When the Axis forces, including the Italian dictator Mussolini, attacked Egypt and Ethiopia, and the Japanese invaded Burma, rumours became rife in Dar-as-Salaam that Hitler had his eyes on East Africa as well and could reach Tanganyika at any time. In fact, when German forces invaded Crete they were in effect already facing Africa and were poised to attack it any time. [*2*]

Bapuji's flourishing medical shop near the railway station had a big veranda facing Acacia Avenue, the main road. Pillars supported a hanging roof over the veranda. This was a favourite nesting place for birds. We spent a lot of time on the veranda, watching those tiny little birds hatch their bald nestlings from tiny little eggs. Chirruping they flew away to unknown zones early in the morning and returned in the evening to feed their chicks. Soon even the chicks were flying all over the place. It was amazing.

One day from this vantage point we saw big convoys of Lorries, full of Europeans being transported to the station; mainly women and children and a few shabbily dressed old men. These unfortunate prisoners seemed hungry and traumatized. It was whispered that these prisoners were Italians, Hungarians, Jews, Poles and even some Germans. Nobody seemed to know from where they had been herded, or where they were being sent. It was shocking to see these ragged men and women crying helplessly while many wept just silently clinging to their children. This went on for weeks on end, and it was all very painful to see, and simply frightful to hear that Hitler had special gas furnaces built to burn the captives sent to camps by the trainload from all over Europe and Africa. [3]

It was said that many of the prisoners we saw passing through Dar-es-Salaam, were Polish, and later reports confirmed that an international refugee organization had sent over 10,000 Poles to Tanganyika for resettlement. Many had died on the long and arduous journey from Europe to Africa, and I thought that those who had survived were almost worse off, their condition was terrible . . . Apart from that another group of Europeans who passed through were the few hundred Italian prisoners-of-war captured by the Kings African Rifles during the battle at Colito in May 1941. They were used as forced labour to build roads all over East Africa. [4]

We also saw many British Navy manwaarias—sailors in Dar-es-Salaam when their manwars, man o' war ships docked in the harbour after their exercises at sea. These smart looking young sailors in their white uniforms came ashore wild with excitement after months of being cooped up on their vessels under wartime conditions and tensions. Many of them were just kids in their early twenties. They would take over a small town like Dar-es-Salaam, drinking dancing, singing and generally having fun wherever they went. And if by any chance they encountered any Indian woman covering her face with her sari pallu as was the custom then, they took it as open invitation to tease her. Invariably one of them would lift the lady's veil, sari pallu and say 'Hauk' with glee. The obvious out come was that the startled woman and her friends would scatter higgledy-piggledy in all directions! We found these incidents very funny to watch while hiding behind our favourite perch in the veranda . . .

This was the time when I first saw a sea-plane which had landed in Dar-es-Salaam harbour. To add to our excitement, it was rumoured that a submarine was in the harbour with its snout bobbing over the water. People whispered that it was on some mysterious mission and thronged on the sea front to try and locate it. It became a guessing game for us all.

All this while, my parents were getting more and more worried about our future. If Hitler, a European, was being so sadistic with Europeans, what would he do to people of other races if he did indeed manage to reach Tanganyika? Bapuji finally decided it was best if for the duration of the war we returned to Jamnagar to live with our grandmother Motiba and Faiba, paternal aunt in the family home. Many of his friends had already left by Amra, Kampala, Karanja, Khandala and other ships. But by the time Bapuji decided on our move, steamships between East Africa and India had been withdrawn because recently, one of these ships had been torpedoed by a Japanese submarine and went down with all passengers on board. One such unfortunate traveller was Maganlal Sir, my secondary school teacher, returning to Tanganyika after spending his leave with his family in India. We heard that he was a good swimmer and had leapt into the sea, but was sucked into the depths by the massive force of the ship as it sank.

Chapter 9

Our Dhow Safari

By 1943 the war was raging on all fronts: on land as well as on sea and by air. Bapuji realized that if we were to reach India safely we needed to leave Dar-es-Salaam immediately. One of the companies belonging to Karimjee Jiwanjee family was the booking agents for the Union Castle line and British India Navigation Company. Their offices were situated next to our medical shop. When Bapuji went to inquire and book our passage, they confirmed that the steamers had indeed been stopped for the moment from sailing across the Indian Ocean, due to German and Japanese submarines lurking around in the Indian Ocean and assaulting any ships that came onto their radar. The only alternative was to travel by dhow.

Call it by chance or providence, Bapuji found one dhow preparing to leave immediately for Bedibandar-Jamnagr. He hired the entire boat so as to be able to select and limit the number of travellers. The dhow was named Bijli and my brother Anant remembers that she belonged to Kasimchacha. She was not even half the size of the steamers, but to me she looked immense and majestic, with all her sails swaying gently in the breeze. Kassim Chacha was her nahoda [captain] sukani [pilot] and sailor all rolled in one. A devout Muslim, he descended from generations of seafarers and had grown up with boats and dhows. Bapuji addressed him simply as 'Maalim' meaning learned one / teacher. They became good friends and had long conversations on board when the sea was calm. From his early childhood Kasimchacha had imbibed seafaring from his father and grand fathers and had many interesting stories to tell.

To keep its balance in the high seas a dhow needs to carry a certain amount of carefully distributed weight, most of it in the form of cargo. Kassim Chacha told Bapuji that since buying a load of cloves and spices from Zanzibar would take time, he should purchase any available stocks of grains from Dar-es-Salaam. There were shortages in Jamnagar due to the war and local drought, and the supply of grain could be sold on the open market in India. The June-July monsoon winds were approaching making our route all the more dangerous for sailing. We needed to leave urgently. Bapuji took this advice and managed to buy about 500 bags of mixed grain and have it loaded on the dhow. He also had loaded on a months' supply of provisions to see us through the dangerous voyage; milk tins, jams, wheat flour, rice, pulses, jaggery, peanuts, potatoes, onions, spices, salt, oil, ghee, coffee, tea and some medicines for common colds, fever and diarrhoea. Water for drinking, the most important item, was stored in huge tanks on board. Two kumbhars, potters, who wanted to visit relatives in India but could not afford the passage money, joined us as cooks and helpers in lieu of their fare. A few other friends of Bapuji's travelling

to their families in Gujarat were also on board with us.
My enterprising parents were confident that despite the
threat of being detected and torpedoed by either German
or Japanese submarines prowling all along our route, we
would make it to India safely. And we children felt secure
in that confidence and never doubted that we would reach
our destination safely.

Dhows set sail or moor in accordance with the
momentum of the waves, so Bijli had to wait for the tide to
come in. It so happened that on the Sunday after loading, a
strong high tide was due, so it was decided that this would
be an auspicious time to start our journey. All passengers
were instructed to be on board by Saturday afternoon. Our
personal belongings packed in heavy tin trunks had already
been loaded. After a short prayer and invoking God's grace,
we bid farewell to our friends and neighbours, locked up the
house and the shop and went down to the old customs wharf
where Bijli was anchored. For us it was a familiar place, with
its corroding jetties and quite a good number of steamers
and dhows always waiting for their turn to load and unload
cargo. We often went there for evening walks; Bapuji used to
regularly supervise the arrival of his shipments of medicines
at the old customs and was on very good terms with the
Askaris and supervisors. They welcomed us like family. We
boarded the dhow, happy and excited with the thought that
we were embarking on our own, 'Sindbad the Sailor' voyage.
No one slept that night. At sunrise on Sunday morning, the
clear sky and the playful ocean were ablaze with ember light
from the rising sun as the full tide surged in. Once again we
conducted a special puja—ritual prayers in which Captain
Kassim Chacha and his crew of six badala-kharwas took
part with enthusiasm. And Ba and the other ladies offered
offered Narial ne saker no pado, coconut and cone shaped

packet of rock sugar to Dariya Dev, the Lord of the seven seas. Anchor lifted, Bijli glided out of the harbour in the open sea.

All through the voyage Kassim Chacha kept an eagle eye on his team of Kharwas who were his family members. They managed to sail the dhow beautifully in calm weather, and bravely when confronted with danger on the high seas. Badala and Kharwa sailors are employed to work as ship's mate on the dhows. Gradually as seafaring went out of business many of these families settled down along the coast of East Africa including Zanzibar, Malindi, Dar-es-Salaam and even as far as UK.

The distance between the coast of Tanganyika and that of Gujarat is approximately 2,200 miles (3540.56 Kilometres.) Depending upon the winds, the length of the route taken and halts on the way, it takes a dhow about a month to make the journey. Longer if conditions are unfavourable or the monsoon sets in, during which the vessel can capsize, get lost or be pushed south to Mozambique or Madagascar, completely off course. In a hurry, we chose to bypass Zanzibar but dropped anchor at Mombasa where Kassim Chacha had some pending business to finish. We were not allowed to disembark and left Mombasa on the same day. In order to avoid the German and Japanese warships Kasimchacha decided to sail nearer the coastline, bypass the ports of Mogadishu and Aden and headed towards Socotra Island.

Until now our sailing had been comparatively smooth. Kassim Chacha was constantly at the helm, following the stars and navigating Bijli towards Socotra Island. He knew the skies and stars like the palm of his hand. At night he pointed the constellations out to us, and quietly narrated fascinating stories about his wanderings around the world to distant lands. No one was allowed to light a candle or even smoke a bidi or cigarette for fear of being spotted by Japanese or German ships and submarines. We were forbidden to listen to the radio or make any kind of loud noise during the day or night. The news from All India Radio every morning at a very low volume was the only concession granted. This added to our general sense of danger and mystery.

Bijli had three sections. The first was the hold, where all cargo, the water tanks and our extra trunks were stored. The second area consisted of bhandakiyu, bunks, with a very low ceiling overhead, for children and women. It had a tiny toilet. The youngest passenger was my cousin Motiben's six-month-old infant son who was unwell. Bapuji had tied a makeshift ghodiu, cradle to a beam, and the baby slept there most of the time, swaying gently to the rhythm of the waves. Her second son Anupam, a toddler at the time and my two-year-old sister Niru followed Ba everywhere through the cramped living space that had mattresses spread out on the floor for our resting and sleeping. One had to crouch to enter the bunks. On the upper deck at the far end of the dhow a strange box-like contraption tightly secured to a rim on board hung dangerously over the sea: this was the toilet for men. At the other end, Kassim Chacha sat with his binoculars and compass working out navigation, while the crew constantly manoeuvred the sails in order to harness the wind. Cooking was allowed only once a day and the cooks prepared simple rotli-shak, with jam or condensed milk as dessert. Apart from these simple meals for lunch and dinner we were permitted snacks of peanuts, gur, dates and dry fruit, so we were quite well nourished. On windy days when the sea was rolling and cooking became difficult on deck, we ate achar and khichdi prepared on a charcoal sagdi securely fastened with ropes.

For most people it takes a few days to get used to the salty air coming from the sea, and the dhow rocking with the waves. We took to it immediately like fish in the water. Some passengers played cards while others conversed or simply lazed around. My favourite place was the upper deck where something or other was always taking place. I was allowed to spend most of the day on the deck and sleep at night under the star lit skies along with my father and brothers. I passed the time watching the incomparable vistas of nature, gazing with wide eyed wonder at scurrying and flurrying rain clouds rolling by. As sunlight filtered through these clouds often a spectacular miracle of colours, a rainbow in the sky unfolded before our eyes. It felt that Bijli was chasing the rainbow but of course the rainbow always stayed as far away as ever in the horizon. Excited we tried to work out if they were sharks or whales when we encountered shoals of sharks and whales with their calves. I marvelled at the force of these magnificent creatures, nuzzling and guiding their young with such immaculate tenderness. Kassim Chacha warned us to be absolutely quiet; if we did not disturb them, they would not bother us. Otherwise they go crazy with fear furious energy, which can even overturn a smaller dhow. They follow a liner or a Dhow, hoping to feed off the waste it discharges, with perhaps once in a way the whole ship or dhow going down and providing a virtual feast for them!

The vast sea had different moods and secrets: sometimes it was playful and teasing, occasionally calm and benevolent and often it was turbulent and threatening. At dusk the moon, stars, clouds and waves would start their own fascinating show. Our fragile, perishable yet indomitable Bijli was but a tiny speck in that immensity. We were all travelling together towards the same destination, and yet each one of us was immersed in his or her own individual world. It was extraordinary, and an overwhelming mystery. Sometimes, absorbed in deep night silence, I would feel infinite, able to touch the clouds, leap to the stars, and gust with the wind and flow with the waves . . . Now, with good number of kilos added and a head full of grey hair I still experience that wonder when I am out on the beach.

There is a beautiful poem by Nirmalprabha Bordoi as translated by Pradip Acharya, She writes;

'Keep a patch of forest in your bosom,

To give you a shade to rest in,

Keep a bit of sky in your bosom,

Where two birds, for once can fly alone.

Perhaps I can even dare to add a line to say;

And where one can dream along!

When the winds were fierce or when it rained, the sails had to be manipulated all the time in order for us to make any headway towards Socotra Island. Full of caves and mountains, it is a much-needed stopover that allows vessels to refill their freshwater supply and travellers to stretch their legs onshore and marvel at Mother Nature's bounty.

According to Kassim Chacha, the island had a very rich marine life, and about 700 rare species of flora and fauna can be found there. The name Socotra meaning Island of bliss was derived from Sanskrit the ancient language of India. At the recently held Mandvi conference cum exhibition, one of the participants from Mandvi, Maalam Shivji Bhuda while reminiscing about his seafaring days describes that on the Socotra Island there was a temple of Sicotar Maa. When a dhow passed the island, similar to the custom of offering a coconut the kharwa sailors would first offer a small replica of their dhow to the Deity and pray for safe journey. [1]

We were all looking forward to visiting this Socotra Island, not realising that nature had the upper hand over man in this matter. It was the winds and the waves fortified by the enemy submarines which would chart Bijli's path across the Indian Ocean and not the seasoned sailors nor the ingenuity of the Sukani, Pilot! As we neared the island the sea became extremely choppy and we weathered the worst storm of our journey. Bijli was tossed about like a tiny cork, and we hung onto the railings and prayed for our lives. The more terrified among us sought shelter below deck, while the rest frantically tried to bale out the flooded upper deck, a useless effort because walls of water were crashing over its deck. One moment Bijli was all but submerged, the next moment flung up to soar on the crests of high waves. We fought our way through that danger. By some miracle our much-battered Bijli did not break apart in those ferocious waves.

Building a dhow is a very intricate art. Few if any nails and iron fixings are used in dhows, as iron begins to rust immediately in seawater; the entire boat is intricately assembled with traditional technology that uses special glues. Bijli was well made and held together, but the storm forced us well past Socotra Island and we could not replenish our freshwater supply.

Our cheer and relief at the storm's abating was replaced by raw distress when the wind suddenly died down completely and Bijli was becalmed and unmoving. It was a perfect target for any passing German or Japanese submarine. Our drinking water was rationed, and everyone started to pray fervently. Up to now our journey had been an exciting adventure, but when Kasmchacha and his mates started praying my parents realised that we were in trouble. There were enemy submarines lurking around, the sun was mercilessly hot, and we were thirsting for water in the middle of the ocean! Apart from the drinking water our food supplies were also dwindling, sails were lying limp and the cheerful sailors looked sad and worried. As children we did not understand the seriousness of the situation. However there was nothing that anybody could do to help. The much needed help could come only from the heavens above!

Thankfully the wind lifted after a nerve-wracking ten days, and we set off again. When we finally sighted land, a great cheer went up and heartfelt prayers poured from every voice on Bijli. We had made it in spite of all the odds against us. Bapuji had worked very hard all his life. He had taken a big risk and decided to travel by dhow during war time. And most of all he was now relieved that we had passed the worst part of our journey without any loss of life or limbs and every body was safe and in good cheer. We had reached the Gulf of Kutch. From there we proceeded to Bedibandar. As we neared the coast, many small fishing boats came up to welcome us and rejoice at our arrival. Young men dived from the fishing boats to retrieve coins being thrown into the sea by Bijli's ecstatic passengers. Kassim Chacha knew some of the men and through them sent a message to his family that he would be with them soon.

It had taken us more then a month to reach the shores of Gujarat from the shores of East Africa. Relying only on a compass, binoculars, small courageous crew and his own deep knowledge of the sea, Kassim Chacha had brought us all safely 'home' across the mighty Indian Ocean.

Chapter 10

Jamnagar

We scrambled eagerly out of Bijli into the smaller boats, and headed for the shore. I was excited and overwhelmed with the hustle and bustle of arriving in Jamnagar safely after our long journey. Now suddenly we were in a hurry to reach home and meet our grand mother Motiba and Faiba, have a good bath, some thing nice to eat and just go to sleep! When we reached the customs house in Bedibandar, another dhow with passengers from Uganda had also just docked. There was complete chaos, everybody was busy searching for their luggage, and red-turbaned coolies were running back and forth helping people. I was disappointed to see the dilapidated condition of the customs building, and surprised to see women working side-by-side with the men. While waiting anxiously for Bapuji to finalise the immigration formalities, Ba got the chance to compare notes with passengers who had just arrived from Mombasa. It turned out that my parents knew one of them, Shree Hargovindbhai Jhaveri whose wife and two small children, like us were new arrivals from Uganda, East Africa. Hargovindbhai's younger brother Kanti had come to receive them. We were introduced briefly and then parted ways. They went to Rajkot, and we to Jamnagar a few miles away. Little did I know that destiny would have us meet again in a setting beyond my imagination!

Home for us was the two storey white washed building with four or five shops on the ground floor. Well maintained and 'Pragrai Nivas' my Grand father's name boldly written on the building it looked cool. And Motiba and Faiba were waiting for us with open arms. My parents were visiting India after a gap of twelve-thirteen years and were very happy to see their mother and sister. They had taken a difficult decision to undertake a hazardous journey and were relieved to see it completed and reach home, while like my siblings I was preoccupied exploring and getting used to the entirely new environment in Jamnagar.

After resting for a few weeks my parents started looking for a school for us and Bapuji quietly began his search for a suitable boy for me. Meanwhile I fell ill with typhoid, a dreaded virus in those days. By the time I recovered and started attending the all-girls school, the academic year was almost over. Sanskrit and Hindi were compulsory subjects. As I knew neither, a tutor was hired to coach me in both these subjects at home and another teacher was hired for music. The Sanskrit/Hindi tutor was a tired old man, worn out from taking on too many teaching assignments. In contrast, the music tutor, though blind, was energetic and very good. Though, I struggled on with the Sanskrit and Hindi now surprisingly I had lost interest in learning music, proving Proust right when he said that, 'Every thing comes about just as we desired but only when we no longer desire it.'

My maternal uncle Ratu Mama was in Bombay doing a solicitor's course. He had a close friend who had just passed the law exam. Ratu Mama thought that this friend might be a suitable match for me, and advised him to visit us in Jamnagar. By an astonishing coincidence, he turned out to be the Kanti Jhaveri whom we had met in the Bedibandar customs house upon arrival from Tanganyika. After his visit I was aware that consultations were going on among the elders about our engagement. All this time Bapuji kept very busy looking after the affairs of the house and family, I hardly saw him. Ba was busy with Motiba and Faiba and left on my own I felt strangely overwhelmed. A short while later our engagement was announced. It worked for us, but looking back after all these years I find it marvellous to see how expectations have changed over the years for our grand daughters, daughters and daughters-in-law as well!

Born in Rajkot in 1921, Kanti was the youngest of four children born to Diwaliben and Shri Laxmichand Jhaveri, Professor of mathematics in Rajkot. After finishing secondary school Kanti joined the local Dharmendra Shihji College. During that time he joined the Quit India movement and took up Gandhiji's call for non-cooperation and non-violent civil disobedience. As an ardent and popular student leader he organised a successful strike in his college, and was consequently arrested and jailed, to the great distress of his mother, now a widow. At home she waited and waited for the whole day and night for him to come home from the College. She had an inkling that trouble was brewing and some thing was amiss. Finally in desperation before even the day break, she went in search of her son, and traced him in the jail. After completing his jail term Kanti joined the Ruiya College in Bombay and then obtained his LLB degree from the Law College in Poona.

After our engagement, my brother Mahen and I visited Rajkot to meet my mother-in-law Diwaliben and sister-in-law Vilasben Hargobindbhai's wife. Her children Vipin and Vinoda were toddlers, I adored them. Another child, Illa, who is equally sweet, was born later. We then visited Kanti's elder sister, my sister-in-law, Savitaben in Drangdhra. She looked after her younger brother Kanti like a mother, and in fact she mothered the entire family. Her husband, late Kantibhai Sheth was general manager of the first soda ash factory in India, built in Drangdhra. Everyone, including his family, addressed him as 'Bhai'. They had four lovely children; Benaben, Babubhai, Kanubhai and Batukbhai. She made me feel completely at home in their spacious bungalow with its big garden.

It was quite a new feeling to be suddenly embraced and accepted and braided into a wider kinship almost without effort, through the single act of my becoming engaged. And it was a novel experience to be addressed as 'Kaki' and 'Mami' by all these new nephews and nieces. They were kids, and I was not quite an adult myself, so we bonded immediately. It is wonderful to still retain the same relationship with all of them, even though they themselves are now grandparents.

After our return to Jamnagar I started attending school again, kept occupied adjusting to the new curriculum and my new status as an engaged girl. Kanti started writing letters and I responded. We tried to tell each about our aspirations and expectations. I in my own fumbling way tried to cope with my newfound adulthood. My parents were now feeling restless and looking forward to their return to Dar-es-Salaam. And I was more then happy to accompany them. It was pleasant meeting Motiba and Faiba, but for some reason I could not understand, I did not feel at home in Jamnagar.

Chapter 11

Brick by Brick and Step by Step

World War II formally ended on 6 June 1944 - D-Day, with Germany's defeat at Normandy. By then Bapuji was feeling restless and yearning to get back to Dar-es-Salaam. As a result once again we bid farewell to Motiba and Faiba, travelled to Bombay by train and then onward to Tanganyika in the SS Amra. We were travelling second-class, in which families had their own cabins. We were supposed to confine ourselves to our own area, not entering either first or third class. But as seasoned travellers by dhow, my brother Mahen and I were soon sneaking into all sections of the ship. The first class was immaculate, with stately dining halls and a library; it was staffed by uniformed cabin boys who chased us away if they caught us playing there. Third class was very congested. Passengers sat, ate, lie down, be sick and interact in cramped spaces cordoned off with tin trunks and bedrolls. Despite the discomfort the atmosphere was friendly. Collective games like antakshari—sing a song games were played, people sang, played cards, told stories and jokes and made friends. Moreover, we were never chased away!

I passed the two-week journey, watching the waves, daydreaming, responding to the meal gong, and indulging in quantities of potato chips and pooris for breakfast. Amra our steamer reached Dar-es-Salaam too soon! Bapuji opened up his medical store once again and we all picked up the threads of our earlier lives. But things were not quite the same for me. Suddenly I found that since I was now engaged Ba would not allow me to go anywhere, even to school, without being escorted by my brother Mahen. This mandate proved to be quite an irritant for both of us.

Meanwhile my fiancé Kanti a vegetarian had gone to London for further studies. Post-war London was a bleak and shattered city, suffering from all kinds of shortages and power outrages. There was strict rationing of food items and electricity. The severe cold affected his health, especially eyes, so he decided to fly back to Dar-es-Salaam. The journey in a Dakota aircraft from London to Dar itself took him four days. Ultimately he did reach Dar. And one fine day I found him waiting at home when I returned from school; the telegram he had sent from London informing us of his intended arrival reached a couple of days later! I had just received my results of the Form 3 annual exams, in which I had done extremely well, topping the class. The next year would be my final year at school, during which I had to pass the Senior Cambridge exams.

But now it was time to get married. Our wedding took place on 19 May 1948. It was a low key simple ceremony in the small compound of the Hindu Mandal building. Initially we continued to stay with my parents while Kanti looked for employment. Fortunately Bapuji knew Mr. Vellani, the

Senior partner in Vellani & Co. an old and prominent law firm in Dar-es-Salaam. Mr. Vellani was not keeping in good health, and needed a young lawyer to assist him. Kanti started chambering with him. After finishing the mandatory six-month internship he joined the firm as a professional lawyer, with a monthly salary of 600 shillings per month.

It so happened that at the time one of his colleagues, Chotubhai Davda's family, was building a block of four flats with shops on the ground floor. We rented the flat on the top floor at 150 shillings per month, and moved in with our beds, a few chairs and mikekas (mats woven of sisal and coconut fibre), some kitchen utensils and pots and pans borrowed from my parents. We economized as much as possible, and I would remind myself of my father's two favourite sayings: 'Cut your coat in accordance with the cloth' and 'If you want to keep warm, snuggle your feet to suit the length of your blanket'

We bought our supplies from Bhikhabhai Rambhai & Co. shop on the ground floor of our building, paying them at the end of the month. I still have one of their bills, No. 2663 dated 26-1-1964: the bill makes pleasant reading as it gives not only the price list but it is a fascinating reminder of those days gone by!

Cooking oil: 4 Shillings per kg
Almonds: 5 Shillings per 500 Grams
Cashew nuts: 2 Shillings and 50 cents per kg
Peanuts: 1 Shilling and 25 cents per kg
Potatoes: 1 Shilling per kg
Mug, moth, tuver dal and other cereals: 1 Shilling and 50 cents per kg
South African apples, 1 box for 10 Shillings
Condensed milk 3 tins for 5 Shillings and 75 cents

Being frugal, saving and furnishing our rooms bit by bit, we even managed to buy our first car, a Hillman Minx. Our home was always filled with young and aspiring lawyers vociferously discussing cases, politics and all kinds of subjects. We had many friends, and among these Shantaben and N.S. Patel, Maduriben and Chotubhai Dawda, Rehanaben and Nurudin Sadikot, Gulshanben and Nurali Sayani, Avatar Singh and Indiraben became close to our family. We all celebrated Diwali and Eid together. They were all contemporaries who had faced challenges and established distinguished careers as lawyers. I loved and respected Jikaka, who was deaf and dumb but he could understand and communicate freely through lip-reading and mime, with a few words mumbled in between. An excellent cook who prepared fine vegetarian food, he gave me a recipe book written in Gujarati as my wedding present that became a cherished personal possession. I still have it, more then sixty years later. Like most girls my age I was a very inexperienced cook, but was fortunate to have my mother nearby. Under her guidance I picked up the skills quickly and began to enjoy creating meals for family and friends.

My most wonderful moments in that flat opposite the Odeon Cinema were the arrival of my son Atool, born on 6 March 1949 and my daughter Abha, born on 22 July 1951. Married with a lawyer husband, I was just 21 years old by the time both my children were born with the result that I often felt like a novice swimmer struggling hard to negotiate the deep Indian Ocean! We had great support from my parents, brothers, and young sister all the way. And my children thrived and grew up with the family's constant love and care.

Soon we moved in a bigger and spacious flat, in the newly built Chavda Building situated on the Morogoro Road near Gurdwara, Sikh Temple. That area still had the ambiance of a small village with trains passing nearby and many people living in small houses with corrugated iron roofs. Our children Atool and Abha loved to watch and wave at the trains, while sitting near the window on the kitchen table when I was cooking. Our landlord Girdharbhai Chavda's wife Kuru was my school friend. Her young sons Pravin, and Vidu, and my Atool and Abha, learnt together to crawl and play.

Around 1956-57 we moved once again to Ramnik Mahal in Sea View, Ocean Road. Atool and Abha had their primary education in Upanga Primary School near our house. Since then the school and its surrounding area have been developed in an Army Cantonment. Atool finished his Secondary school education from the newly built Azania Secondary School and Abha from Jangwani Girl's School.[1]

Kanti habitually bought several Indian and English magazines regularly every week. I looked forward to them and enjoyed reading them as they opened up new worlds for me. My children quickly picked up the practice of reading, especially since each Saturday my brother Mahen took both of them to the Kanti Printing Press belonging to his friend Amrit Patel that adjoined the old post office. At the press, they bought Beano, Dandy and many other comics and children's books. So come Saturday and Atool and Abha waited eagerly for their Mama my brother. He used to arrive at lunchtime in his red pick-up, and they would be hiding behind their favourite sofa, getting more and more excited as he approached it. Whistling as he looked for them, apparently not knowing where they were hiding. Once discovered, a riot of hugging and shouting erupted, and he would go off with them for the weekend having fun with the whole family. It was one of the best relationships my children have experienced. Even after Mahen got married they continued with the same happy relations with his young bride. Very soon new additions of nephews and nieces joined in the family.

Now the focus was on studies, sports, Universities and Awards. And we all remained preoccupied facing these new challenges. Time just flew.

Chapter 12

A Brief Glance over Uganda

A different sequence of events was unfolding right across our border in Uganda. My brother-in-law Hargovindbhai-Motabhai to us, had migrated to Uganda from India in 1936 when he was about 25 years old, settling in Jinja where he opened a photography studio and bought a sugarcane farm near the Kakira sugar factory. Similar to Tanzania, Uganda is endowed with fertile land and harvests are usually good. This fact enabled Motabhai to simultaneously manage both farm and studio.

Facing the spectacular Ripon Falls, Jinja at that time was a small town on the shores of Lake Victoria near the source of Great River Nile. This was our favourite picnic spot whenever we visited Jinja. The vistas were indescribable, simply breathtaking. When the Owen Falls dam was built there in 1954 to supply Jinja and adjoining areas with a continuous supply of water and electricity, Ripon Falls was submerged. With it went the gorgeous roaring cascades of water, with thousands of leaping fish and fishermen in their small boats.

Jinja had been established by the British in 1907, and according to accounts of early travellers some Indian traders began arriving there in 1910. Prominent pioneers among this first group had migrated from India to East Africa by dhow when they were young teenagers: Meghji Pethraj Shah, Muljibhai Madhvani at the age of fourteen and Nanjibhai K. Mehta when barely thirteen years old. After gaining some experience by working with earlier settlers they opened their own dukas. Bit by bit they progressed, and slowly opened up the whole area by starting large-scale farming and big and small industries, turning sleepy Jinja into a commercial hub. In the process they became renowned businessmen, entrepreneurs, industrialists and philanthropists.

Motabhai and Bhabhi had spent more than fifty years in Jinja, raising three children, making lifelong friends. My widowed mother-in-law Ba had also joined the family there in 1948. On 4 August 1972, the brutal and volatile dictator Idi Amin 'Dada' suddenly expelled all Asians from Uganda. His action affected us all in East Africa in one way or the other, as we all had family members and friends spread out in Tanganyika, Kenya and Uganda. To this extent, as an aftermath of this upheaval in Uganda people in East Africa as a whole experienced material losses and emotional upheaval.

It so happened that on that particular date—4 August 1972 Vinodaben, our niece from Jinja, had arrived by early morning flight from Kampala for a short holiday in Dar-es-Salaam for the first time. We went to receive her and were surprised to see that she was having some problems with the immigration formalities and was not permitted to leave the airport terminus with the other passengers. Upon inquiring we were told of Idi Amin's order expelling the Asians from Uganda. We were also told that the airport officials were waiting for instructions from the Ministry of Foreign Affairs with regard to whether passengers from Uganda sould be allowed to enter the country or not. We went from desk to desk explaining that Vinodaben was a visitor who can leave the country after a day or two with us. The immigration officials replied that she had to leave by the same flight, back to Kampala because at the moment all Ugandan Asians were persona non grata in Tanzania. This decision was taken in order to prevent future diplomatic wrangles. They added that in fact it was advisable to leave in the hope that some solution to the Asian 'problem' might be worked out in Uganda.

At that time the Dar-es-Salaam airport restaurant was closed for renovation, and no food or drink was available for people in transit. After making sure that no flights back to Kampala were available immediately we Left an anxious Vinodaben in the terminal and rushed home. I quickly mustered up some snacks and tea to take to her and we rushed back to the airport. Due to our appeals and frantic efforts to convince the authorities we were given one concession, Vinodaben was allowed to leave on the last flight going out to Uganda; to a country she could no longer call home. Not sure what she would face, she handed me her pouch containing her jewellery for safekeeping. I returned her purse when we visited her in London later on.

This was not the end of her story. She describes the rest of her journey in one of her mails. She writes "Here is the account of my feted journey to Dar-es-Salaam. In May 1972 Suresh having his work permit expired in Uganda had left the country to settle down in the UK and I was to follow him after he had settled down with a job and a place to stay. In August 1972 my friend and neighbour Kanta Jani and I decided to visit you and Kaka in Dar-es-Salaam via Nairobi—my very first holiday ever. We made a coach journey from Kampala to Nairobi without any incident. We met Kanta's sister and family in Nairobi and spent a couple of days with them touring the big city. We then took a flight to meet you and Kaka and also enjoying my very first experience of travelling by Air, completely unaware that, after we had left Uganda, President Idi Amin had announced his plan to expel all British Asians from the country within 90 days. When we landed in Dar-es-Salaam, there was a big delay at the immigration. To my surprise my friend was allowed in the country as she had Ugandan Passport but I was not permitted having a British passport. They thought that if they let me enter the country I would never leave again as I was a British Asian from Uganda. No amount of pleading will convey to them that I was on a short visit to the country to see my family. They said I had to go back to Nairobi where I had boarded the flight from. I was very disappointed and nervous. Thanks to your and Kaka's efforts they let me stay with you till the last flight of the day. It gave me some relief and breathing time to reflect. I was glad to spend some time with you and Kaka but I found it very upsetting that I couldn't come home with you. I consoled myself that every country has their laws and they have to be obeyed. I took the last flight back to Nairobi not knowing what to expect in Kenya. But my nightmare was beginning once again with more vengeance. My friend had decided to come back with me as well. At Nairobi Airport the Immigration people took my passport away from me and said they will return it in the morning before I boarded the flight back to Uganda. We spent the night at Nairobi Airport. The next morning they told me that they had misplaced my Passport and I will have to wait until they locate it. I inquired about my luggage, and they said that it was put on a flight to Germany. It took them nearly two days to find my Passport and I was put on the first available flight back to Uganda minus the luggage. Now I was very nervous in case the same ordeal was repeated and I was not allowed back in the country. At the Kampala Airport there was no problem as I was a teacher and I was allowed to disembark at the Entebbe Airport. The professionals like Doctors, Teachers etc were exempt from the 90 day notice. All over Uganda the situation was getting worse because of big army presence and a lot of assaults on the innocents were going on. Jinja were I was staying with my parents was no exception. Ba and Papa thought it was not safe for me to stay there any longer so they booked me on a flight to UK. My ordeal was not yet over. At the Entebbe Airport I was searched at gun point and they took all my paperwork and all my jewellery away. I was not allowed to take any money out of the country either. The tragic and most frightening part was that I lost all my certificates and all my official papers. I was very nervous as I boarded the flight at midnight and thought that at last it was going to be a new beginning, but that was not to be! The plane started to circle on the Runaway and all of a sudden there was a big explosion. We all thought that was the end but they said it was the tyre that has burst. All the passengers were asked to get down and go back to the terminal and wait for further instructions. They would not put us on any other plane. We had to wait at the Airport till they got the replacement tyre from some country. We were not allowed to go back home either. It took them two days while lots of other planes were leaving with British Asians. It was like a never ending horrible dream. I was feeling extremely scarred as time passed, and Ba and Papa were also equally worried. At last we boarded the plane and flew to the safety of cloudy, cold, damp, dark, depressing and miserable UNITED KINGDOM in search of a new life.

I have given a lot more information then intended, but writing just about my visit to Dar-es-Salaam seemed incomplete as all these happened in such a short period during the same trip. It had robbed me of my confidence and my country.

This happened over forty years ago but I still remember it vividly. I do not think that I will ever forget it!"

Ultimately before the ninety days notice expired, Motabhai and his family including my mother-in-law who was 95 years old at the time, also left Uganda with 80,000 other Asians, and settled down in Britain. Late Motabhai and Bhabhi used to talk often about the kindness and care given to them by the British people when they arrived in UK. Especially he used to remember fondly that even close family members would not have been able to look after Ba so lovingly.

All these years apart from a visit to Dar-es-Salaam my mother-in-law, Ba had stayed with Bhabhi and Motabhai. Her life was itself a series of migrations. Born in Sakhpur in 1877, she followed her husband to Rajkot at a young age. After his death she travelled to join Motabhai's family in Uganda around 1948, and following the Amin diktat in 1972 migrated with the family to UK, where she died peacefully in her sleep in 1981 at the age of 104 in RedBridge-Ilford. Hers was an eventful journey by any standards. Vinodaben recently retired after working all these years with Kodak LMT. Vipinbhai a Banker, who was Departmental Manager in Barclays Bank Kampala, opened his own little corner shop in Letchworth, prospered and opened Stores in London. He is now retired. Illaben qualified as a Nurse initially, continued her education in Banking and Insurance while earning and raising a family and now is holding a senior position in Insurance Company. They all own their own properties and life goes on. In retrospect, those enterprising Ugandan Asians expelled by Idi Amin and forced to build new lives for themselves in Europe and the West, thank the despot Idi Amin for creating the crisis which allowed them to settle down and prosper through fresh beginnings in the developed world.

After the Ugandan Asian communities were arbitrarily expelled, their farms, houses, businesses and industries were randomly appropriated, mismanaged and ruined beyond salvation. Economic and infrastructural disaster apart, under the absurd and bloody rule of Idi Amin his henchmen carried out systematic genocide, butchering anyone he considered an enemy or a threat. It is alleged that, so many victims of government atrocities were dumped in Lake Victoria that drifting corpses regularly blocked intake channels at the Owen Falls hydroelectric dam. Looting, raping, gory killings at will and dumping the dead bodies in rivers, lakes and by the road side to rot was the order of the day, his password! Drunk on perverted fantasies of power he attempted to annex the Kagera province of Tanzania. This led to Uganda-Tanzania war that Amin lost, leading to the fall of his regime in 1979. He fled for political asylum first to Libya, and then to Saudi Arabia where he died in 2003.

Grand father Laxmichand Becher Jhaveri

Sitting; Atool, Abha, Urmila, Ba, Vilas Ben,
Illlaben, Vipin Bhai,
Standing; Kanti Jhaveri, Vinodaben, Niru,
Hargovindbhai Jhaveri

Gandhi Family; Mahen, Niru, Urmila,
Bapuji, Abha with Ba, Jhaveri
Standing Anant with Atool

Ba, Faiba, Motiba

Mahen with Abha and Atool

Mahen
Atool, Tarala, Aruna, Anant, Niru-Abha
At the old Customs House JETTY.

Niruben and Dr. Navin Vibhaker at their
wedding reception.
Standing Kanti Jhaveri, Baa, Urmila, Lilam
Mami, Ratu Mama & Babuji.

Abha.

Atool.

Atool and Urmila when he was
leaving for London

Ba, Bapuji, Abha, Jhaveri, Urmila, when Abha
was leaving for London

Chandrika and Atool

Nitan-Abha.

Nitan, Abha, Atool, Chandrika

Rohaan, Ratna, Roohi, Meera.

Ratna, Meera, Roohi.

Rohaan, Ratna, Meera, Roohi

Jhaveri and Urmila

Picnic in Bagamoyo, with family and friends.

Part II

Chapter 13

Travel back in Time Divisions

I grew up in Dar-es-Salaam in Tanganyika. At that time I had never realized that it was an environment in which we were living in small racially bound compartments. Most of all, our lives were controlled by extremely stringent rules imposed by the British Colonial government. In Tanganyika, they were not as cruel as the Germans but they ruled with an iron hand nevertheless. Under their regime the Europeans, Asians and Africans were systematically isolated in three grades. The Europeans occupied the highest position, the African were in the lowest rung, and Asians occupied the middle buffer zone. Moreover there was no social interaction whatsoever between these communities. As if this was not enough, many other extra boundaries were self imposed and jealously guarded. There were Hindus and Muslims, Goans, Ceylonese and Parsees; amongst the Hindus there were casts and sub casts like Patel, Lohanas, Wanias and so on, and there were Ismailis, Ishnasheris, Sunni, Shia and other sub casts amongst the Muslims. Intercast and inter community relations remained cordial but the rivalries and misunderstandings between the Hindus and Muslims flared up from time to time. People took it all in their stride and continued to lead their life automatically bound by their own self imposed conventions as well as the restrictions set by the Colonial government.

As time went this realization prompted me to look at the history of Tanganyika especially during the colonial rule under which I grew up. Not with the idea of flogging a dead horse but by way of introspection, at least to verify the facts about our collective lives and understand our past as it happened.

To my surprise I found several research papers and books looking at the subject, confirm that housing, medical facilities, schools, general education, employment, entertainment in fact all facets of our life in Tanganyika were governed by the colonial government through manipulative and strictly racist policy.

Professor Ned Bertz, a distinguished Scholar and our very good friend in one of his well researched Dissertation, details this aspect of our historical and social background during the pre and post independence era in Tanganyika. For me, his report has proved to be an indispensable source of information and official records in writing this chapter.

As stated above, all facets of our life in Tanganyika were systematically manipulated and governed by the colonial administration's racist policies. People tended to take this embedded injustice for granted as a fact of life, reflexively and mechanically functioning within it, and so preoccupied with daily survival that they rarely thought through its long-term implications. As scholar Susan Geiger had pointed out in the mid-1950s, 'racial segregation and discrimination were firmly entrenched throughout Tanganyika and in Dar-es-Salaam. In particular, from the earliest days of colonial rule the European, East Asians and African populations were divided hierarchically in all spheres of life: residential areas were racially exclusive; schools and hospitals were separate and types and grades of employment were racially categorized.'

I remember as a child the only Europeans whom I saw from a distance were those who came to my father's medical store for medicines, or those who were going about performing their duties; they were always the boss. The Africans also came to the shop to buy the medicine or just ask for advice. However they were more visible as clerks, farmers, small shop keepers, cleaners, labourers and Askaris, policemen. And the Indians were fellow shopkeepers, clerks, teachers, doctors, neighbours and others.

An obvious example of this division was the European Swimming Club in Dar-es-Salaam near the ferry that did not admit people of other races. Indians and Africans were not even allowed to cross the demarcated line on the beach that absurdly extended out into the sea and was a Whites-only preserve where Europeans swam. All cleaning was to be finished by the African cleaners before the club's opening time. And so, in the late 1940s or early 1950s, Bapuji and some of his enterprising friends decided to raise funds to build an inclusive swimming club. They successfully established the Dar-es-Salaam Swimming Club, a modest building built right next to the European Swimming Club and the Hela Tatu Ferry that took farmers and picnickers like us to Kigamboni on the opposite side of the creek.

Bapuji loved swimming. He traversed the creek every morning from the newly built Dar-es-Salaam swimming club, and taught my son Atool to swim on this stretch of waves rolling in from the Indian Ocean. Even now old-timers swim with ease across the creek early in the morning, and if a newcomer manages the feat, tradition demands that he treat all the members of the club to hot jalebis and ganthia, sambharo and masala chai on Sunday morning. The water was pristine and the shoreline near the harbour entrance was beautiful; we often waved and wished 'Karibu and Kwaheri' 'Welcome and Bon Voyage', to friends and relatives either travelling for further education to UK or coming in from and sailing to India on those mysterious steamships. The Club, created in order to defy racial segregation, continues to be a lively place. And after more then half a century families still gather in the evenings to socialize and walk on the beach. Ironically, there is now no sign of the European Swimming Club. In its place stands a huge fish market built by a Japanese firm. It teems with fishermen and women selling all kinds of catch, fish large and small, dry and wet, cooked and row, few octopuses and a fascinating variety of seashells harvested from distant shores. But due to poor sanitation that area is reeking and filthy, dangerously polluting the entire harbour environment that once was pristine, picturesque and enticing.

The phenomenon of colonization and racial segregation by the British Government had started taking roots when after the First World War, the League of Nations decided to place East African countries, Kenya, Uganda and Tanganyika under the British rule through the Peace Treaty of 1919. Thus the British Government took over their mandate in 1922. From then on their system of governance was designed exclusively to fortify their rule over East Africa and Africans for ever by any means.

Strict segregation was enforced through out the urban area of Dar-es-Salaam, and indeed throughout the country.

For instance Dar-es-Salaam was divided into three zones. The most fertile land and the best locations were reserved for Europeans only. Their fine houses, schools, playing fields and hospitals were built within these zones, and non-Europeans could not live here. Nor could they move freely through these areas.

The Indian section where we lived was ever growing and developing into another reserved area. It was the main commercial zone where traders, artisans and government employees lived and run their shops and businesses in well-planned double-storey buildings, on lanes and by-lanes and at least a smattering of roads. Often these houses were built side by side with the small squalid tin-roofed houses where water for drinking was drawn from wells and kerosene lanterns provided light. Some of my childhood friends lived in such dwellings.

In contrast the housing facilities for the Africans which included Tanganyikans of all tribes was hopelessly neglected and over crowded. Time was when they lived mainly on the periphery of the towns and settlements, and even in a city like Dar-es-Salaam, these areas lacked the most basic facilities like sanitation, piped water, street lights even minimal transportation system or any development programs what so ever. The Arabs lived in the area reserved for the Africans but in a better locality within this area. They retained their separate identity. This section of Dar-es-Salaam was known as Native Town or Kariakoo.

The original people of Tanganyika were referred to generally as Africans. A few of them were employed in the government offices in junior positions but mostly they worked as domestic help in Europeans as well as Indian homes, as sweepers and cleaners, and doing heavy work carrying the loads and so on. Many of them were small farmers, who were required to carry an identification pass known as kipande. This system was used to control and restrict the movement of Africans throughout the country. The indignity of the situation was that they had to pay the 'tax' for this kipande, and if they were caught without this identity card they were hunted down, caught like criminals and conscripted for hard labour. In addition their housing facilities were congested and neglected. Those who could afford to do so would build four to six rooms with a common courtyard keep one or two rooms for personal / family use and rent out the others. For many people this is still a preferred means of earning monthly income.

At the same time it is interesting to note that, the Indian zone was a mixed area of various communities. People from the subcontinent historically settled in Tanganyika and those who had migrated here prior to Partition were generically and collectively referred to as 'Indians.' These included Hindus, Muslims, Sikh, Parses, Christians and Buddhists and they lived peacefully side by side. After India Pakistan divide in 1947, enmities and rivalries began to fissure the existent harmony between Hindus and Muslims; and when Ceylon and Burma emerged as independent nations the term 'Indian' became more specific. Thus all sub continental immigrants to Tanganyika then fell into a new category; 'Asiatic or 'Asian.' This 'Asian' section continued to develop as the main commercial zone for many years.

During those days all medical facilities were also segregated and patients were treated in accordance with the colour of their skin. The European hospital was built by the Germans on a strategic point facing the sea. Managed exclusively by European doctors and nursing staff it was reserved for whites only. Indian and African nurses and staff were restricted to low-level and cleaning jobs. John Hatch, a member of the British Labour Party who visited Tanganyika in 1955, had commented, "When I was told that the first African District Officer has been refused admission to a European hospital after a car accident I realized that racial discrimination has not by any means entirely been destroyed in this country." [1]

In 1949, under the British this hospital initiated a policy of token admittance of patients of other races, a slight improvement on the stark segregation in other establishments. Our son Atool and daughter Abha were born in the European hospital in 1949 and 1951 respectively. For medical reasons I had to be hospitalized for some time after the deliveries, and I found the British nurses very compassionate and dedicated despite the colour bar that was going on in the hospital. My experience in the hospital confirmed my faith in the inherent goodness of human beings. Both my children were born early in the morning, and I remember resting on my bed and feeling absolutely fulfilled and content as I watched the sun rise over the Indian Ocean. After the Independence the hospital was expanded and converted into Ocean Road Referral Hospital; and since then it has been declared a national heritage building.

Indians in Dar-es-Salaam used their own community clinics and hospitals within racially allotted areas, and Africans used the Sewa Hajji Hospital built by the well-known philanthropist and pioneer trader in East Africa Shivjibhai Haji Paro, popularly known as Sewa Hajji. It was said that he made his money from many things including selling armaments and guns.

He was Born in 1851 in India and died at an early age of 46 in 1897. He was one of the early Khoja settlers who immortalised their names in East Africa within a short time, by contributing large sums of money for the construction of local hospitals in Zanzibar, Dar-es-Salaam, Tanga and Bagamoyo. These facilities were used primarily by Africans and Indians. [2]

Some excellent German doctors worked in Sewa Hajji, but here too there was discrimination between the Africans and Indians. They were allocated separate timings and clinics for check ups and medical dispensation. Sewa Hajji Hospital now has been converted into the huge Muhimbili hospital complex.

In addition several white missionary groups had built clinics and small but well-maintained hospitals in different parts of the country to serve much needed medical treatment mainly for the Africans, where patients of other races also received medical treatment with equal care and love. In many rural areas these centers were the only available medical services for people in distress.

Another means of racial discrimination by the colonial regime was to control and manage cinema, the chief mode of public entertainment, through a completely segregationist Censorship Board. We were occasionally taken to the cinema as a treat by our father, Bapuji, who was very passionate moviegoer and frequenter of all the cinema houses in Dar-es-Salaam as they came into being one by one. The Empire Cinema was the first cinema house built in Dar in late 1929 by Hassanali Adamali Jariwalla. That was before I was born. By the middle of 1930s the show at the Empire Cinema was being run by Babubhai Vadgama.

The ticket price was 1 Shilling for the front rows and 1 and 50 cents for seats further back. There was even a Zanana show one afternoon a week only for women and children. I loved the little Alice in Wonderland, and the Wizard of Oz, Tarzan films and thrilling Bombay blockbusters such as Hunterwali and Toofan Mail starring Fearless Nadia in all kinds of fantastic stunt filled movies. I was about five-six years old and used to get very excited and scream with all the other kids, when Nadia jumped up the top of the train tops and land on her white horse whip in hand galloping along with the train. She battled for every good cause with all types of criminals, triumphed against any odds and in the end was always reunited with her Prince Charming!

Each show began with a newsreel often showing British Royalty. This was followed by Tom and Jerry cartoons and then the main feature. At the end of the show it was mandatory for the audience to stand while the British national anthem was played, and a picture of the Royalty was projected. First it was the King George the Fifth when he was alive, and after him they showed young Queen Elizabeth sitting side saddle on her white horse. She looked regal and remote as well!

It was apparent to us even as children, that there was no question of Europeans, Asians and Africans being a joint audience in cinemas. Occasionally, if Indians and Arabs were allowed to view a particular show, Africans would not be permitted to attend that showing. Professor Ned Bertz has noted that, 'this brazen policy of discrimination resulted in protests by educated Africans, and way back in the 1930s a delegation from the newly formed African Association met the authorities to demand equal access to films shows open to other races.'

In 1931, the new Provincial Commissioner acknowledged that existing cinema policy "gives rise to a feeling of resentment among educated Africans at a regulation which they consider to be clearly discriminatory in nature. In practical terms it meant that Africans are inferior persons in comparison with others, and should not be allowed to watch movies along with them" [3] The administration on their part not only admitted this anomaly but on the contrary, continued with racial manipulations and also looked at other social and economic instruments such as regulating the price of admission, to restrict access of Africans and Asians to cinema halls. [4]

One outcome of this segregation was the Amana cinema, built in the late 1940s in Dar-es-Salaam's Kariakoo area primarily for African audiences. It was inaugurated by the Governor, Sir Edward Twining, with much fanfare; the price of admission was deliberately kept low one-third of that charged at the very popular Empire, Avalon and Empress cinemas where English and Hindi movies were regularly screened for non-Africans.

The most ruthless application of segregationist logic was practised in the area of education, with discriminatory policies systematically implemented in order to thwart the progress and further the subjugation of both Africans and Indians. As explained by scholar Ned Bertz, 'The first world war necessitated the closure of all schools in the war zones. The teachers in these schools were dispersed and the German missionaries were expelled.'

By now the British Government had taken over the mandate of East African countries from the vanquished Germans. And by 1920 they had already appointed a Director of Education. Their discriminatory approach is exemplified in this 1925 comment by the Director of Agriculture, who was of the opinion that a mere five percent of African children were "sufficiently intelligent to profit from academic instructions." [5] Moreover, many colonial officers actually believed that that Africans were incapable of handling professional jobs.

This distorted rationale was constantly being put forward in different forms by all government agencies. In

1925 Britain disseminated a continent-wide memorandum on 'Education Policy in British Tropical Africa', and a first education conference was organized in Dar-es-Salaam the same year. The conference adopted the policy of Education for Adaption. Through this elaborate framework the Colonial Government connived to limit the scope of the education and progress of the Africans by any means. They planned; "for the African students providing only basic reading, writing and accounting skills in support of the indirect rule system, and the transfer of vocational agriculture skills to develop only subsistence peasant agriculture . . ." In addition in 1927 an Education Ordinance was passed, stipulating among other things that the colonial authorities would establish separate committees on education for each of the three racial groups to determine curricula and staff requirements, and construction and maintenance of school building would be done from the individual budget for each group. By this means the British administration further separated the races in schools and imparted a different system of education to each group. [6]

The problem of segregation was also complicated by intra-group tensions. To illustrate, the Government Indian Central School, where I studied in early 1940s was founded in 1920 as Lokmanya Tilak School. It was open to children of all Indian communities. According to Professor Ned Bertz, the 1927 Education Ordinance concretized the tripartite racial education, and extended grants-in-aid to qualified Indian schools like the Ismaily ventures; some of these schools had already received German and British funding. However, at this stage, it was British colonial policy to dispense an educational grant-in-aid to only one Indian school in a given town, and in Dar-es-Salaam the grant went to pan communal Lokmanya Tilak School. Unfortunately this triggered the old rivalries and disagreements among the leaders of the two main communities; it displeased both the local Ismailis, who voluntarily donated significant funds to operate their own schools, as well as the Aga Khan, who himself contributed about half of the recurrent budget of the Lokmanya Tilak School. Eventually the school was taken over by the government and re-established in 1929 as the Government Indian Central School. [7]

To consolidate and compound the matter further the British used their very famous, divide and rule policy amongst Africans and Asians. Colonial unease with regard to the possibility of empowering both Africans and Indians through education, as well as other anxieties about local schooling systems, can be seen in this 1925 memorandum by Mr. Rivers-Smith, Director for Education, to Chief Secretary of Tanganyika: "There is the political aspect which in all schemes of education should be kept constantly in view. With the knowledge of political development in India during the last few years, we cannot afford to ignore the possibility of an unfortunate African political repercussion in future years as a result of the development of a closer liaison between the two races which might be the result of co-education. At present we have a healthy rivalry and a growing race consciousness amongst the Africans and a certain feeling of resentment that the Asiatic get so many of 'plums'. In my opinion co-education might conceivably weaken this healthy and natural rivalry and eventually lead to making common cause for political ends. [8]

Again in 1929 while responding to a suggestion by some educators, to send qualified African students to study at a technical college in Uganda, an institution which eventually would develop into the famous Makrere University, Tanganyika's Assistant Director of Education, cautiously noted that, "Mr. Rivers-Smith, however, is of the opinion that there is an element of danger of sending them to Kampala where he understands the type of political thought prevailing amongst Africans tends to be of somewhat extremist nature, and he wishes to make certain that the men would return schoolmasters and not versatile political agitators, before considering further the details of this proposal".[9]

By 1951 Uganda's Makerere University had become an example in East Africa of a progressive institution open to students of all races. But in Tanganyika, despite the long-standing demands for a strong academic curriculum and integrated education all branches of the colonial administration continued to block and delay any steps towards implementation of these demands, fearing that an educated populace would prove difficult to control.

These ongoing manoeuvres to control the development of a major section of society continued without respite through all branches of the administration. Ironically, it was the very denial of such educational opportunities to Africans that catalyzed the momentum of nationalism in Tanganyika. [10]

Nature has a way of bringing a change and Destiny often deals a sharp hand to those who are blindly bent on their own selfish motives. This is exactly what happened when a young man who was born in a grass mud hut, Julius Kambarage Nyerere the central figure in the national movement challenged the Colonial Government and started the Independence struggle in Tanganyika.

He was one of 26 children of Nyerere Burito, Chief of Zanaki WA Butiyama; Zanaki tribe of Butiyama. The Chief had married twenty two wives. Julius Nyerere was born on 13-April-1922 to the Chief's fifth wife Christina

Mgaya WA Nyang'ombe. After finishing secondary school education, Nyerere received a scholarship from the Colonial Government for further studies and qualified as a teacher from Makerere University. On returning home, he taught for three years in Tabora as required. He then received second scholarship and joined the University of Edinburgh; the first Tanganyikan to pursue higher education in a British university. After returning from Edinburgh he took up a teaching post in Dar-es-salaam, but the call of nationalism was too strong for him to resist. He became a politically active and was elected President of the Tanganyika African Association - TAA. Later its name was changed to Tanganyika African National Union, TANU. The organization's main objective was to achieve Independence for Tanganyika; and Nyerere soon initiated a nationwide membership drive to strengthen TANU's influence. This came to the notice of the colonial authority who threatened to dismiss him from his teaching post if he continued with his activities. For him now there was no going back. Boldly Nyerere resigned from government service and from then on devoted all his time and energy to creating political awareness and continued fighting for people's rights.

Education was naturally one of Nyerere's central interests, and he challenged the administration's policy of allocating educational funds to Tanganyika's three main racial groups on equal basis, i.e. providing the same amount of financial support to Europeans, Asians and Africans, ignoring the huge disparity in the number of students belonging to each group. Nyerere remarked with caustic ire in 1955:

"Disparity of educational expenditure per head of the population in each racial group is always there . . . [But] this particular disparity is aggravated to the point of absurdity . . . Even if the whole population had accepted the proposition . . . that quality makes members of the minority groups deserve more money per head for their children's education, one would at least have expected the authorities concerned to have considered NEED. For lack of education is one thing in which the African can claim undisputed superiority over the other racial groups." [*11*] Nyerere also protested vehemently against the administration's reluctance to start coeducation in schools as repeatedly recommended by visiting U.N. delegations in 1948, 1951 and 1955.

In spite of all the protests, criticism, recommendations and appeals by national and international institutions and individuals, the Colonial government continued unabated to pursue its racist policy and became more repressive. Similar to Kenya and SA, they used all kinds of intimidation in order to retain their tight hold on the country. Their word was the absolute law and no other considerations applied. The future looked bleak as the arguments and protests against the injustice and racial discrimination continued with more vigour and determination. Ultimately it resulted in full fledged struggle for independence.

In conclusion, these few deliberately selected, incidents and salient items of official correspondence regarding our day to day life do tell its own story. Yet, it can never take away the charm of the yester years; the whole life time happily spent with high hopes for the future!

Chapter 14

Pre-Independence

The 1950s and 60s were volatile years in East Africa. The British colonial administration was still reeling from the repercussions of its forced departure from India in 1947 after a final atrocious political spasm: the genocide bloodbath of Partition and now in Kenya they were embroiled in the violent Mau Mau uprising which was becoming more gruesome day by the day. It is well documented fact that, as the Mau Mau uprising progressed the response of the Colonial Government became so violent and unjust that the Mau Mau uprising is considered the bloodiest uprising against the British in the whole of Africa.

Its roots were planted more then a century ago soon after the First World War (1-July-1895) when Kenya was proclaimed as a British Protectorate. Its status was changed again to being a British Colony soon after the Second World War in 1920. Similar to South Africa, the British Government's primary interest in Kenya also was to acquire by force the richest agricultural land with the best climate and hand it over to Europeans.

They thus accumulated about 7,000,000 acres 928,000km of most fertile hilly regions of the Rift Valley Providence by force, and reserved it exclusively for white farmers. It was later known as White Highlands. In the process they arrested, tortured and massacred thousands of the original indigenous land owners. This onslaught on innocent tribals led even Churchill, to express concern about how it would look if word got out: he said "It looks like butchery. Surely it cannot be necessary to go on killing these defenceless people on such an enormous scale."

Apart from the land the white farmers also needed cheap labour and so the government of the day in Kenya introduced measures that compelled the tribal's to submit to wage labour. They further established the Reserves for each ethnic group, preventing the natives from growing cash crops and passed Hut and Poll Tax, The Masters and Servants Ordinance 1906, and an identification pass known as Kipande in 1918.

Through all these and several other repressive measures they converted the former indigenous land owners in a big army of cheap farm labourers and so called squatters in their own land. By early 1920s, despite the presence of 100,000 squatters and tens of thousands more wage earners there was still not enough labour to satisfy the white settlers need. So the Colonial government introduced The Ordinance of 1939 finally eliminating squatters remaining rights. This atrocious law permitted settlers to demand 270 days free labour from squatters who were actually the original owners of the land! The situation for these unfortunate natives deteriorated rapidly. Not only they were deprived of their land, made to work under harsh conditions without pay, they were being flogged and even killed for any odd reason.

Finally the Kenyans, lead by the members of the Kikuyu tribe said enough was enough. They rebelled openly and took up gorilla warfare against the Colonial government in 1952.

The British immediately declared a state of emergency in October 1952 and began moving army reinforcements and unleashed a regime of terror in country. The emergency lasted unto 1960. According to Wikipedia encyclopaedia; just 32 white settlers were killed in the eight years of emergency. It also cites the following report by The Kenya Human Rights Commission which says that 90,000 Kenyans were executed, tortured or maimed during the crackdown, and 160,000 were detained in appalling conditions. [1]

This more then a centaury old history, of greed, looting, shootings and Mau Mau revolt is impossible to describe in a short chapter, but this was the environment all over East Africa. Tanganyika was also passing through similar situation as it was facing the same Colonial system and people were now fretting to break free from their old shackles. Fortunately, compared to the British Government's horrific record in Kenya, Tanganyika's transition to nationhood was relatively peaceful, though not without danger and uncertainty.

To start with, similar to Kenya in Tanganyika also, commodity exports and all foreign trade were state-controlled, and most rural people survived against the odds on subsistence agriculture. The farmers were not allowed to cultivate any cash crops. And all aspects of farming, type of crop and planting, harvesting schedules, ownership and breeding of livestock, and even where the farmer can built his hut, were decided by the bureaucracy headed by Regional and

District Commissioners. Media, entertainment, education and medical facilities were also entirely state-administered. Tanganyikans were being pushed systematically by the government through ordinances and declarations into tight compartments and corners, with only specified roles to play as colonial subjects. In addition, to consolidate their hold on the people, tribalism in Tanganyika was actively nurtured by the colonial government; first as inherent to their elitist divide-and-rule policy. And second, as a weapon to terrorize people into submission through granting special powers to individual chiefs.

In this repressive environment TANU, Tanganyika African National Union was officially founded as a political party in Dar-es-Salaam on 7 July 1955, with a core membership of about 17 members. Julius Kambarage Nyerere was endorsed as party President. [2]

Right from TANU's inception Mwalimu was the guiding light for his people. He started mass mobilization of members, by actively taking into confidence the chiefs, elders and ordinary people in the street. He visited remotest part of the country at personal risk, persuading people to support TANU and explaining to community leaders the importance of being united in a struggle against an unjust colonial government which denied them, security and basic human rights. Mwalimu was subject to scrutiny all the time and the government monitored his every move with mistrust. He had to continually push through people's fear and resistance, because even the merest suspicion of political interest or involvement could result in the government ordering that a person be dismissed from his job at the very least, with dire threats of further punishment. However, since most women worked from their homes they were self-employed and consequently they were able to associate with TANU party unnoticed by the government. Quite soon they began to play an important role in party-building through quiet word-of-mouth mobilization, recruiting and registering new members, holding and hiding men's membership cards, carrying messages and helping to organize meetings throughout the country.

Mwalimu himself was a prolific writer from his student days in Makerere and Edinburg, and used his pen effectively to protest against the government's oppressive and discriminatory practices. He found a loyal and passionate supporter in Randhir Thaker, one of our neighbours in Dar-es-Salaam, who on 15 of April 1959 launched a daily newspaper in Swahili language called Ngurumo meaning 'The Roar'. The newspaper's aim was to reach and mobilise the masses, and explain to them TANU's fight for independence in the language which they understood. Randhir was born in Dar-es-Salaam where he finished his secondary school education. He went to India and after graduating as a science graduate Randhir had joined the police training academy in Nasik. It was considered one of the toughest training establishments in India; he was awarded the Sword of Honour for his accomplishments there and remained very active in the Indian freedom struggle before coming to Tanganyika to join his family. With this fire burning in his heart, it was natural that after a chance meeting with Mwalimu, Randhir plunged into the Independence movement in Tanganyika. He became Mwalimu's close friend and comrade, and Ngurumo became a voice for TANU. Randhir and his younger brother Surendra Thaker, who was his Senior Editor, worked 16 hours a day in order to bring out the newspaper and despite government harassment and financial difficulties Ngurumo was very successful. It was deliberately priced at 10 cents only, to be affordable for every social class. TANU party leadership started to subsidise Ngurumo. As time passed by, Ngurumo became the daily with the broadest newspaper distribution throughout Tanganyika in the early 1970s, when its circulation reached 40,000

Tragically, Randhir died young, shot by a neighbour after some petty argument. His death was a great personal shock to all of us, particularly Mwalimu. TANU was now entering a very important phase in its history. Mwalimu continued to focus all his energies to achieve full Independence for Tanganyika. At that time, in spite of the strong divide that existed between the Hindu and Muslim communities due to India Pakistan conflict the Asian Association which had a mixed membership, came forward and gave Mwalimu wholehearted support throughout the freedom struggle.

I remember Association meetings were held late into the night at our house, and Mwalimu would often join the members in their attempt to work out feasible strategies to counter the colonial government's delaying tactics. Occasionally he would be accompanied by Mzee John Rupia, Bhoke Munanka, Rashidi Kawawa and others. I usually prepared a variety of snacks for the meeting and then remained in the adjoining room, trying to read but they were discussing important matters which would affect all our lives, and it was impossible for me not to listen to what was being said. Consequently I had the benefit of close knowledge of these urgent political issues, and a strong sense of the risk involved. Occasionally, some of our acquaintances warned us that we were playing with fire and would get into serious trouble with the Colonial government. Occasionally, to show his displeasure at these meetings our landlord would have the parking space in the garden blocked so that cars could not be parked inside the garden.

During all their deliberations, D.K. Patel, Habibbhai Jamal-Amir Jamaal's father, A.A. Adamji, Diwan Singh, M.A. Khimji, and Tara Singh, were respected as the wise old men of the group and members took their advice seriously. K.L. Jhaveri adds in his book, 'Marching with Nyerere' that Habibbhai Jamal was also a member of the Managing Committee of the Asian Association and became a political bridge in uniting various Asian communities in order to create Tanganyikan Nationhood. Today while reading the files preserved by him, I come across the following documented information about the Association.

"In 1950 leaders of the Dar-es-Salaam Indian Association, after very careful consideration, decided to change over from Indian Association to Asian Association. The main reason for doing so was that the sub-continent of India had become India and Pakistan. And the Government of Tanganyika now recognized only three categories of people in Tanganyika; Africans, Asians and Europeans. They had appealed to all their upcountry branches as well, to make the necessary changes and function as Asian Association Branches."

'According to Mr. H.R. Dharani, the Association's first Secretary-General, 'originally the idea of Asian Association was conceived by the Late Dr. Malik to counter the suicidal fissiparous tendencies among people of Indian origin after the partition of India' [3]

Where by it was Mr. D.K. Patel who was former hard core member of the Indian Association and the President of the Indian Merchants Chamber, who successfully guided the transition through his persuasive diplomacy and subsequently became the founder member of the Asian Association. It was formerly launched in September 1950; and the Association's constitution was adopted by a public meeting held on 22nd December 1951 in the Bohora School Hall in Dar-es-Salaam under the chairmanship of Mr. D. K. Patel. At this meeting, Mr. M.A. Khimji was elected President of the Asian Association.

The Association believed in equality for all, common inter-racial schools and hospitals, equal opportunities and equal pay for equal work for all in the Tanganyika civil service, open land and urban policy, and election through universal franchise as opposed to nomination or limited representation. [4] The list of the 61 members who were present at this meeting proves that in spite of the India-Pakistan divide there were many leaders from all sections of the Asian community who joined hands to work for the betterment of society as a whole. [5]

From the beginning, individually and collectively, members of the Asian Association played a pivotal role and remained steadfast in their whole hearted support for Mwalimu and TANU. This helped to stabilize to a great extent the complicated relationship between Tanganyika's Africans and Asians during that highly sensitive period.

Later a few members of the Association shifted their loyalties to other political groups, due to differences of opinion or change in ideology or personal reasons. And there were members of the Asian community who right from the beginning had opposed the Association's close collaboration with TANU. Notable among these dissenters was V.R. Boal, known as Boalkaka, proprietor / editor of the Tanganyika Herald, a small bilingual weekly in Gujarati and English languages published every Thursday and sold at 5 shillings per copy. Boalkaka relentlessly had his guns trained towards The Asian Association and fired the missiles from the front pages of his newspaper with full force all the time. His and some other Asian's main contention was that the rights of the Asians as a group were being ignored by the Association.

In 1954 a U.N. delegation was visiting Tanganyika once again, intending to gauge the people's mood and mental readiness for the dramatic changes of Independence. Public sentiment of that time is exemplified in the comment of 80-year-old Mzee Chamuenye, who came to meet the delegation all the way from Kisiju. He declared, "I was not born under German rule. I was born during the Arab period. When the German came I fought him and our elders fought against the Germans because they did not want to be ruled. You know we were ruled by force due to lack of weapons. The Germans fought the British who took over the country. Now we the elders are prepared and ready to rule ourselves . . . ."

After completing 'fact-finding' interviews around the country, the delegation submitted its report to the U.N. This led to the first visit of Mr. Julius K. Nyerere to the U.N. Assembly in 1955, when this crucial and path breaking report was scheduled to be discussed by the Trusteeship Committee. He attended this meeting in his capacity as the President of TANU party, to represent the people's voice. All his travel expenses were raised through fund raising by his friends in collaboration with TANU. The official team representing the government consisted of one African, one Asian and one European member. They were lead by the Chief Secretary of the country. This dissenting team argued that Nyerere was the only political leader who wanted Independence at that time. "We are not yet ready to govern ourselves," declared Justin Mponda with force, the African member, interestingly was a former friend of Mwalimu. The Asian member, Iqbal Chand Chopra, Q.C. a prominent lawyer from Mwanza, put forward the same viewpoint. As recorded by Jhaveri, 'It was during this visit that Mwalimu called for the Asian Association's support to indicate that we, as the only political body of the Asian community in Tanganyika were supporting the political aspirations of the people of Tanganyika for complete Independence under the leadership of Mr. Nyerere. History will duly record, as the national songs of the people of Tanganyika have already done, this timely and valuable support which the Asian Association fully and immediately gave, upon Mr. Nyerere's request. This support was essential to disprove the stand of the Asian nominated member as well as the African member who had been sent along with the other European member to argue at this crucial meeting.' [6]

At that time the position of the Colonial Government was that it would consider the question of granting Independence to Tanganyika in about 20 to 25 years time. They argued that Tanganyikans were not yet ready for self rule! As usual Mwalimu had succinctly pleaded for immediate independence.

As soon as Mwalimu returned home the war of the nerves started in earnest. The Government intensified their policy of closing down TANU branches and intimidate the populace indiscriminately. According to Simon Ngh'waya, staff writer and reporter with Mwafrika Newspaper, "TANU was in the process of organizing a nation wide strike if the Government did not agree to grant Responsible government by 1959. TANU was just four years old at the time, its President Julius Nyerere had declared that this strike was the war cry to begin our independence struggle. For this reason the colonial government conspired to break Julius Nyerere's strength and destroy TANU and the unity of the people at all costs. In fact in another incident at the time they had jailed two editors of Mwafrika Newspaper allegedly for 'inflammatory writing and inciting people" [7]

Soon Julius Nyerere was charged with anti-government libel and sedition. Briefly, the first charge against Julius Nyerere alleged that on May 1958 Nyerere unlawfully by print, published matter in Sauti ya Tanu concerning F. B. weeks, the D.C. at Musoma with the intent to defame him. Similarly the second count was based on the allegation of defaming the D.C. of Songea Mr. G. T. L. Scott, and third charge alleged that on the same date defamatory matter against both Mr, Weeks and Mr. Scoot was published in Sauti ya TANU.

The case began in Dar-es-Salaam on 9 July 1958, before the presiding District Court magistrate Mr. L.A. Davis. Mr. John Summerfield, acting Solicitor General and Mr. N.M. Dennison comprised the prosecution team while Mr. D. N. Pritt Q.C. led the defence, assisted by Mr. K. L. Jhaveri, in charge of the legal aspect of the case as pertaining to Tanganyikan law and Mr. N.M. Ratansi, in charge of the evidence aspect. As Jhaveri notes, "The Tanganyika's laws differed in some aspects from the British Laws at the time. We knew that the case was complex and complicated."[8]

At this stage, a brief synopsis of the case may usefully describe the case proceedings and illustrate the ideology, logic and operations of the colonial administration in Tanganyika.

In 1957 the government had planned to establish district councils called 'Baraza la Mseto'—multi-racial councils, based on parity of members of all three communities viz a viz, African, Asian and European regardless of any other considerations so as to control the day to day life of the villagers. The council of tribal chiefs opposed this concept, fearing it would not only reduce their own authority but enable the Europeans as well as the Asians to dominate Africans. The district commissioner Mr. Weeks was on his part determined to persuade the council of chiefs to accept the idea. He had asked Mr. Makongoro, a very senior Chief who had been a Chief for thirty two years, to tell the Council of Chiefs at Mzumbe-Morogoro that the Chiefs at Musoma had accepted the idea of district councils based on racial parity and tell the Musoma Chiefs that the Council of Chiefs at Mzumbe Morogoro had accepted the same. Chief Makongoro refused to participate in this trickery and told Mr. Weeks that the notion was unacceptable not only to the chiefs but also the people of those areas.

The next thing that happened said Mr. Pritt was that in early 1958, Chief Mohamad Makongoro was arrested and charged in the District Magistrate's Court with various offences including the cooked up charge of official corruption. He pleaded guilty to the charges concerning hunting without a game license, of failing to record game animals, failing to surrender his expired license, and using unlawful methods of hunting for which he paid the fine and pleaded not guilty to four other charges including that of official corruption. He was fined some more and sentenced to six months jail for each of the last two charges of official corruption. He paid all the fines and appealed against the jail sentence for official corruption. The appeal was heard in the High Court in Dar-s-Salaam before the Chief Justice who acquitted Makongoro because in his opinion, "the evidence of the prosecution was riddled with inconsistencies and contradictions and the Crown witnesses themselves were obviously lying in respect of material facts."

And yet after he was released, he was not allowed to return home to his people even after a group of 12 elders met the authorities and requested them to allow their Chief to come home.

Mr. Weeks then called a public meeting which was attended by a thousand members of the Waikuzu tribe. He started the meeting by accusing Mr. Hamed who was the sub Chief, of collecting money for Mr. Makongoro and TANU. This was denied by Mr. Hamed. In spite of that the sub Chief was not paid his salary for the month of January as punishment. Mr. Weeks then informed the crowd that Chief Makongoro was in jail and even if he was released he would not be allowed to continue as a Chief, and the administration was appointing Mr. Marehant most probably junior officer in the government as chief in his place, along with two other sub-chiefs. The people questioned and objected to this arbitrary dismissal and appointments of their tribal leadership. The infuriated Mr. Weeks then accused the people of collecting money for TANU and Chief Makongoro. Similar harassment was endured by a man named Hassani Ngunyunka of Songeya, a Native peasant who came from a small village and whose only crime was that he was holding a TANU membership card. He reported this matter to TANU Branch in Songea that on 19 March 1958, the police drove up to his farm and asked if he was a member of TANU. Seizing his membership card, they said, "We are arresting you." When he asked why, they replied that it was due to his forcing people to join the organization. Hassan denied it vehemently. The police then casually asked a bystander if he too was a member of TANU. The man affirmed that he was, upon which he was thrown into the police truck along with Hassan and remanded in police custody. After spending twelve days in jail the father and son duo were charged in the district court. Latter the case was dismissed for lack of evidence. It was the same story of threats and arrests all over the country side, in Gaita, Musoma, Mahenge, Mara, and Songea: wherever a TANU branch was oppened ordinary members, sub-Chiefs and even Chiefs were harassed and dismissed and these branches were being closed down by the administration under any number of flimsy pretexts.

These disturbing incidents were brought to Mwalimu's notice when he visited Geita a small town at the time in Gaita district and he wrote a scathing article in Sauti ya TANU-Voice of TANU no. 29 published on 9th May 1958 about Mr. F.B. Weeks D.C. Songea and another district commissioner called Mr. L. T. Scott. D. C. Musoma. This article led to Mwalimu being charged with three counts of criminal libel, to which he pleaded not guilty.

During cross-examination by Mr. Summerfield, Mwalimu confirmed his authorship of the article about the two District Commissioners Mr Weeks and Mr. Scott, stating that it had been written to draw the government's attention to the serious discontent prevailing in the Geita and Musoma areas.

In his submission, Mr. Pritt Q.C. Defending remarked that a large section of the population felt unjustly treated, as described in Mwalimu's article in Shauti ya TANU. The people felt that whenever they protested state injustices, only occasionally investigations were carried out by the authorities and that resulted in penalization not of the concerned government officials but of the protesters who reported these incidents.

However, instead of responding to these arguments the prosecution closed its case without calling any further witnesses. This prompted Mr. Pritt to remark caustically that he did not think Mr. Summerfield "had the 'remotest knowledge' of who was on trial; it was in fact Mr. Weeks and Mr. Scott and a certain part of the territory that were on trial" in this "case of utmost seriousness" whose outcome could affect eight and a half million lives.

The case thus continued amidst many legal counter-arguments, objections and adjournments. As a result some charges were dropped and some amended. And ultimately Mwalimu was fined 1000 shillings on the first count against him and 2000 shillings on the second. Both fines were accompanied by an alternative of six months imprisonment in default of payment. Nyerere was given forty eight hours to pay the fines. The case provoked a strong public reaction. As Jhaveri noted in Marching with Nyerere, before daybreak on the day of verdict 11ᵗʰ August 1958, "hundreds of people were already crowding around the small courthouse in Dar-es-Salaam. Some had come from distant villages with Blankets and cooking utensils, as if for a camping holiday. Police constables lined the street round the court and a riot squad stood ready, in case of trouble. The court was packed . . ."

The depth of collective esteem for Mwalimu was attested by the fact that Mzee John Rupia the Vice-President of TANU and Bibi Titi the women leader were able to collect money for the fines from the assembled crowd outside the court within a short time.

Even though the fines were relatively small, their imposition had great political repercussions. The case against Mwalimu provided crucial momentum to the process of Independence from colonial rule. From this point on, events started moving fast. There was a groundswell of open public support for TANU,

And the colonial administration had no option but to take note of the people's mood if they were to avoid a Mau Mau-sort of bloody uprising on their hands. TANU branches and sub branches were now allowed to function with out much hindrance. The party took the opportunity and moved forward swifly. Mwalimu laid the foundation stone of TANU's new Headquarters on Mnazi Moja site with fanfare while Mr. Kambona, the Secretary General of the party left for UK to study Law.

By this time the UTP, United Tanganyika Party and the ANC African National Congress had also begun to develop a political presence in the country; interestingly, ANC was established by Zuberi Mtemvu, a trusted friend of Mwalimu and at one time Secretary-General of TANU, who had left the party because he felt TANU had too mild a policy towards non-Africans especially Asians. As I understood it, apart from his opposition to some of the policy matters, Zuberi Mtemvu's main point of contention with TANU and Mwalimu was that the indigenous Tanganyikans and Asians immigrants, even those born in the country form a separate category. As such they cannot be treated as equals in the eyes of Law. He and some other members from within TANU wanted this distinction to be recognized by the Government in its policy planning. On the other hand Mwalimu declared that those Asians born and brought up in Tanganyika and for whom it was the only home should not be treated as lesser Tanganyikans. They were just one of the tribes of Tanganyika. And members of all tribes were equal in Tanganyika.

Chapter 15

Travails and Triumph

In January 1957, after a heated debate within the party TANU had agreed to take part in upcoming 1959 national elections which were based on 'tripartite' voting system, in an effort to prove party strength and as an important step forward to internal self-governance. Under the tripartite system, each constituency was to elect one African, one Asian and one European candidate, and voters were required to vote simultaneously for all three candidates as their representatives from the same constituency. As the majority of voters would be Africans, it was explained that this method was formulated specially to ensure that non Africans had the chance of winning an election. This system also turned out to be a blessing in disguise for the Asian members as it provided them an opportunity to be seen and heard. The Asian Association was TANU's partner and collaborator in this national Endeavour. It was mutually agreed that TANU take up the mandate of proposing the

136

names of African and European candidates, and the Asian Association Managing Committee was entrusted to select the names of Asian candidates in consultation with TANU.

Dar-es-Salaam, where Jhaveri was contesting, was different from other constituencies in the country. Its residents traditionally lived in close-knit communities, and apart from being the country's commercial and political capital it had the highest number of non-African registered voters as Africans comprised only one-third of the total number of voters. The second glaring point was that, from the beginning the members of the Ismailia Community had maintained a separate political identity. Most of them, with a few notable exceptions had declined to join the Association. And as the community had a big presence in Dar, its potential voting power was also substantial in Dar-es-Salaam.

As a consequence of this environment many members of the general public, who were sitting on the fence were now keen to join Asian Association. Not only that almost every eligible politically minded member of the Asian community aspired to be nominated as a candidate from the Asian slot from Dar-es-Salaam. Eventually, after a long drawn process of discussion and selection the Managing Committee of the Asian Association derived a list of some eight to ten serious candidates aspiring to stand for election. These names were shortlisted and finally out of these names two names remained; M.M. Devani and K.L. Jhaveri. Both were good friends, and we were neighbours . . .

The Managing Committee of the Asian Association met again in December 1958 to finalize the selection. Jhaveri describes the moment, 'We were invited to ascertain briefly our views and then asked to leave as they continued their deliberations. We both went together for a drive and in about an hour or so we returned to the meeting which was being held in the Asian Association premises in Acacia Avenue (present Samora Avenue.) Shortly there after, we were informed that I was chosen to be the official candidate of the Asian Association. Manubhai Devani was the first person to congratulate me and wished me success. Everybody present warmly congratulated me and expressed full support.' I was very happy to see that soon in 1958 Manubhai Devani was elected the Mayor of Dar-es-Salaam.

There was excitement, expectation and challenge in the air! All these arrived in quick succession and the action started immediately.

Dr. G. M. Daya, who was born in Kenya in 1923, had just joined the Asian Association in Dar-es-Salaam. He came from the powerful Ismailia community and being a doctor he was well-known in Dar-es-Salaam. He had friends in high places including the incumbent President of the Association Mahmud Rattansi, Amir Jamal and it was believed even Julius Nyerere.

Dr. Daya was also one of the aspirants for the Dar-es-Salaam seat. After careful and lengthy process of consideration and evaluation of all the names of aspiring candidates when Jhaveri's name was announced by the Asian Association, Dr. Daya felt strong umbrage at being left out and opposed the Association's official candidate vehemently. So much so that he then challenged the Asian Association Managing Committee by giving them an ultimatum publicly to either nominate him or face opposition. Soon brickbats starting flying in the air and the leading newspapers in Dar-es-Salaam, Tanganyika Standard and The Sunday News came out often with screaming headlines 'Doctor expelled' 'Expelled candidate hits back' 'Doctor held a pistol at our head' 'Wind up Association,' and on and on and on.

Late Mr. H.R. Dharani a prominent Lawyer born in Dar-es-Salaam in 1912, where his father was a Customs Official in the German Government, differed from other lawyers and shunned political involvement. However he had always remained an outspoken critic of anything he perceived to be wrong. He wrote a long letter putting on record the history of the Asian Association and its aspirations and concluded his letter succinctly by saying that "Dr. Daya pointed the pistol at the head of the Association, though holding it at the wrong end." This letter was published in Sunday News dated 18th January-1959, Dar-s-Salaam. [Note-1]

Regrettably the good Doctor and his mentors had failed to read the writings on the wall. He persevered with community based politics for the success of his political debut; he stood for election as an independent member and continued his virulent attacks on the Asian Association.

Eventually Jhaveri's election campaign also started in earnest and led by the dedicated TANU activist Joseph Nyerere, public meetings, private consultations and various other preparations commenced in Dar-es-Salaam constituency. Joseph was the mainstay in helping to organize the election strategy and became like a brother to me. Jhaveri kept busy campaigning, day and night approaching and meeting members of all communities. His personal records of people's actions and reactions at these meetings provide a fascinating word picture of the racial environment prevailing in Dar-es-Salaam at the time.

By this time fortunately Jhaveri's Associate Advocate Mr. D.N. Parekh, who was reading in his chambers at the time had taken over the bulk of their professional commitments enabling Jhaveri to devote all his time to the election campaign. Furthermore unknown to him, Mzee P.N. Kotak and his group of volunteers from the Vyayamshala were out in the field helping to organize these election meetings, canvassing for votes and providing transport to the elderly and infirm. Miss Lilu Asher one of our friends, warm hearted and spirited went door-to-door requesting the voters to go early to vote; in Dar it was unheard of for women those days to go out canvassing for votes. And my cousin brother Himat Gandhi distributed posters and stickers, tirelessly checked that these were pasted in every shop and on every car bumper, often missing his meals in the bargain. These committed volunteers never expected us to offer them even a cup of tea. In fact Mzee Kotak treated them all to a party after the election results were declared. Majority of them are no more with us. It is true that people come in our life for a reason, a season or a life time. They are there for what ever purpose that we need them to be there. And then without any notice they depart. Our need is fulfilled and their work is done. We bid them au revoir and move on with time: I do so with a prayer and thanks in my heart for all our lovely friends and fellow travelers past and present.

At home there was a continuous flow of visitors and meetings. I did not take active and official part in the meetings discussing the politics of the day as such, but without even realizing it I was very much part of the whole process taking place around us. Besides Atool and Abha were still very young and I remained fully occupied running the house and looking after my kids.

Elsewhere in the country this exercise in all round partnership with TANU continued smoothly through out the election campaign. Ultimately, it turned out that all but six candidates proposed through tripartite system were declared elected unopposed. Interestingly, among these six was party president Mwalimu himself.

(a) He was opposed by Chief Kunambi in the Eastern Province.

(b) In Southern Highlands Lady Chesham faced I.C.W. Bayldon head of U. T. P.

(c) John Keto was opposed by Zuberi Mtemvu, the President of African National Congress in Tanga Province And

(d) In the Northern Province the only Asian lady Mrs. Sophia Mustafa was opposed by five men; H. K. Virani, N. M. Mehta, M. D, Patel, D. Behal, and S Mohamed. Indomitable lady that she was, she routed them all and won her constituency seat with flying colours.

(e) Nearer to home in Dar-es-Salaam K. L. Jhaveri was being opposed by Dr. G. M. Daya

(f) Mr. D. Heath by Tom Tyrrell who was former mayor of Dar-es-salaam while the third candidate Rashidi M. Kawawa was elected unopposed.

During the election campaign Mwalimu was kept busy addressing public meetings in support of TANU candidates all over the country. In Dar-es-salaam the final and very well-organized public rally was held at the site of the old airport on 8 February 1959, the last day of the campaign. A high platform was built in the centre of the ground, and it was connected by loudspeakers so that Mwalimu's speech could be heard in every corner of the ground. Posters were put up everywhere, even on the platform, with Jhaveri and Heath's photographs and the words 'VOTE FOR JHAVERI' and 'VOTE FOR HEATH.' Hours prior to the meeting the ground was packed with people: this rally was different from all other TANU gatherings because it was in support of an Asian and a European member of TANU who had the courage to stand for office with an African member, in the face of strong opposition by some members from within the Asian community on communal ground.

Also, until then members had been nominated to the Legislative Council by the Government, and the public had no say in the process at all. So the idea of being able to elect a representative caused a lot of excitement. This was also the first time all three TANU candidates Rashidi Kawawa, K.L. Jhaveri and D.F. Heath were sharing a public platform. Most of all, Mwalimu himself was to address the meeting, and people expected him to give his frank opinion with regard to impending political changes.

There was intense excitement and expectation in the air, and the people were already chanting and singing national songs when Mwalimu arrived at the rally. With him on the dais sat Rashidi Kawawa, Mwalimu's trusted companion who was earlier declared elected unopposed, D.F. Heath, K.L. Jhaveri, Mzee John Rupia, Bibi Titi Mohammad and Joseph Nyerere. Young and old, men and women, stretched as far as the eye could see and beyond: Asians, Africans and even a few Europeans, sitting shoulder to shoulder. The Swahili newspaper *Baragumu* of 12 February 1959 estimated the crowd to be over 50, 000.

The three candidates soon finished their short speeches, and then Mwalimu rose to address the meeting. "*UHURU!*" he called out. The sky reverberated with a passionate roar from tens of thousands of throats: "*UHURU!*" He called it out twice more, receiving the same response. He then surveyed the crowd looking up at him in mesmerized silence, eager to hear his words. It was electrifying moment and a pin drop silence pervaded the whole ground. Without mincing words Mwalimu proceeded to spell out his demands to the government; elected members as a majority in the

Legislative Council; the abolition of the tripartite system of representation which required voters to vote for three candidates, one each from African, European and Asian community from the same constituency; and universal adult suffrage. He reminded the gathering that "Freedom does not come by violent means," and further emphasized that "One of the peaceful means is by voting, and if you don't vote tomorrow, it means you do not want freedom . . ."

On 19 February voting took place without any incident, and the results were announced from the balcony of Arnatoglu Hall at about 1 a.m. the following morning. The waiting crowd of several thousand was already in a festive mood, and erupted in cheering and waving when it was announced that both candidates had won, Jhaveri with almost twice as many votes as his opponent Dr. Daya. According to Mwalimu, "In other places TANU's victory in the election had been taken for granted, largely because the majority of voters were Africans. Whereas in Dar-es-Salaam the scenario was different, as out of more then 8,000 registered voters the African voters were fewer then 3,000. The result of the Dar-es-Salaam elections has proved beyond all doubt that the majority of non-African voters agree with TANU demands." [1]

In effect this also meant that majority of voters had refused to communalize the election process and chose to vote for candidates on the basis of merit rather than race or ethnicity.

From then on, true to expectations memorable and important changes took place in quick succession in Tanganyika.

On 17 March 1959, amid pomp and ceremony accompanied by a police band, Abdulkarim Yusufali Alibhai Karimjee took the oath of allegiance as Tanganyika's first

Parliamentary Speaker. His family's journey had started way back in 1825 when Mr. Jivanjee Budhabhoy, a trader from Cutch Mandvi in India sailed to East Africa and settled down in Zanzibar where Abdulkarimbhai was born. By the time his great grandfather Budhabhoy died in 1898 the family had established trade connections with Europe and continued to expand. In 1943 they established their offices in Dar-es-Salaam headed by Abdulkarimbhai, where he continued to reside.

A businessman, philanthropist and social worker in his own right, Abdulkarimbhai had also served as Mayor of Dar-es-Salaam. His family had been living in East Africa for five generations. They are major donors to educational and social institutions all over the country. Gracious and friendly Batulben and Abdulkarimbhai entertained a lot. Their tables were always filled with gourmet fare, and their house hosted delightful company. Their spacious bungalow was across the creek on the other side of the Selender Bridge in Oyster Bay, facing our house in Sea view. In those days we could see the lights in their garden glimmering like a beacon. Abdulkarimbhai used to often warn me in jest that he could keep an eye on me from his home, and I used to joke in return that I could do the same from mine!

Sir Richard Turnbull, Governor-General, was present in full regalia at Abdulkarimbhai's swearing-in ceremony. All the new elected members, including Jhaveri, also took oath as parliamentarians, thus forming an opposition party in the Legislative Council. Mwalimu was brimming with confidence of a much loved and trusted leader. As expected, Sir Richard Turnbull outlined far-reaching proposals for constitutional advances towards the country's Independence, warning that these directives, now and in the future, would depend on the proper maintenance of law and order. The situation was quite volatile, and Mwalimu, as leader of TANU, appealed for public calm and restraint, declaring that the national movement had the backing of all Tanganyikan tribes and their chiefs, and members of all races; and that it was any country's fundamental and legitimate right to attain self-government and Independence. And he added forcefully, 'we the people of Tanganyika are demanding our legitimate rights.'

On 20 October 1959, the Governor Sir Richard Turnbull announced that the general election would be held in Tanganyika the following year that is, in 1960 and not in 1962 as earlier stipulated by the colonial regime. And the much desired abolition of the racial parity system of representation was already on the cards.

Party work began enthusiastically, and this time TANU was going to nominate all the candidates, Africans, Asians and Europeans. In a sense it could be said that the influential Asian Association was bowing out, enabling TANU to take the lead as the majority voice. Predictably, there was very strong opposition to this from a section of the Asian community. And the more Asian Association tried to explain its stand; the critics lead by 'Tanganyika Herald' newspaper became more vitriol. Their main demand was that Asians as a significant historical minority group that had contributed greatly to Tanganyika in all sectors should be given special rights. This demand had no place in an atmosphere vibrant with promise of majority rule and the expectation that TANU would now open its doors to non Africans when the time was ripe. And ultimately, grant citizenship to people of Asian origin. Being a Member of Parliament from Dar-es-Salaam constituency and a lawyer, it was a trying period for Jhaveri as he had to face these objections directly all the time.

A believer in Gandhian philosophy since his student days Jhaveri had always believed in racial equality. And as for me I remember sitting quietly as a child in fading sun light listening and talking to Bwana Shambha, and watching Bi.Tatu cook maize meal Ugali. When I got married, our home was a meeting place where every body was welcomed happily. On my part I found it difficult to understand this clamour for special privileges by a certain section of the society by virtue of their race and felt irritated and thought that those members of the Asian community who were clamouring for special rights also had failed to realize the fact that times had changed and there was no place now, for racial or tribal politics in Tanganyika.

While this debate was still going on at various levels, nominations were announced on 18-July-1960; 57 TANU candidates for the general election were declared elected unopposed. Only in 11 out of 50 constituencies was there any opposition to TANU candidates. This sweeping mandate ensured that TANU, led by Mwalimu Nyerere, was invited by the Governor Sir Richard Turnbull to form the next government. On 1 September 1960, Julius Kambarage Nyerere became the first elected Chief Minister of Tanganyika. It was reported that, this was the first instance in the history of Commonwealth countries that a national election was won without a single vote being cast.

As CM of the nation he now needed to train more of his party men to take up new responsibilities. He persuaded Joan Wickens whom he had known since his 1950 student days when she was then working for the Commonwealth Department of the Labour Party, to come to Tanganyika and help establish the Tanganyika Education Trust and the Kivukoni College in 1960s. In fact she was the guiding force behind both these institutions. Mwalimu's aim was to provide working knowledge to his party men who had missed getting formal education. Joan Wickens continued selflessly working with Mwalimu as his Personal Assistant, speech writer, mentor and friend through out his life. She died in December 2004 in England.

Apart from that right from the beginning Julius Nyerere had a trusted team of colleagues helping him to run TANU and coordinate the freedom struggle. He appointed some of these men and women to his cabinet; others were elected unopposed to the new Legislative Council; and some remained in charge of strategic posts within TANU. These loyal comrades came from different backgrounds. Some were well educated and socially privileged while others were grassroots activists who had suffered at colonial hands and learnt their lessons while participating in the freedom struggle. They were all committed to a common goal: to attain full Independence and develop Tanganyika as a nation for the benefit of all based on the principles of democracy.

This time Jhaveri was elected unopposed from Dar-es-Salaam constituency, and once more our house became an animated hub for MPs from upcountry regions, as well as politicians and interesting personalities from around the world.

On 27 March-1961 the Tanganyika Constitutional Conference was held at Karimjee Hall in Dar-es-salaam, attended by Colonial Secretary Ian Maclaud. It was unanimously decided that by 1 May 1961 internal self-government was to be granted to Tanganyika, followed by full Independence to be formally declared on 9 December that same year. On 1 May Julius Nyerere took oath as the first Prime Minister of Tanganyika and began negotiating and working out the modality of the departure of the British. And setting up his administration and initiating nationwide development programs, even as he kept a vigilant eye on the mood of the people. Especially at the time of independence the situation was dire, as up to now the administration was strictly governed by archaic laws which kept the European at the highest positions, Asians in the middle and the Tanganyikans themselves on the lowest rung of the society. As a result of this discriminative policy there were no Tanganyikans in the civil service manning the higher posts. Just to give some idea there were only two African lawyers in the Judiciary and out of 515 registered doctors only 14 were Tanganyikans. There were only twelve African graduates in the whole country. All of them including the doctors and lawyers were holding junior positions.

It was the same in all branches of government. Mwalimu was determined to reverse this situation through the expansion of training facilities at all levels, and through a policy of actively Africanizing the civil service. Jhaveri was appointed to the Civil Service Commission as a member and later on he joined the Africanization Commission when it was formed to handle this very sensitive subject. The Civil Service Commission under the guidance of Chief Marealle was charged to oversee the administration of government Civil Service viz a viz, recruitment, training, discipline, promotions, transfers, retirement, pensions and any other matter that needed their attention and change the prevailing situation methodically.

The Africanization Commission on the other hand had the mandate of reassessing and overhauling the entire system and to ensure that qualified Tanganyikan officers took their rightful place in the administration of the government bureaucracy. This was done through retirement and pensions, promotions, in-house training, foreign study trips and courses, and inviting expatriates on short term basis to help in training and running the government smoothly.

Africanization was a very sensitive subject at the time. Hon Maswanya was appointed the Chairman of Africanization Commission and Mr. J. Namata as Secretary. The others were Hon K. L. Jhaveri M.P. Mr. Salehe Kibwana, O.B.E. Chairman of Tanga Town Council and Mr. Magogo, Secretary General of the Tanganyika Union of Public Employees. Up to now the British Government had assured with an iron fist that the Tanganyikans themselves did not progress at all while the Europeans occupied the highest position. The Asians were in the middle buffer zone. And they were the first casualties of the Africanization drive as it meant premature retirement for some of them and promotions for their junior officers. Bearing in mind this point, the whole exercise required judicious and just implementation on the part of the Commission so that no officers suffered injustice. The Commission worked diligently to rectify the anomalies existing in the administrative branch of the government. They examined and evaluated the whole Civil Service structure, and laid a solid foundation by putting in place various training schemes for the Tanganyikan officers who were appointed to man Government administration as envisaged.

In 1971-73 Finance and Management Institute of the Finance Management was established to train people in Banking, Finance and Management. Chandubhai Chohan helped set it up as its first staff member & Executive Secretary. He was also with the Treasury—ministry of finance as a Pensions Advisor for the Parastatal organization pension scheme and was the main person to negotiate and then get it through the scheme where by, the UK Government took over paying the pensions of about 3750 mostly

Asian pensioners who were in Colonial British service in Tanganyika, and who were retired under the new policy. Some of them had opted for early retirement while others were replaced and pensioned off due to Citizenship issues. The white civil servants were already looked after in an independent agreement. That agreement / arrangement benefitted many in India and UK etc whose Tanzanian shillings were not going far and pensions paid in pounds & indexed improved their situation. Born in Mombasa in 1921, Chandubhai Chohan was awarded MBE in the Queen's Birthday Honours list of June 1958 at a very young age of 37 years. He retired from Civil Service in 1971 after working selflessly for 33 eventful years in Tanganyika-Tanzania.

In Dar-es-Salaam, by now The Faculty of Law was functioning well and the plans for establishing the University of Dar-es-Salaam were taking shape in full swing.

It was a heady time and people were optimistic about the future of the country, especially the members of the TYL (TANU Youth League). In an over-enthusiastic attempt at social reform, TYL set out to cleanse the nation of colonial-era 'vices' including prostitution, one of the oldest professions on earth! One such enthusiast was Hasmukh Pandya, a very active member who had joined TYL even before finishing his secondary school education. One of seven brothers and four sisters, he was born on 24th-January-1942 in Dar-es-Salaam. According to his reckoning, his grandparents Mohanlal Gangaram Pandya and Shantokben had arrived in Zanzibar roughly 150 years earlier. His own parents had migrated from Zanzibar to Dar at a young age; they were very poor but were helped by the Karimjee Jiwanjee family, who from their trust fund gave his grandfather a two-storey building in the Kisutu area. His grandmother started a school on the first floor teaching Gujarati, and the family opened a guesthouse called Arya Sukh Shanti Hindu Lodge on the ground floor. It was informally known as 'Moti Vishi'—big hotel, and from it Bapuji used to buy jalebi, ganthiya, papaya sambharo and chatni-kachori for our breakfast every Sunday morning.

One evening Hasmukh was on his watch in the streets along with two of his TYL comrades, Thabit Shabani and Omari Ramadhani, when they noticed a *mkiwa* (prostitute) entertaining two drunk European sailors. Obviously this called for stern action on their part. The three youths stepped forward and told the *mkiwa* she was too young to be engaging in such behaviour and that too in public. "No problem, I will go upstairs," she responded. They went upstairs in a nearby hotel where the mkiwa locked herself into a toilet with one of the sailors.

Thabit and Omari kept watch on this new development while Pandya went to look for a policeman. He found two Askaris on patrol and brought them to the spot. One of them rapped on the toilet door with his baton. The first to emerge was the mkiwa, bare breasted, followed by her half naked client. The Askaris marched the young woman and the sailors to the police station to record the incident, taking Hasmukh, Thabit and Omari along as witnesses. However, the first action taken by the assistant superintendent, a Goan, was to lock them all into one cell, despite the Askaris protesting that the three boys had not committed any offence. The next officer on duty, a Sikh, continued to detain them but released the original culprits the sailors. Hasmukh, Thabit and Omari were freed from custody the following day only after the personal intervention of Joseph Nyerere Malimu's younger brother who was Minister for Youth and George Kahama, Minister of Home Affairs,

Upon their release Randhir Thaker, the owner / publisher of Ngurumo and Bhoke Munanka Mwalimu's trusted associate and friend published a front-page story with the headline "*Mzungu kajificha chooni*" meaning 'European hides in the toilet'. This seemingly derogatory story upset many Europeans and they insisted that the three TYL youths involved in having the sailors arrested must be taught a lesson. Hasmukh, Thabit and Omari were picked up again by the police, taken to the Kivukoni Court and charged with criminal trespass, creating a disturbance and taking the law into their hands. Hasmukh was born on 24th-January-1942 in Dar-es-Salaam, and at the time he was under 18 by one month. Hasmukh who quite school after Standard Eleven in 1956, boasts of knowing ten languages fluently and says he was crazy!

The magistrate before whom the trio appeared was our friend Late Bashir Rahim, who had studied with Hasmukh's brother. He knew Hasmukh was underage and did not want to try the case. He excused himself, claiming that he was unwell. The case was taken over by a European magistrate who had Ngurumo newspaper in his hand. Hasmukh addressed the magistrate boldly: "We have been called bastards by the police, but we see ourselves as freedom fighters. We called on the police to intervene, but the senior officers are not interested in justice. If you want to send me to prison, I do not mind." A nail that sticks out immediately gets hammered hard.

And accusing Hasmukh of being the ringleader, the magistrate promptly sentenced him to 18 months imprisonment. Decades later, while talking to the newspapermen Hasmukh Pandya recalled his ordeal and what followed in an interview published in Daily News, 13 October 2007;

"I was sent to Ukonga Prison, and then on to Uyui, Tabora where I was assigned to break stone aggregates in the orchards and continued to be obedient to the warders. When finally the 18 months were over I reported to Tabora TANU Provincial Secretary Idi Ligumba. They received me with fanfare and the TANU members even raised 1500/— Shillings for my fare from Tabora to Dar. In Dar-es-Salaam TANU Headquarters, as Uyui Prison graduate I took up new duties and soon was offered a scholarship. I left immediately with a team of 12 TYL members, four women and eight men, to join military training in Israel. Returning home after graduating, our group was instrumental in establishing the Mgulani camp under the Israeli commander Major Ben AmosYeffet. We were also founder-leaders of the Adult Education Campaign.

Meanwhile rapid changes were taking place all over the country; Tanganyikans were in up—beat mood. Many of them were also getting restless and now actually expressing anti-Asian feelings, giving vent to prejudice, fear and resentment which had accumulated over the years. In villages and small towns there was open talk of how they were going to take over Asian shops and businesses, and freely marry Asian women of their choice. In addition several irresponsible leaders in the hinterland began to interfere in the daily affairs of people. By the same token, some Asians lacked faith in the new government and continued to be locked into a parochial mentality that denigrated Africans, for whom they often used the derogatory terms like golo, kalio and looked suspiciously at the changes that were taking place in the country.

It is also a sad fact that apart from some Asian families, who had good brotherly relationship with the Tanganyikans, there were not many social contacts on equal terms between the two main sections of the society. And people felt cosy and safe within their own tiny communal boundaries and continued with their old habits.

Mwalimu was highly aware of the danger of racist attitudes and discriminatory social practices prevailing in the country. He issued stern warnings about consequences if there was hooliganism and lawlessness anywhere. At the same time he issued strong reminders to non-Africans: "Whether or not the non-Africans cooperate, that is the vital question . . . If freedom and Independence is won with the willing cooperation of immigrants, Tanganyika is bound to become a happy democracy and an example to rest of Africa."

During that period, the government newspaper Tanganyika Standard often came out with headlines such as "TANU Self-Seekers Warned: Duty to Public Comes First, Says Nyerere"; "Mwalimu Warms Officials Who Break Leadership Code", and so on. His biggest challenge came after Independence when his government proposed to grant citizenship to non-Africans who were legally entitled. Many Africans were not happy with this idea, and their resistance was reflected in parliament through strong opposition to the Citizenship Bill. Mwalimu, however, declared emphatically, "A man's colour is no sin in Tanganyika . . . When we formed our nationalist movement, we set out to do one thing; unite people. And the people of Tanganyika . . . immediately began to think of themselves not as Europeans, Indians and Africans, or even as Wasukuma, Wamasai or Wanyamwezi, but as Tanganyikans. It is that unity which has made it possible to reach this stage peacefully." [3]

All these not withstanding opposition to the bill continued. Up to now Mwalimu's word was accepted by his people without a murmur. And so in a way this was his first acid test, done by some of his own more radical party men and MPs. The debate became so heated that one morning, while parliament was in session Mwalimu even offered to resign. Coming home that day for a quick lunch, Babubhai Laxman, Sophia Mustapha, Dr. Krishna, Barbro Johanson, Thankiji and Jhaveriji were in a sober yet agitated mood because Mwalimu's resignation would have meant the dissolution of Parliament itself. Ultimately, Mwalimu overcame all opposition to his policy through personal determination and adherence to his ideal and principles regarding citizenship for non-Africans. The relevant legislation was passed, but this did not mean that all Asians were granted citizenship overnight; nor did it mean that all Asians trusted the offer and took it up wholeheartedly. Some opted to hold on to their British passports and thereby lost their right to Tanganikyan citizenship, while many families, including ours, renounced our right to British nationality and immediately chose to apply for Tanganyikan citizenship. Many Asian couples worked out a strategic and practical compromise. They chose to benefit from both options by one spouse retaining the British passport and the other obtaining Tanganyikan citizenship. This enabled them to not only deposit money in the UK but also to migrate there should the need arise. [Note-2]

As the date of Independence neared, the euphoric atmosphere was underscored with palpable community tension, so much so that the Minister for Home affairs directed the following confidential circular, dated 28 October 1961, to all members of the National Assembly:

So far Tanganyika had a magnificent peaceful record and to date all the joyous days which have marked Tanganyika's progress towards Independence have been unspoiled by any unpleasant incidents. Our aim must be to ensure that this record remains unbroken. From my own and from information available to me, it would appear that there is a great deal of uneasiness in the country and it is in such conditions that unpleasant incidents are likely to occur. I believe however, that if we all co-operate it will be possible to avoid them. I would particularly request your cooperation in achieving this aim, which I think should be taken in two parts. The first thing is to impress upon all your constituents the necessity from refraining from any remarks or actions which would incite racial animosity or cause uneasiness among the immigrant communities. Secondly the immigrant communities must be persuaded that there is no cause for alarm. In an atmosphere of tension an ill-considered or stupid remark, made possibly in a state of drunkenness, could well spark off trouble of some magnitude, where as the same remark made in a relaxed atmosphere to a person who is not expecting trouble would most probably be disregarded. Since, therefore, it is obviously impossible to ensure that such remarks will not be made, it is essential that by Independence Day we achieve a state of tranquility and racial harmony. Government ministers will be touring the country as much as possible between now and Independence, but their efforts alone will not be sufficient unless all members of the National Assembly cooperate by putting over to their constituents the Government's wishes in this respect, I am sure that I can rely on your active cooperation in this respect. [3]

Fortunately in Tanganyika the people's ingrained love for peace and harmony prevailed. And as the Independence Day dawned there were great expectations, aspirations, and celebrations through out the country. People had chosen to forget and forgive the past and move on to a bright future.

Looking back at that tumultuous time in our life, Jhaveriji and I feel it was a great privilege and honour to have been a part of this historical moment. All rhetoric notwithstanding, here in India in the evening of our lives we still deeply cherish our Tanzanian nationality, symbolized by our Tanzanian passports and the TANU and UWT cards that we have carefully preserved. The cards evoke our patriotism and decades of meaningful political and social activities, but it also signifies something much deeper. It brings forth a profound sense of belonging to Tanganyika.

Chapter 16

Uhuru—Independence

The Independence Day dawned on December 9th 1961. Tanganyika was emerging as a new Nation, the youngest to join the Commonwealth. The country had achieved this goal without any bloodshed. It was a unique day in the history of Africa as well as the world where violent uprising, against subjugation was the order of the day. The Colonial Government's mouthpiece, The Tanganyika Standard dated 9th Desember 1961 came out with a long Editorial entitled: Birth of a Nation, ". . . . Today a new Nation was born. This is a historic and happy day, made even happier by the fact that the transition has taken place not in an atmosphere of recrimination but of universal goodwill. That this has been possible is due to in no small measure to the enlightened political leadership of the Prime Minister Mr. Julius Nyerere and the close and friendly understanding established between him and Tanganyika's first Governor General Sir Richard Turnbull . . . ."

The main ceremony of hoisting the new flag of Tanganyika was to take place at exactly at one minute to midnight on Saturday 9th 1961. But the celebrations started early in day with a March-past and a Youth Rally. Amidst great excitement, from early morning onwards on 9th December 1961 women and children, young and old, all colorfully attired, waving flags and singing trekked in a steady stream towards the newly built National Stadium four miles away from Dar-es-Salaam city centre. They went on foot, bedecked bicycles, buses, Lorries and whatever other mode of transport they could muster. There were Askaris everywhere, shepherding people along briskly, firmly and pleasantly, so that the people could reach the stadium in time for the morning parade. The program started with Nyamwezi dancers singing "Wahangaluka"— 'How are you?' while dancing the popular Msanja dance. They were followed by the Wasukuma group dancing with their huge pythons and snakes to rapid percussion. The crowds were visibly mesmerized by the enormous reptiles raising their heads and flicking their tongues. Soon people's attention was drawn to a group of brightly costumed Indian ladies performing Dandiya Ras, the familiar sprightly Gujarati dance, led by the youthful Padmaben Anantani. I was instrumental in organizing this group; we had been practicing for weeks, and I was very happy to see the Indian dancers celebrating side by side with various ngoma groups from different regions of the country. This was followed by a choreographed mass display by schoolchildren, and a march-past by men, women and children, saluting and singing patriotic songs.

I missed my children, who would have really enjoyed the spectacle. They were with their grandparents at home. Jhaveri and I were caught up in the whirlwind of Uhuru celebrations, going from event to event, morning and evening, returning home only to dress suitably for the next function; An official banquet at the State House, a garden party, a state ball, sundowners, conferences, openings, pageantry at the National Stadium and so on. We were often accompanied by Babubhai Laxman, Member of Parliament from Mwanza, and his wife Shardaben, and Dr. Krishna, Member of Parliament from Tanga, and his wife Dr. Satyaben. One such afternoon we came home after lunch for a quick change. To give me a break Dr. Krishna insisted to make tea for us all and Babubhai offered to help him. All I had to do was to point out tea, sugar and they would take out the milk from the fridge. It was as simple as that. They assured me that, the tea would be ready in no time at all! But obviously instead of milk they used 'chash'—yogurt milk and the tea got curdled! We had a good laugh at their expense and I served them tea and snacks.

In the evening the official flag hoisting ceremony at the National Stadium was to start at 10.49 p.m. on the same day that is 9th. December 1961. In high spirits we reached the venue well before time and were shown to our seats in the enclosure reserved for newly elected Parliamentarians. We had a superb view of the proceedings, and it was absolutely exhilarating and unforgettable experience. The evening festivities began with the arrival of the Duke of Edinburgh, who was given a royal salute and a guard of honour mounted by the King's African Rifles. This was followed by a floodlit military tattoo, with soldiers in smart white uniforms, young cadets, police dogs and their handlers all displaying their skills. At one minute to midnight, as the last notes of British national anthem hung in the air, the National Stadium, with 80,000 people gazing into the illuminated arena, was suddenly plunged into darkness. The silhouette of palm trees on the distant horizon could be seen in the radiance of huge flashing tropical stars. There was a total hush; overwhelmed, people held their breath and the moment of suspense seemed to extend infinitely. Suddenly there came the quick clear slapping of halyards against the flagpole; then a swift descent, felt rather than seen, of the British flag; then a crisp command: "General Salute—Present Arms!" All the stadium lights came on with blinding force and slowly, to the notes of the Tanganyikan National Anthem, our black, green and gold national flag was hoisted, soaring above the royal box with its three main dignitaries; Prince Philip The Duke of Edinburgh, representative of the Queen of England, Sir Richard Turnbull, Governor-General of Tanganyika, and the African leader on whose slim shoulders rested the faith and future of independent Tanganyika Prime Minister Mr. Julius Kambarage Nyerere, known fondly as 'Mwalimu' Teacher.

A free African nation was born, as a triumphant roar rose from multitudes of throats and fireworks burst across the sky in an exuberant display. The ceremony concluded with a huge coloured portrait of Mr. Nyerere being raised; simultaneously a torch was lit on Mount Kilimanjaro by Captain Alex Nyerenda, shown live on a giant screen while native drummers and the police band entertained the crowds. Recalling the energy of that unforgettable night quickens my pulse even now, over half a century later.

Sir Richard and Lady Turnbull were now leaving the country. Thousands of people lined the coast to watch their departure cheering the unofficial escort of private yachts and motorboats that raced seawards to accompany the H.M.S. Loch Ruthven as it sailed out of Dar-es-Salaam harbour. The couple stood high on the frigate's bridge as small boats and launches circled the ship, sounding their hooters and sirens. A 21-gun salute boomed from the shore, and the ship responded with a similar salute. Finally the signal "Goodbye and thank you" was flashed from the Loch Ruthven and signal station on the harbour front flashed the same message back. Tanganyikans were not only bidding farewell to Sir Richard and Lady Turnbull who had been highly regarded by the public, but in effect pronouncing "Kwaheri" Goodbye to the colonial government itself. It was amazing to witness how smoothly the British managed to wind up the harsh and unjust colonial institutions in Tanganyika, where they had officially ruled from 1920-62. And yet they departed on a note of goodwill with aplomb and friendship. In addition, amazingly they still retained a strategic presence in the country through control of the National Army, Tanganyika Rifles Army as firmly as ever.

Now it was time for Mwalimu to be installed as the President of the Republic. He took oath as the President of the Republic of Tanganyika in a magnificent ceremony based entirely on African traditions and culture. A thunderous drum roll from the Royal House of Mwami Ntare Theresa Chieftainess of the, 300,000 strong Ha tribe heralded the arrival of His Excellency President-elect Nyerere with his wife Mama Maria Nyerere at the National Stadium. He was welcomed by Chief Pedro Itoshi Marealle. Witnessed by national and international leaders, on behalf of the citizens of independent Tanganyika, Chief Mzengo assisted by Chief Marealle, formally presented Mwalimu with a robe to mark him as the Father of the Nation; a spear as a symbol of courage and protection; and a shield as a symbol of defense. The arena reverberated once again with the sound of exploding fireworks, drums, police bands, a tattoo, march-past, salutes and ngoma dances, broadcast live by Radio Tanganyika. [1]

On 9 December 1962, exactly one year after attaining Independence, Tanganyika under Mwalimu's leadership was welcomed into the Commonwealth of Nations as a sovereign state. A man of strong principles and high ideals Mwalimu always led by personal example, which distinguished him from other world leaders. People trusted and adored him; he had managed to lead them and the country towards full independence, without violence or bloodshed.

One of his first actions was to establish Swahili as the national language, which as a cultural mechanism effectively united the country's 126 or more diverse tribes, many with their different dialects. Gradually English was replaced. In fact Tanganyika was the first East African country to declare Swahili as its National language. Later on it was also declared as one of its official languages by the United Nations.

His socialistic policies mandated that health and primary education were made free for all citizens, and he continued to visit the entire country, constantly viewing and reviewing conditions for himself. He initiated many self-help development programmes in rural and urban areas. "Uhuru Na Kazi!" Independence and Work "Uhuru Na Ujamaa" Independence and Socialism "Uhuru Na Upendo Independence and Brotherhood" these rousing slogans were mantras for his particular concept of national progress. At a personal level Jhaveri and I together with Mr. and Mrs Gopalan, Mr. and Mrs Avatar Singh and many of our friends enthusiastically took part in several self help schemes to build low-cost housing in Dar-es-Salaam's Magomeni locality. The atmosphere all over the country was filled with dynamic leadership and surging enthusiasm.

I have always considered Julius Nyerere to be very honest, sincere and friendly person. Surprisingly I often felt tongue-tied and awestruck in his presence, which was against my nature! We used to meet regularly at UWT and TANU meetings, Tanganyika Law Society Annual Dinners when my husband was the President of the Society for fifteen years and at various social gatherings. One particular incident that I remember vividly is when we were attending the State Ball at the Diamond Jubilee Hall in Dar-es-Salaam in celebration of Independence. I was sitting on our allocated table with my MP husband. Julius Nyerere came and joined us, one of the official dances was just going to be announced, I realized that he might ask me to dance, I have never danced western or any Indian dance like garba even as a child. I panicked and asked my husband in Gujarati, what should I do? He said just that you do not know how to dance. Julius understood, laughed and left our table before the proceedings started. And to my utter regret I lost the rare opportunity and the pleasure of dancing with the President of my country Tanzania. I still feel the disappointment of the moment!

Chapter 17

Where are the Women?

In June 1955 John Hatch, the Commonwealth officer of the British Labor Party was visiting Tanganyika on behalf of his party. An experienced Civil Servant and a writer, he had written extensively about Africa including Tanganyika. Noticing the stark gender imbalance during his meeting with TANU leaders, he pointedly asked them: "Where are the women . . . ?"

At that time TANU was facing very hostile Colonial Government and was still trying to evolve and transition itself into fully functioning organization. All this while even though women had been active in its formation, mostly behind the scenes, and in spite of the fact that the party constitution formulated in 1954 included a women's wing, the latter had yet to be launched officially. Now TANU leadership took up the challenge and hastily pulled together a selection of women representatives, among whom Bibi Titi Mohamed was their obvious choice as the leader of this group. A meeting was arranged for the next day. However, at that time the social environment was such that, even party elders were unable to arrange this meeting without first obtaining permission from her husband to do so. Finally to their relief he was persuaded by his brother to agree to this meeting and granted his permission. [1]

Accompanied by some of her friends for moral support, Bibi Titi was introduced to John Hatch as the 'leader of the women's section' of TANU, and thus the women's section came into being officially.

Bibi Titi was born in 1926 in a devout Muslim family. She studied up to Standard IV in a government primary school. Outgoing and energetic, she was the lead singer of the ngoma group Bomba, a position that requires not only outstanding musical talent but also a strong and charismatic personality. She had them both in abundance. These proved very useful when she got involved in TANU's activities. At that time there were several ngoma associations in Dar, as it was common practice of many talented women of her generation to affiliate with singing and Ngoma dancing groups. Some of these had exotic names such as Good Luck, Safina, Submarine, Snow White, British Empire, and so on. Taking the support of her friends and party elders, Bibi Titi approached and successfully mobilized all these women. Most of them joined TANU and the freedom struggle with enthusiasm and as they were self-employed they did not have jobs at risk. Neither were they cowed down by the ire of their husbands because a lot of men opposed the women of their families taking on dangerous political work.

Under colonial rule, men were under threat of losing their jobs if found in possession of party membership cards. Even for women it was fraught with risk and danger, but they quietly took over the membership drive in their localities by convincing the men to join TANU, act as their agents, pay their subscriptions, and hold and hide their membership cards. Simultaneously, they continued to help organize the party meetings without arousing the government's suspicion. Slowly branches of TANU began functioning in some places and meanwhile the women's wing of the party also began to flourish as thousands of women joined in party activities.

The solid contribution of Tanzanian women was crucial at this stage of the freedom struggle. Bibi Titi accompanied Mwalimu everywhere, captivating crowds with her powerful singing and strong presence at mass meetings. One of her favorite songs was "Hongera mwanangu wee hongera, hongera wee Na mi hongera wee, hongera . . ."

TRANSLATION:

Congratulations my child

Congratulations to you, and to me also. Congratulations, congratulations my child . . . , [2]

It is a lullaby about the strong bond which exists between mother and child and it became her theme song. When she sang it at public gatherings the crowds responded as one, with all the women swaying and humming along and the whole atmosphere became charged with emotion.

Umoja WA Wanawake WA Tanzania, UWT started functioning as a section of TANU, under Bibi Titi's leadership. I was invited by Bibi Titi to join the Central Committee of the UWT; the only organization representing all the women of Tanganyika under one political party ideology in the country. I felt honoured to be a part of UWT Central Committee, at the national level from its early days. From the beginning Bibi Titi had the full support of Mwalimu and the entire party machinery. Her husband divorced her because of her involvement in party politics, but this had no impact on her commitment and energies.

As time passed she became a formidable leader with a mass following, and was a Nominated Member of Parliament. It was believed that Bibi Titi fell out with Mwalimu when she disagreed with the Arusha Declaration, and leadership code. She was one of the accused with Oscar Kambona and other high profile personalities of the time for being involved in Tanganyika Rifles Mutiny in 1964 and subsequently to stand trial in the now famous treason trial. That she ultimately lost her place as a respected leader in the party Annals is now history well known. She is no more with us; may God grant her peace.

Before I became a member of the central committee I was already an active member of the UWT Regional as well as District Committees in Dar-es-Salaam. The organization was still in its infancy having teething troubles but there was great and infectious enthusiasm and thirst of the women for development on all fronts.

To channel and guide this energy and establish appropriate development programs with limited resources was a challenging task inherited by Prime Minister Rashidi Kawawa's wife Mama Sophia Kawawa—the next Chairperson of UWT. She was down-to-earth and compassionate, and never minced words when it came to fighting for women's rights and dignity. Over the years we became very good friends. Other memorable Central Committee members I had strong bonds with included Thekla Mchauru, Lucy Lamek, Gertrude Mongela, Martha Bulengo, Sara Lusinde, Nargis Dasture, Janet Kahama, Sara Nyerenda, Lea Lupembe, Mama Asha Ngoma, Mama Adam Sapi, Mama Kunambi, Bi Hawa Mafta, Mama Mwasaburi Ali, Baya Mwankema Thekla Gumbo, Beatrice Mansoor . . . It was a distinguished gallery of wonderful women who were also achievers in their own professions.

We were like a family, striving to achieve the same goals. Despite being the Prime Minister's wife, Mama Sophia Kawawa did not expect any special privileges and was just like one of us. During our fieldwork we shared living space, food, ideas, and arguments. We sang and danced together whenever and wherever the opportunity arose, and occasionally even vociferously agreed to disagree. Major Hashim Mbita, a young budding foot soldier in TANU at the time, helped us to organize UWT Head Quarters as a functioning unit before Thekla Mchauru took over as the Secretary General. When our discussions turned contentious, as was frequently the case at animated group meetings, Thekla used to scratch her head, with her kilemba—headscarf askew would cry out in frustration, "Kula waya!" Each time her outburst had a different import and intonation, but it invariably caused us all to burst out laughing and our tension dissipated at once.

The urgent need of the hour was for us to go into the rural areas, meet the women and learn at first hand how best they could be assisted, and what mode of 'development' would be most useful to them in their particular environment. But before we could make any progress in this direction, we had to start first of all to sensitize the women themselves about their plight and predicament. It was a long and bumpy process but if we wanted the women to take their rightful place in society we had to begin at the beginning.

We started by visiting regularly and holding our general meetings in upcountry branches. After the meeting we split up into smaller groups and spent time in the surrounding areas visiting women's groups. This gave me a rare opportunity to visit the remotest parts of Tanzania and meet women who lived bound by social taboos and customs without practically any modern amenities available to them.

Theirs was truly a harsh struggle. We stayed in many villages where water had to be fetched from a distance, homes were thatched huts and toilets were a hole in the ground, open to the elements but sheltered by a makuti roof away from the main hut. We were advised not to go out of the main hut after dark unless we wanted to confront wild animals and snakes dangling from the makuti roofs. If we needed to use the toilet after the evening hours, then the trick was to go near these open huts in groups with sticks and torches in hand, talking noisily to frighten off lurking animals and reptiles. Even then the slithering snakes managed to show up in unexpected places with equanimity.

In many village families were in a state of disorientation and despair because during those early Ujamaa days entire communities had been forcibly moved from their homesteads by over ambitious Government officials, with promises of resettlement that included schools, hospitals, electricity and running water. Instead, they were moved onto land next to the jungle where no such facilities existed, and told to farm it as cooperative farms. In this unfriendly environment people were feeling rootless and unwilling to begin tilling the land which did not belong to them. As a result the green revolution did not materialize overnight, nor did the promised facilities.

Besides this, rural women were even more downtrodden and marginalized. The majority of village women were not allowed to step out of their homes without their husband's permission. Wife-beating and other forms of sickening domestic violence were commonly practiced. It is a universal problem for women all over the world, of every race, religion and ethnicity. Whether black, brown or white, they face similar social and financial oppressions. And male-oriented, male-dominated and male-run legal systems and social constrains offer them very little protection.

In Tanzania, as elsewhere in Africa, it was the women of the family who traditionally farmed the land, raised and harvested the crop, and simultaneously bore children and looked after the family. A typical instance of this dual responsibility is seen in the cashew nut farms of the Mtwara-Newala regions, worked mostly by women. Customarily, the men take many women as wives for purely practical reasons, to create a labour force to work in the fields. The men participate only in the sale of the crop, and keep all the profits. They spend most of this money, earned through their wives' backbreaking labour, on drinking and womanizing. Even in present times, many women face these problems in spite of the fact that they are mainstay for their family's survival. If the wife complains, the man easily divorces her in the traditional manner with the three words "*Talaq, Talaq, Talaq*", leaving her without support or security, and just as easily takes another wife.

This was the environment we were endeavouring to change by educating both men and women, and creating awareness about women's rights. Our goals were to push for women's emancipation by initiating small-scale projects to enable women to earn, open kindergartens and nursery schools, convince the government to begin adult education programs in villages and build classrooms, especially for girls' schools. At the same time in collaboration with the village committees and TANU branches, we were also trying to get the state to develop an efficient system of water supply and easily accessible health clinics in these areas.

Prior to this, in order to make any progress at all in rural areas it was important to establish UWT branches in the villages, mobilize the village women and their leaders and support their collective voice. Fortunately we had the full support of President Nyerere. It was his practice to attend our meetings whenever invited to do so, and we took full advantage of that. I remember him as being very focused, observant and helpful at these meetings. We had his attention and commitment, and with Mama Sofia Kawawa's persuasive arguments, many of our recommendations led to appropriate action being taken by the government. As expected, on their part the women also responded enthusiastically, especially in terms of joining adult education classes. It was a joy to see grandmothers and mothers sitting next to their children to learn the alphabet and later take the magical step of actually writing their own names.

In 1962-63 the UWT office in Dar-es-Salaam district used to receive handicrafts made by women's groups from upcountry centers. This shop, situated in the foyer of Avalon Cinema building, was running at a loss and the stock was getting ruined. I took formal charge of the shop. Mama Mgeni, District chairperson, Grace Msungu, treasurer, and Agnes Nshiku, District secretary, were on the shop committee in their official capacity. We employed a salesgirl, and after a while the shop once more became a viable income-generating UWT project. By next year we were invited to participate in the Saba Saba trade fair as an example of a successful social / developmental initiative. I like to believe that the revival of the shop and our success at the Saba Saba trade fair encouraged many of our members to start cooperative groups for poultry and vegetable farming, tie-and-dye units, sewing, handicrafts and soap-making ventures in the city as well as in many of our upcountry branches.

We often visited those rural branches by bus. On those long journeys, invariably members carried mihogo (cassava), mahindi (corn), dried fish and some even live chicken for their relatives in the upcountry centers. I carried thepla, batetanu shak, chevdo and ganthia. We shared our food, singing, joking and gossiping while seated precariously over baskets full of dried fish and screeching fowls. At times we travelled by slow and halting trains, with entire third-class coaches booked for us. Once we were travelling to Kilosa. We reached Morogoro at night and after a short stay at station we left early in the morning. After about half an hour the train seemed to be going slowly backwards towards Morogoro. There was commotion near our coach as one of the junior clerks, who had one too many during the night was missing. Obviously he had fallen down some where on the track and promptly fell fast asleep right there in the jungle teaming with wild animals. He was still dreaming when the train reached him, in effect saving him by a whisker. The poor man got so scared that he did not touch even a glass of Bia-Beer during the whole trip!

Attending the meetings away from home meant for us late nights talking, joking, singing, sharing experiences and drinking beer and Fanta. Many of our older members were Muslims who had formerly belonged to ngoma groups that were open to all, regardless of religious and tribal affiliation. Occasionally there was mock posturing of visible tribal accents amongst the members like Wachaga and Wasukuma resulting in merriment all round. Swahili was the common language that bound our understanding. I had grown up speaking Swahili, and became fluent through using it continuously at UWT meetings and on long journeys to remote regions. It helped me to reach out, make friends, and find my own tiny little place in the lives of the village folks.

Apart from discussing African traditions and current socio-political realities, many women talked about colonial times. A frequently told story was how men were tethered with ropes, beaten up and jailed for not being able to pay the required colonial passi, tax, or for any other alleged offence. These prisoners were tied up together in pairs, so if one wanted to use the toilet the other had to follow him. One mother wept as she recalled her son's return: "I worked very hard and saved enough to pay for his release. And when at last he came home dirty and hungry, I cleaned and wiped his swollen face and legs with hot water and fed him uji with my hands. He was crying silently and so was I." "How can I forget it? It happened to many of us too often. It takes time for these wounds to heal, and it takes fore ever to accept inhuman treatment and forgive the loss of one's dignity. Even today I am finding it difficult to forget; those experiences stay clearly etched in my mind." She said still crying.

On the lighter side, once we were being welcomed by a priest who had just taken charge of the parish in one of the villages in Mwanza District. Missionaries are very good at learning quickly local dialect and customs. Being enthusiastic he was in a hurry to prove that he understood the culture of African hospitality, and started by saying, "I am disappointed to know that you are not sleeping with us tonight . . . and went on a long winded speech in the same vein to welcome us . . . ." We could hardly suppress a smile but had a good laugh afterwards at his expense.

On these journeys I wore as usual my simple cotton saris, and was conspicuous even in large crowds. It was known that I was a vegetarian, so while on these visits to upcountry branches, initially Thekla would kindly ask if I would like to stay with a local Asian family. But I refused, preferring to be with my colleagues even while I did occasionally accept an invitation here and there. Even remote places offered staples like mcicha-spinach, kunde-cow peas, maharage-beans and cabbage with ugali, maize meal or rice. Breakfasts were substantial uji, bread, butter, jam and tea. Normally we ate in the mess hall either in a school or any other hall available as organized by the UWT branches where we were meeting. But often we were also invited to village feasts where the food was served in big round enamel plates piled high with ugali or rice in the middle, a meat dish and any other vegetables in season. We sat on the ground in traditional Tanzanian style in groups of five or six and shared the food, my friends were always careful to keep the meat away from my portion of ugali. It gave me a profound sense of happiness of belonging and fellowship. I would not have exchanged those meals for any gourmet repast in the world.

Nargis Dastur one of the CC member, was not keeping in good health, so it was often the case that I was the only Asian woman on these upcountry tours. While I stayed immersed in women's activities during the 1960s as a member of the UWT Central Committee, I also asked myself why Dar's Asian women were in general so reluctant to attend our meetings or participate in our social empowerment projects, despite being so active within their own particular communities. I approached Asian women's Organizations and also spoke at length to personal friends. After detailed consultations we started the UWT Kisutu branch under my chairmanship. Our members were diverse and representative: Hindus, Muslims, Goans, Christians, Bohras, Ismailis, Parsis, Sikhs and so on. We raised funds for our work through fun fairs, food bazaars, and larger cultural events. For example Harjibhai Arya who was a well-known personality in Dar, had organized an East African tour for Kamal Barot and her troupe of artists from Mumbai. They were scheduled to perform in Dar-es-Salaam. Kamal, my friend from schooldays, was a prominent and busy playback singer in Bombay. They kindly agreed to present a musical program in aid of UWT projects. The tickets for the event, which was held at Diamond Jubilee Hall, were sold out within a week. Our chief guest was Mama Maria Nyerere. The performance was a roaring success, with the group singing and dancing to the tune of some popular Swahili songs including "TANU ya njenga nchi" TANU builds the Nation.

Kisutu Branch's first project was to establish a class for Standard VII girls who had failed to secure a place in secondary schools. It was very important to keep these 12 to 15 years old girls off the street and keep them gainfully occupied by training them in making some handicrafts. Tarlaben Valumbhia, Shakuntala Gopalan and Viduben Patel, were exceptionally talented with their hands and taught the girls sewing, embroidery and how to make household items from scrap and discards. The girls enjoyed it, realizing that these classes might be the first step towards self-reliance. In fact, a couple of our trainees were able to later start their own successful arts-and-crafts shops on the Main Street of Dar-es-Salaam.

This was the time when UWT CC members were also busy meeting national and international women's leaders. This gave us many opportunities to share experiences and expertise and plan our future programs together.

Some of these women leaders from far away left a strong impression on my mind. One of them was Nelson Mandela's second wife Winnie Madikizela-Mandela. I met her whenever she visited Dar-es-Salaam, when Mandela himself was in jail. She was a very forceful speaker, danced energetically, sang with a booming voice and by and by became a powerful and much feared youth leader. Another member whom I remember well is Garca Machel. She was married to Samora Machel, the former Mozambican President and ANC leader who was later killed in an air crash. ANC had their base camps for freedom fighters in Tanganyika, and Samora Machel and his wife Garca Machel used to visit Dar often. She was also a freedom fighter, very soft spoken, rather shy but very effective personality. She later married Nelson Mandela on his 80th birthday in 1998.

At one time Sonia Gandhi was visiting Dar-es-Salaam with her husband Rajiv Gandhi. We were organizing a day's program for her. To give the women from Dar-es-Salaam a chance to meet her, we organized a public meeting for her to address. The Arnatoglu Hall was filled to capacity with members from UWT branches from around Dar-es-Salaam. Most of these members had walked a few kilometers from their homes early in the morning to reach the venue on time. To our disappointment Sonia Gandhi was so remote that there was no chance of interacting with her by any of our members. Thus at one level when I was meeting these distinguished personalities I was learning as well. My best moments came when I was visiting the hinterland and meeting the women from all over the country and interacting with them. I felt equally excited to hear Mariam Mabeka the famous South African singer singing her world famous song, 'Malaika nakupenda Malaika.'—'Angle I love you Angle,' and applause Bi Kidede from Zanzibar when she serenaded the absent lover with her haunting Tarab songs,

During that period I was involved with the Asian women's groups as well. Many Asian women from these groups were enthusiastic and wanted to take part in joint projects. UWT Kisutu Branch was a good example of this solidarity between the women of different communities.

But I did encounter non-cooperation from the leaders of communal groups. They often claimed personal as well as communal leadership roles and found objections and created obstacles if this was not forthcoming. These vicissitudes did not deter me as I realized that, their negative response was perhaps due to the fact that I was not happy to work with the communal tones and equations. Eventually, I continued with my activities in my own small way but with more vigor!

While people were thus preoccupied with development projects, drastic changes in the political field were in the offing within Tanganyika and in Zanzibar, Kenya and Uganda.

These resulted in far reaching decisions being taken by the government of Tanganyika and Zanzibar. From within a short span of time not only the policy but the Constitution of the country had to be changed. And by and by the Tanganyika of yester years came to be known as Tanzania of today!

Chapter 18

Zanzibar Revolution

During the Sultan's regime under the British umbrella, Zanzibar was considered to be safe heaven; a melting pot of many nationalities living in harmony. Nobody bothered to lock up their doors and the cupboards were kept open. Even the shop keeper while out on this and that errand did not bother to lock up his shop during the day time. Women and children moved about at all hours of day and night without any fear. Even though people lived within their own community groups they lived amicably with a feeling of brotherhood all round.

All this changed on 12th January 1964 when there was a revolution in Zanzibar. It overthrew ad hoc the Afro Shirazi government, including the Sultanate and established the Revolutionary Government led by Sheikh Abeid Amani Karume.

Speculation was rife; we kept on hearing many rumours about the Revolution in Zanzibar especially because during those days the media were heavily censored, and the information and the news travelled underground. In effect this acted as the main source of information in Dar-es-Salaam. By all accounts it was a horror story about arrests and people being killed on the slightest suspicion, forced marriages and dhows full of escaping parents with their young daughters capsizing in the Indian Ocean in the middle of the night. While others, managed to cross the high seas and reach the shores of Tanganyika or Kenya and some lucky ones even took the ten minutes flight by air or an hour's ride by a speed boat to reach Dar-es-Salaam. There were murmurings about the whole communities vanishing mysteriously over night during the Revolution. [*1*]

However, by early 1990s the Government policy had changed; the newspapers gradually got their independence to report news as it happened. Many newspapers mushroomed and made their way on the streets writing about matters, which formally would have resulted in reporters being arrested. These reports provide the missing links in the historical events taking place in the country.

In Zanzibar after the Revolution Sheikh Abeid Amani Karume emerged as the new leader. It was he who led the second phase of the revolution which changed the future of Zanzibar and Tanganyika as a whole. Sheikh Karume had taken over the reign of Zanzibar with popular acclaim and true to people's expectations he changed the entire social structure prevailing in Zanzibar by boldly declaring that all land belonged to the people and not a few individuals as before. In addition he directed that all public services including water, health and education be given free. And he granted every citizen 3 acres of land for farming and shelter purposes. These changes granted equal opportunities to all and boosted people's confidence in the new Government.

Sheikh Karume also started and enforced mixed marriages between Africans, Arabs and Asian communities. People holding high positions just went around the schools and selected girls even more then one to suit their fancy."

William Edget Smith in his book, 'Nyerere of Tanzania' on page 152 also corroborates that, "as a result of this, one of the outcome was that in 1966 Karume under the pretext of removing colour decimation made a law by which he took away the right of the parents to refuse to give their underage daughters in marriage to whoever wanted to marry her.

Because of this many young girls specially, the Arab girls were forced to marry older men whether their parents agreed or not and parents were jailed." The girls simply avoided going to school and there was panic exodus of parents by small dhows from Zanzibar in the middle of the night at great danger to their lives. Many Asian parents also left the isles by this route.

Initially, it was believed that Karume led the revolution, latter on it was said that on that night Karume and Mohamed Babu, both were safe in Dar-es-Salaam. And the leader was actually John Okello and his revolutionaries who were mainly unemployed members of the Afro Shiraz Youth League. Okello was a Ugandan who had arrived in Zanzibar from Kenya in 1959. He had served as Branch secretary for the ASP in Pemba. According to some news papers reports he claimed to have been a Field Marshal for the Kenyan rebels during the Mau Mau uprising but actually had no military experience."[2]

Though Okello vanished from the scene as mysteriously and suddenly within a short period, the Revolution in Zanzibar changed the destiny of Zanzibar-Pemba and Tanganyika. It was considered to be the shortest war of the time in which a government ruled by a hereditary Sultan with over a century of absolute power was toppled in less then a day. Nonetheless it was a bloody revolution and its ripples could be felt far and wide for a long time.

The whole saga of Zanzibar Revolution is fraught with hair raising elements of danger, doubt, suspense and bravery. Greatly outnumbered and poorly armed, the Revolutionaries were a motley group of young men with one goal in mind. They had wanted to remove the Sultan's rule from Zanzibar come what may. And the only weapons available to them were their pangas-machets, bows and arrows, and sharpened bicycle chains while the Sultan's army under Colonial rule was well armed and well trained. All that notwithstanding, these young revolutionaries had been holding secrete meetings for quite some time to plan for the revolution. They saw their chance to strike, when a large number of people were to assemble in and around the Stone Town to celebrate a popular religious holiday where it was easy for them to mingle with the crowds unnoticed.

On the night before the celebrations all Zanzibaris were in celebrating mood. And in anticipation of enjoying themselves they had happily set up tents or just slept under the swaying palm trees and waited for the morning festivities to start. Scattered amongst these revellers, a large numbers of young men were waiting to carry out their plans and overthrow the Sultan's regime. Gabby Mgaya, a senior staff writer with Daily News as well as other reporters have written a series of articles about the Revolution. According to his report, "The Revolution began earnestly as planned the night before 12th January 1964, when hundreds of gallant Revolutionaries accompanied by about 250 men of the 4th Battalion marched in the dead of night on the Ziwani Police Barracks Armoury. At 3 am an order was issued to the men to cut the wire surrounding the fortified compound.

The moment was fraught with danger, suspense and fear." Armed as they were with bows and arrows, home made pangas and bicycle chains, the revolutionaries were out to battle with solders armed with automatic rifles and machine guns. All but forty men baulked at the prospect of crawling through the wire and left the success or failure of the revolution and even their own safety, hinged on the shoulders of those forty young men.

Valiantly the remaining men crawled within 25 meters of the barracks building. Here they found only two men on guard duty as the rest of the paramilitary solders were sleeping on the upper floors unarmed in keeping with the standard peacetime army regulations. But those two downstairs minding the gate were armed!

Gabby adds "The revolutionary forces rushed at these guards. Automatic fire rang out and the three of the 4th battalion men went down. However, one of the sentries also fell, downed by an arrow shot by a revolutionary named Albert. By then another revolutionary had closed on the remaining sentry. It was here that the deciding moment of the revolution occurred.

The revolutionary got hold of the gun. They fought and the revolutionary managed to hit him in the cheek with the gun butt." the firing stopped. The men were now at the gates of the armoury where hundreds of modern weapons were locked up."

As expected the doors of the armoury gave way against their combined force. Soon every man was armed with a modern automatic rifle. Besides that by the end of that fateful day, three battalions of solders together with thousands of young men who were waiting in the adjoining areas had joined the Revolutionaries. They were also issued guns and automatic rifles; the Freedom fighters, who had started the night, armed only with most primitive weapons were now the best equipped force on the Island. They unleashed a ragging fire of unspent anger over the Isles and took over the remaining police posts and the communication centres without much resistance. In the process many innocent lives were lost.

The Revolutionary solders had now seized the Island of Zanzibar and successfully toppled the Omani Sultans' dynasty that had ruled the islands for over 133 long years. Consequently before even the day was out Sultan Jamsheed bin Abdullah fled from the Isles with his family and entire cabinet in tow, leaving the populace at the mercy of the national and international political winds blowing fiercely in the Isles.

By some strange coincidence the Zanzibar Revolution was followed soon by National Army revolts in Tanganyika, Kenya and Uganda in quick succession. In Dar-es-Salaam Tanganyika, the date set for the Army Mutiny was January 20th 1964.

Chapter 19

The Tanganyika Rifles Mutiny

On 20 January 1964 we woke up to a quiet morning as usual. Just a week after the Zanzibar Revolution the day had started like any other day. However, we sensed a peculiar atmosphere around our house. Lorry loads of troops and armoured vehicles were moving on Ocean Road, Radio Tanganyika had stopped broadcasting and rumours proliferated that a big problem of some sort was brewing, and that soldiers of the Tanganyika Rifles had mutinied. Panic began to build up. Asmani, our old house help, said that even public figures such as Bibi Titi and Joseph Nyerere had been slapped and roughed up. President Nyerere and Vice-President Rashidi Kawawa had gone into hiding. No one knew where. Some said they were in Nairobi while others said Mwalimu was hiding in a prison, disguised as a mad woman.

That day our children did not go to school. At about 10 a.m. we heard gunshots in the vicinity of the nearby

Sea View hotel. Hearing the commotion, our neighbour Umedbhai wanted to leave by car with his wife and four kids and wanted us to follow him. He said, "Challo apne jaladi bhagi jaaye, come on let us run away from here." But to escape where, he did not have any idea. Fortunately he realized the futility and the danger of the situation and remained at home.

It was rumored that soldiers were looking for Mzungu-European Brigadier Patrick Sholto Douglass, the Commander of Tanganyika Rifles who had taken over as the Commander of the Tanganyika Rifles when the British left Tanganyika. This was confirmed by a surprise visitor to our house—a shaken Harkishanbhai Shah, the then President of the Hindu Mandal with equally surprising and strange story to relate.

He told us that his guest, Vinood from Bombay was visiting, He had borrowed Harkishanbhai's car and driven that morning to Sea View hotel to have coffee with some of his friends. While they were having coffee, there was a commotion as soldiers entered the hotel in search of "somebody high up". Noticing the tense atmosphere, Vinood decided to leave, and as he was starting the car a few soldiers came up and asked him to take them to Colito Barracks. Vinood complied in fear, but as they approached the Selender Bridge he pleaded that he was new to Dar-es-Salaam and did not know the roads; the soldiers could take the car, and he would find his way to his host's house on foot. The soldiers agreed and drove away the car. And Vinood walked back home as fast as he could. Now Harkishanbhai wanted Jhaveri in his capacity as MP from Dar-es-Salaam to help retrieve the vehicle! Surprisingly he did get his car back after a few days.

As Jhaveri described in his memoir 'Marching with Nyerere' published in Feb, 1999, traumatic violence was raging all over the city. That same afternoon Jhaveri received a phone call from Mr. Tara Singh of MECCO who had called us frantically, saying that some Sikh boys had been picked up outside the local Gurdwara. He further explained that shots had been fired near the Mnazi Moja grounds and people had been advised by the Field Force through loudspeakers to remain indoors. However, as soon as the shooting stopped those Sikh boys, including the advocate Manmohan Singh Sukla, a junior partner in Jhaveri's chambers, went out to see how many bullet hits were made on the walls of the Gurdwara, Sikh temple. As they were counting the holes, a Field Force unit van arrived, rounded them up and took them all to Msimbazi police station. Their families were in great fear and distress, and Mr. Tara Singh requested Jhaveri to help in getting those boys released.

Jhaveri called the police station and with some effort managed to get through. The officer in charge told him that hundreds of people including the Sikh boys had been rounded up for not obeying police orders to stay indoors while the shooting was in progress. No one would be released until he got direct instructions to do so from his superior. Jhaveri rang the distraught Mr. Tara Singh, and explained the situation to him. There was nothing they could do that night so next morning he picked up Mr. Singh early from his house in Sea View as well as Sukla's sister from her home near the Gurdwara. She had a list of all the Sikh boys who were in custody. They reached the police station shortly after 8 a.m. and met the Regional Commissioner of Police who advised Jhaveri to get permission from the Commissioner of Police before taking any further action. In his capacity as a Parliamentarian Jhaveri knew the Commissioner of Police

Ulanga Saidi, quite well, and their meeting that morning was very cordial. The Commissioner immediately gave Jhaveri a signed note for the RC, on which the names of the Sikh boys were to be entered ensuring their immediate release.

They then returned to the police station to find the RC in fierce argument with three European reporters whose cameras had been seized by the police. Jhaveri, Sukla's sister, and Tara Singh waited on the terrace. On the terrace Jhaveri met the President of the city's Arab Association who had come to take custody of a child, the only survivor of a gruesome incident at Magomeni. This had happened the previous day when a soldier who entered an Arab shop was shot dead by its frightened owner. In retaliation other soldiers had set fire to the shopkeeper's house and the family was burnt alive, except for this four-year-old daughter. Terrified, the pretty child clung to a uniformed African policewoman as if she was her mother. Just then the radio in a nearby room started blaring that some Arabs had begun shooting all Africans in the vicinity of Arab Street. Immediately the RC ordered all Police personnel to go to Arab Street and he himself also rushed there. The Police station was almost deserted. Glancing down from the terrace they saw hundreds of Arabs rounded up the previous day, huddled in the police station compound, unaware of the escalating ethnic tensions.

Meanwhile a rumour spread that Europeans were being attacked in Kurasini, one of the Suberb's of Dar-es-Salaam. The European residents from there began rushing for safety to the city, while the Europeans in the city began rushing for safety elsewhere. The panic was indescribable, and the best policy at that moment was for everyone to reach home as soon as possible. Jhaveri dropped Mr. Tara Singh and Sukla's sister both at Mr. Singh's house, and drove back home to find that our landlord, Magan Kaka, had locked the gate and was unwilling to come out to open it. After repeated requests and reassurances from me, he threw the keys into the compound; I opened the gate and Jhaveri drove in safely.

That night the President spoke on the radio, describing the events of the previous day as disgraceful. On 22 January he made an appearance on the streets of Dar-es-Salaam, accompanied by Mama Maria Nyerere and tried to reassure the Victims, of the terrible day-long rioting, looting and killing in the city's Indian and Arab quarters by the rampaging soldiers. The local residents were relieved and responded warmly but with obvious tension. Shattered glass covered the sidewalks and most shops were boarded up to remind the President of the havoc caused under his watch by the mutinous soldiers.

Mwalimu called a press conference that afternoon in order to clarify the cause of the violence and announce the steps he was taking to ensure law and order. It so happened that the Cultural Society had arranged a lecture at the Karimjee Hall in honour of the late Dag Hammarskjöld, on that very same day. The dapper Secretary- general of UN, Dag Hammarskjöld was killed in mysterious circumstances when the plane carrying him crashed near Ndola in British run Northern Rhodesia on September -18 -1961. President Nyerere was scheduled to deliver the main address at this meeting. Jhaveri and I attended this function. A packed audience of all races was waiting to listen to Mwalimu, who arrived looking haggard and deeply sad. People of all races whether Europeans, Africans or Asians were still under shock; it was unimaginable to think that a mutiny actually took place against President Nyerere's Government. This incident and its consequences was the only subject on everybody's mind. The President talked briefly. And all I remember is that he paid a tribute to Dag Hammarskjold expressed his displeasure and distress at the events of the past week and left immediately.

Next day, Thursday was uneventful and 24 January dawned quietly. But at around 10 a.m Jhaveri heard rumours that a British naval ship had been sighted on the coast. Fearing aerial bombardment, people began to rush home from their offices and shops. Jhaveri also closed his office and told his staff to go home. Reaching the house, he enquired about our kids. Abha was at home but Atool had gone to Shankerbhai's saloon for a haircut riding on his bicycle. Atool had wanted to go for a haircut, and I did not see any harm in it thinking that the mutiny was over and every thing was back to normal. President Nyerere was back in power, we were all safe now and Atool can have his haircut! But Shankerbhai knew better. As he had also heard the roumers about the British that morning, he was closing up his saloon and promptly sent Atool back. At home we panicked and Jhaveri rushed back to the haircutting saloon. When he reached the corner of Sea View he saw our son riding back on his bicycle unaware of any danger. Atool always went to Sankarbhai regularly for his haircut since he was a kid. For once Atool came back without his haircut and for once I was really scarred out of my wits!

Meanwhile people were trying to store up emergency provisions. Jhaveri said that there seemed to be some sort of serious problems and it may take a few days before normal situation may prevail. He also went to get some milk and bread from Ocean Road Petrol Station shop near our home. At that time it was being run by our friend Chandubhai Popat and his brother Shantu. After waiting in the queue for more then half an hour Jhaveri realized that by the time his turn came they were bound to finish all their supplies. My husband came back empty handed.

The next day Saturday we woke up just before 6 a.m. to the sound of gunfire, apparently coming from the vicinity of the lighthouse. At that time the Sea View area, where we were living had very few high rise buildings. This offered us a clear vista of the ocean. We saw British naval warships moored far away ready to enter the harbour and there appeared to be firing going on in the vicinity of the light house. Soon at about 9 a.m. we saw helicopters in the sky carrying what looked like huge Lorries. In fact these were armored vehicles. Some of the copters were just doing rounds flying very low. It was obvious that some military action was in progress. We did not see any soldiers parachuting in our area but soon heard that they had landed some where near the University where Lugalo Barracks was situated. Initially civilians were moving around, but as the rumours spread persistently, people expected aerial bombing to start any time. Everybody, Asians Africans and Europeans rushed to the safety of their homes and remained indoors, watching silently from their windows and balconies. Finally it was announced over the Radio that the British troops had landed in Dar-es-Salaam to restore law and order in the country.

During this period the British press, especially the *Daily Telegraph*, had been reporting extensively on the Tanganyika Rifles mutiny. In addition during all these years since then, this episode has been extensively studied by political analysts and historians, and by those directly or indirectly involved in the mutiny. Later President Nyerere himself challenged the officers of his armed forces to write an account of the rebellion. Their detailed report was published in a book form by the University of Dar-es-Salaam Press. Titled "Tanganyika Rifles Mutiny 1964." It records step by step the whole saga of the military formation of the colonial-era; the establishment of King's African Rifles and its later derivative the Tanganyika Rifles—the National army of Tanganyika, and the causes, manifestations as well as outcomes of the mutiny.

Briefly very briefly, according to these reports, The King's African Rifles K.A.R. battalion in Tanganyika had been established in 1917 in Morogoro to assist the British government to conquer and rule over the Colonial East Africa. During political disturbances they served as a controlling, intimidating and repressive force, and during peacetime they provided spectacle and ritual theatre through parades and ceremonies designed to impress the subjugated population. African troops were considered good foot and frontline soldiers, but Colonial policy ensured they were deliberately kept on the lowest rung of the army, in poor working conditions. As a result of this policy the units in Tanganyika were small, ill-equipped and operated with a subsistence budget.

Later on, The Tanganyika Rifles was created from these units when Tanganyika became independent on 9-December 1961 under the same Colonial set up. In practice this meant that instead of being led by African officers under better a scheme of service, and being regularly given due promotions and benefits as expected, they continued to be poorly paid and shabbily treated while their prospects for achieving commanding positions through Africanization remained virtually non existent. This discriminatory practice did not change even after the transfer of power from the British to the Nationalist Government as the British officers were still in charge of the army and the working environment of the solders remained the same as before.

To make matters more difficult, it seems that at that time there was no proper communication or reliable army platform for hearing and redress of soldiers' justified grievances. This left an impression that the government was blissfully unaware of the dimensions of prevailing conditions and unrest in the army; and the spirit of independence had yet to enter the Army Head Quarters.

A similar scenario was unfolding in Belgium Congo.

On 30th June 1960 Congo gained independence from Belgium. Similar to East African countries where all the officers were British, all the officers and senior non-commissioned officers in the Congo National Army were Belgians. In this incidence as well, the resentment raised its head in the army when the newly elected PM Patrice Lumumba decided to raise the pay of all the employees except the military whose privates and NCOs saw little opportunity for their advancement. Consequently on 5th July 1960, the garrison mutinied against its Belgian officers and armed bands of mutineers roamed the capital looting and terrorizing the white population.

This had prompted President Nyerere to profess publicly his complete trust in his army. At that time he had stated empathetically that there was not the slightest chance that the forces of law and order in Tanganyika would mutiny in the way soldiers had rebelled in Congo.

During the whole of this period Mwalimu remained preoccupied with Organization of African Unity. Under his leadership the headquarters of the Liberation Committee was established in Dar-es-Salaam in mid 1963. From then on Tanzania committed full activist support to liberation struggles taking place in Africa including Mozambique and South Africa.

On 12 January 1964 there was a revolution in Zanzibar, led by John Okello, which overthrew the regime of Sultan Jamshid within a day or two and established the

Revolutionary Government there. Okelo was an ordinary solder with little education. Yet he proceeded to declare himself Field Marshal immediately after the revolution. Knowledge of similar successful revolts in other African countries also may have encouraged the Tanganyika Rifles troops to feel resentful about their own maltreatment by the British officers of the army.

In addition, the newly independent government in Tanganyika had not redefined the defence and security of the new nation and as such they did not intervene in any way into the running of the Army. Later on while writing about the mutiny President Nyerere recalled, " . . . at independence the government inherited the structure and philosophy of the King's African Rifles. Other then that the only sign that changed was the name, from K.A.R. to T.R.—, and it was not the strategy of TANU to infiltrate the Army." [1]

Most probably he wanted to avoid the onset of party politics and tribalism in the army and deliberately left the affairs of his army entirely in the hand of the British expecting them to train and maintain an impartial army with the the right equilibrium. But then perhaps the British Government was pursuing a different agenda. To most of us what actually happened is still a mystery. We may argue, deduce, induce, but all this debate is like the definitions given by the blind men who touched different parts of the elephant and each one gave his own partial definition of it!

Paradoxically however, the harsh reality was that a lacuna in communication between the Government and its Armed Forces had developed some where down the line and President Nyerere's Government tripped in it uncharacteristically. Unknown to him, now an idea of mutiny was already floating in the air!

Final Rebound

Various newspaper reports, the 1970 Treason Trial records and the book Tanganyika Rifles Mutiny January 1964, compiled by Tanzania Defense Forces and published by Dar-es-Salaam University Press reiterate that, there was a compact committee of well seasoned men who masterminded, meticulously planned, and stage managed the plot to oust the British and take charge of the army.

To recall briefly from the above reports, Sergeant Frances Hingo Illogi was one of them. He was born in Bukene, Tabora in 1937. That makes him 37 years old when he took the leading part in the mutiny. Relatively well educated he had experience of working in several departments at Colito Barracks including the transport office and was familiar with its working and locations. Also to his advantage, he was education instructor in the army and knew his students well.

Their strategy was set and all plans were in place by the night of 19th January 1964, when action started in earnest soon after the core group's final briefing under a tree in Mbezi. That night as planned, the soldiers advanced swiftly first of all to capture the armory from the guard room where the arms were locked up.

For Second Lieutenant Makaranga, the Orderly Officer on duty that night it was business as usual. He inspected the guards at the State House and other locations and proceeded to his base in Colito Barracks. He made sure that all procedures were followed as required and the guard room was locked up securely. He then went to sleep after midnight. All was quiet in Colito Barracks as usual. Soon three soldiers stealthily entered his room and ordered him to remain quiet and follow instructions under threat of death. Half dressed, he was he was ordered to open the guard room immediately. From there he was pushed into the adjoining cell and locked up. The soldiers then armed them selves with the rifles which were kept in this room. Now it became easy for the mutineers to take their superiors by surprise one by one, and order them at gun point to march at the double to the guard room cell and be locked up.

On that same night Captain S. M. A. Kashmir also had completed inspecting the guard at the strategic points in town. He went to the State House to check the guard there. After satisfying himself that all was well he headed to Colito Barracks for the same purpose. When he reached the Barracks he too was roughly disarmed, marched at gun point and locked up unceremoniously in the guard room cell with others by one of his junior cadres.

By around 1.00 p.m. the mutineers had thus managed to paralyze and take over the security arrangement at the Colito Barracks.

Next, they set off the fire alarm. Hearing it the soldiers and officers, some half asleep and some alert and worried scrambled to report. The soldiers were ordered back to their quarters but the officers especially the British were mobbed and locked up with others in the guard room by force of the gun.

The mutineers were now in charge at Colito Barracks. They then dispatched teams to town to take over key areas in Dar-es-Salaam such as the Tanganyika Broadcasting Station, the State house, Cable and Wireless Station, the Banks, Government stores, Diplomatic, commercial and residential areas. They also took over and blocked the roads to the airport.

A unit of about 25 soldiers led by Sgt. Hingo Ilogi was on their way to the State house. But before they could reach the State House Emilio Mzena, the Director of Special Branch had been alerted that, trouble had broken out at Colito Barracks and an armed unit of soldiers was heading for State House. Emilio Mzena being a hard-nosed professional immediately recognized the threat approaching from round the corner and instructed his men at state House to evacuate the President to safety. Mzena was alerted about the mutiny at around 2.00 a.m. By 2.30 a.m. the President accompanied by the Vice President Mr. Rashidi M. Kawawa had reluctantly left State House through the back door.

Mr. Kawawa recalls, '. . . I was told to go to the President's House. What had happened?' The security officer said there was trouble at Colito Barracks. We consulted over the matter and reached a decision that we should go into hiding. We left immediately for Kigamboni where a Good Samaritan sheltered us," [1]

The President's escape beat the solders by a split second. When the solders reached the State House they found Mzena hovering around appearing to be one of the aids. He gained the soldiers' confidence and was told that all the British officers were under arrest, and now they wanted to discuss their problems with the President.

In order to parley and buy time, Mzena advised them first to see Mr. Kambona Minister of Defense and Foreign Affairs, and offered personally to take them to see him. But he could not possibly take them all in a car designed for four people, now could he! Ultimately it was agreed that he would take three soldiers including Sgt. Hingo Ilogi so as to be able to spare one seat for the Minister.

Mzena drove the group to pick up Mr. Kambona from his residence. On returning to the State House Mr. Kambona managed to persuade the army men to return to Colito Barracks for serious negotiations.

When they reached Colito Barracks apart from recounting their grievances to the Minister the soldiers spontaneously and by popular acclamation promoted each other to their anticipated ranks. For a start Sgt. Hingo Ilogi was promoted to Lieutenant Colonel and became Commanding Officer while many received higher positions and others became commissioned officers. Ironically many of those who were promoted out of turn were called out from the guard room where they were locked up. This exercise went on until dawn.

Next the British officers' names were called out. One by one, they came out from the guard room where they had spent a sleepless night squatting on the floor with others. They were all ordered on the army truck.

Captain Kashmir was called out as well and ordered on the truck but the Captain was very much a Tanganyikan like everybody else. In fact he was amongst the first Tanganyikans officer to join Royal Military Academy Sand Hurst. That not withstanding after being stripped of his hat, pips, shoulder straps and belts he was taunted boastfully that he was being packed off to Bombay. In the end he too had to join the hapless British Officers on the truck.

And unceremoniously the thirty British Officers with Captain Kashmir were taken straight to Dar-es-Salaam airport from where they were flown to Nairobi and onwards. Their families followed them the next day. [2]

During this period Mr. Kambona came on the Radio a couple of times to reassure people that there was a misunderstanding with the army and matters were being worked out. Mean while Mikidadi Mdoe the Director of Radio Tanganyika managed to reach the President and Vice President in Kigamboni and recorded the President's massage which was broadcast from Radio Tanganyika that very same day.

But that was not enough. People wanted to see their President in person taking charge of the country's affairs.

Often it is asked, 'who can police the Police! For that matter who can police the army?

By now the soldiers were worked up and trigger happy and the situation was tense. In Dar-es-Salaam they went on a rampage, looting shops in the Indian Bazaar, shooting Arabs, blockading Banks, Diplomatic missions and threatening one and all.

In addition motorized units of soldiers went to take over the police posts around town. After efficiently immobilizing Korya Police Station they took Chang'ombe, Msimbazi and Oyster Bay Police Stations in quick succession without any incident. However the capture of Central Police Station was not that easy due to one plucky lady WP Corporal Esta. She had deftly hidden the keys to the armory in her briefs and was beaten up mercilessly for her valiant efforts. [3]

By this time the TR Units at Tabora, and Nachigweya had joined the mutiny. In Tabora the pattern of mutual promotions, rampant looting and shootings was repeated perhaps more violently. It took Captain Sarakikya quite an effort and a while to get the drunk with power, mutineers back in the Barracks. From here also the British Officers with their families were packed off on their way to Britain.

In Nachigweya fortunately there was no looting and shootings save a few isolated incidents. But the mutineers did manage to kick out the British officers on their way back to Britain.

It is important at this stage to note that only 8 days after Zanzibar Revolution, the TR Mutiny in Tanganyika took place on 20th January. This was followed in quick succession by mutinies in Uganda on 23 January and at Langata in Kenya on 24 January 1964. Both these governments had requested the British Government for help, to quell the rebellions in their respective countries on the same day and the Britiish troops had managed to bring the situation under control in Kenya and Uganda within a short time.

This was the situation faced by President Nyerere when he came out of hiding and went round visiting the areas in town most affected by the violence committed by the unruly soldiers and other hooligans when he had remained incognito.

In the end after holding out for four days, the President was also constrained to request the British Government to disarm the mutineers on 24th of January. The British army was more then ready to do so as their Navy ships and battle ready troops were virtually waiting in the wings, on the outskirts of Dar-es-Salaam harbour for this eventuality. Within hours they mounted Operation Floodtide with the legendary British military precision. Their helicopters landed in the football field adjoining the Barracks from where British troops managed to disarm Tanganyika Rifles without any causality under the direction of Brigadier Patrick Sholto Douglas the British Military Advisor to the Tanganyika government and the Commander of the Tanganyika Rifles. Boastfully the Brigadier had told President Nyerere that he knew his men well and could disarm them within half an hour. They were nearly there; reportedly they had taken 45 minutes to do so!

No doubt that the Tanganyika Rifles mutiny of 1964 was a litmus test for President Nyerere personally and perhaps it was the worst crisis of his political career. But then on the other hand it turned out as a blessing in disguise for the country.

In Tanganyika the mutineers over and above every thing else had demanded in no uncertain terms that the British officers should be replaced with African officers. They had successfully managed to accomplish this. Not only they got rid of all the British officers in one go, they installed their own men and took charge of the army.

Without any delay President Nyerere took control of the country's affairs once again. Under his decisive and firm guidance Tanganyika Rifles became Tanzania People's Defense Forces with a new batch of loyal officers in charge. Captain Sarakikya took over as their newly appointed Commander in Chief. And by and by TPDF was firmly integrated in the national grid at all levels. As a result of this policy, presently the Army men hold high positions in National and International institutions and share in the running of the government.

Simultaneously, TANU Youth League was established and two years compulsory National service for all youth after they finished their secondary school education was introduced.

Lastly but not the least as a result of the Army mutiny the Treason Trial was held in 1970 in Dar-es-Salaam. Oscar Kambona was tried in absentia as he was already in London while several well known personalities of the time including Bibi Titi and others who were arrested from Dar es Salaam and Nairobi had to face the law of the land.

As this case has been serialized and reported in several National newspapers argument by arguments and blow by blow, I do not propose to go into it even though it contains some hair-raising information about the plot to subvert an elected government and the duplicity of human nature.

Having said that, it is imperative to put on record the Lawyers names who took up the briefs of those accused and untiringly and diligently defended them; Ferozshah Dastur, Late Murtaza Lakha, Bashir Versi, Late Mahendra

Raithatha, Shyam Jadeja and Nurali Velji. They all were my husband's colleagues and are our family friends. We remember them fondly.

The trial lasted for 127 days at the end of which most of the accused received lifelong imprisonment. Bibi Titi was one of them. After spending seven years in jail, she was pardoned and received publicly by President Nyerere himself. Many others were also pardoned and released at a latter stage. In fact Kambona came back to Tanzania and tried to establish his political party in Tanzania with out any success.

The Japanese Sages say that, 'The bamboo that bends is stronger than the oak that resists.' President Nyerere proved this to be true. The mutiny must have been harrowing experience for him but in spite of it he established a solid army base for his country and came out stronger after the Tanganyika Rifles Mutiny.

Chapter 20

The Birth pangs of a New Nation

One of the most enigmatic questions in the whole issue of the mutiny of Tanganyika Rifles and the Revolution in Zanzibar concerns the rapid succession of similar events in the whole of East Africa. When these rebellions occurred, Uganda followed by Kenya asked for and received British army help to quell the rebellions on the same day. Tanganyika held out until 24th when it also decided to invite the British to intervene and disarm their army.

The British forces managed to accomplish this task smoothly within a short period. And each of these young Nations treaded its own path after that.

However, in Dar-es-Salaam the Zanzibar revolution and TR mutiny were followed by strong rumours of foreign Governments being involved in the power play to gain a foothold especially in Zanzibar. Some reported that communist countries including Cuba, China and East Germany had their eyes on it, while others theorised that this was the British and American Governments' doing. By all accounts it was clear that all the attention was focused on Zanzibar because being an island it was in a vulnerable position. This made the situation in East Africa at the time more fragile and fluid.

Consequently, Presidents Nyerere and Sheikh Abeid Karume who was also the Chairman of the Zanzibar Revolutionary Council decided to establish immediately the Union between Tanganyika and Zanzibar as a first priority. Thus Tanzania was born under the guiding light of the then President of Tanganyika, Mwalimu Julius Nyerere and the President of Zanzibar, Sheikh Abeid Amani Karume on 26th April 1964. Tanganyika and Zanzibar now were jointly known as Tanzania. And their political parties merged and became Chama Cha Mapinduzi—CCM.

Unfortunately both these leaders were polls apart in their thinking, working style, and temperament. They were a study in contrast; President Karume started to work as a stevedore, and a trade unionist. He joined politics and ultimately became President of Zanzibar. He was a man who brooked no opposing views. Where by President Nyerere had graduated from Mkrere University and University of Edinburg and was articulate and ever ready to explain his policy to the average man in the street.

From the beginning these differences in their temperaments resulted in many pitfalls and became an impediment for the smooth running of the Union.

Various Newspapers were always coming out with these reports regularly from time to time.

Tanganyika Standard of March 1st 1968 reported that; ". . . . by 1967 people were terrified of Karume because of his excesses. Nor would he listen to Mwalimu's words. Time and again he used to openly make fun when told that Mwalimu would disprove of his undemocratic ways, and even threaten Mwalimu that if he is not happy we will break the Union. It seemed that it was always Mwalimu who had to suffer all kinds of outrages in the name of the Union . . . ."

Another leading newspaper, 'Rai' was also forthright in its comments and reviewed the problems facing the Union bluntly in their issue dated 12-5-2007. Excerpts; ". . . . Sheikh Karume was uneducated and oppressive. During his government Zanzibar did not follow any Constitution. It was governed through Presidential Decree . . . ." In short, the report also said that President Karume's often repressive methods, especially his 'Kamata Kamata' campaign; indiscriminate and arbitrary arrests resulted in creating fear and resentment amongst the people in Zanzibar.

Travelling for any reason, anywhere even to Dar-es-Salaam was difficult for Zanzibaris. While others were trying to leave by any means, Wolfgang Dourado a lawyer by profession decided to stay back in Zanzibar.

He had joined the Colonial Zanzibar civil service in 1947 as a clerk, gradually rising to the position of permanent secretary in the ministary of Home and Legal affairs in 1963. Immediately after the Revolution he was appointed the Attorney General of Zanzibar. To his credit Durado survived as Attorney General in Zanzibar for 13 long years during the most difficult times immediately after the 1964 Zanzibar Revolution. At one point during this perilous period he had left his important personal files with my brother Mahen for safe keeping; he was afraid that he was being followed by the C.I.D. Police and might be arrested any time. He collected them only after he thought it safe for him to do so.

As lawyers Jhaveri and Dourado were friends. One evening Wolfgang Dourado came home for tea. They were both advising Pravin on some legal matters.

Having spent all his life in the Isles as a major player in the political transition of Zanzibar he was like a walking encyclopedia of Zanzibar history. It was also obvious that he has seen and been through many upheavals and hazards, during his career as the Attorney General in Zanzibar. I thought he was very brave to remain in Zanzibar when everybody else was leaving and said so. His argument was that he believed that if all qualified chose to leave at the same time and left every thing into the hands of inexperienced and radical Revolutionaries, the situation would be much worse. For this reason he had chosen to serve the Revolutionary Council of Zanzibar by seeking to make changes from within. Besides that, Zanzibar was his country, his home!

His forefathers had migrated from Portugal. They had been living in Zanzibar for the past three generations. Wolfgang Joseph Dourado himself was born in Zanzibar on September 20, 1929. In 1958 he married Yvonne Agnes.

Despite all the difficulties that he faced as the Attorney General immediately after the Revolution he remained very close to Karume. He pointed out that Karume had some good ideas but he was not following the right procedures.

Some time after the Revolution, Zanzibar Government had decreed that no private lawyers were to be allowed to practice in Zanzibar. This order resulted in bizarre situations where Durado as AG had to appear for both the sides in the same litigation. Especially after President Karume's assassination, Dourado served both as Prosecutor as well as Defense Lawyer for the accused during the Treason Trial in Zanzibar.

Another serious situation that arose at this time is also reported by Charles R. Swift in his book 'Dar Days, The Early Years in Tanzania.' The Author writes about his interview; "Dourado was worried and depressed. He looked furtively behind him. He was under intense pressure from both Karume and the Revolutionary Council to sign an order doing away with English system of Justice on the Isles, to be replaced with, 'People's Court' Dourado had refused to sign the order. At that time he submitted his resignation and was told by Karume that, "You are too useful to me." With tears in his eyes Dourado told me that he would welcome being put in detention because his present position had become untenable."[1]

By a strange twist of fate Dourado was detained for a day during another spat with Karume. This turned out to be equally traumatic experience for him. He describes this in his usually forthright and frank manner while replying to the 'Guardian' Newspaper's Deputy Managing Editor Bernard Mpalala who interviewed him in great detail earlier in May 2007.

In this interview Bernard asked many probing questions and received equally honest answers from Durado. One of the questions he asked was 'You won the trust of Founder President Abeid Amani Karume up to the time he was assassinated. How close was your personal relationship? Dourado replied 'We were very close even if he flogged me and his son Amani.'

Q; He flogged you? Why did he flog you and his sons also?

Yes indeed, that was a crucial question; Dourado was the Attorney General of the country. Why should he a lawyer be detained and flogged with a whip? The crux of the matter was that Dourado had opposed forced inter racial marriages in 1970. He was not only against these forced marriages but he had offered his sage advice to Ali, Karume's younger son against it. So he was detained and got Viboko—whipped. And Amani, Karume's eldest son was whipped and thrown out of the house for good measure for professing his trust in Dourado's good intentions!

Next day Karume went to see Dourado in prison, and when Dourado asked him, 'Mzee umefanya haya—Sir you did this to me?' Karume reply was "Even though we do not agree with you in this matter, we shall still support you to continue holding your position of Attorney General in Zanzibar. So now you go back to your work. The whole saga was preposterous; quietly Dourado went back to his work!

Even after Karume's assassination Dourado gave a fiery anti-union speech at a meeting organised by the Tanganyika Law Society in Dar-es-Salaam and it was believed that he was detained again for some time.

After his retirement as Attorney General, Wolfgang Dourado was appointed a Judge of the High Court and also the Chairman of Land Tribunal in Zanzibar. He passed away at his Vuga residence in Zanzibar on March 19-2012 in the presence of family members and was laid to rest in Zanzibar.

Apart from that on the national front, a sore point that used to crop up from time to time between President Nyerere and his Vice President Karume was the question of holding General Elections simultaneously in Zanzibar and in Tanzania mainland. According to Tanganyika Standard of March 1 1968 Sheikh Karume promised that there will not be any election in Zanzibar for the next 50 years from 1964. He declared that ". . . . election is a ploy by the imperialists to oppress the people . . . ."

Elections in Zanzibar were held when the new leaders took over after the Tanzanian Vice President Karume was assassinated one evening while playing cards with his cronies in the Party Headquarters in Zanzibar.

After Sheikh Karume's assassination his son the very same Amani Karume who was whipped by his father for questioning him became the President of Zanzibar. Recently Amani Abeid Karume completed successfully three terms as President of Zanzibar. He retired after holding successful elections as required by the Constitution of the Union Government. A gentle person, he has given the much needed healing touch to Zanzibar and Pemba and put it firmly on the road to Democracy and progress for all.

Simultaneously, since 1964 many changes have taken place in Tanzania; and the Union continues to evolve by trying to streamline the rough patches and rectify its Constitution step by step. This process is still going on almost fifty years down the line. In fact at present intense debate on another set of proposed Constitutional changes is going on earnestly in Tanzania.

It is now envisaged to bring major changes in the Constitution of Tanzania. One of the proposed recommendation redefines Zanzibar as a State formally known as The People's Republic of Zanzibar with it's territory composed of Unguja, Pemba and all the surrounding islands as was before 1964 merger with Tanganyika. With autonomy to join international as well as regional organizations, and the ownership of any petroleum reserves found in the region.

Whether these recommendations if passed, will bring in the highly expected global investment to the Isles, and not just a few rich Arab countries once again back to Zanzibar is also a big question mark. Constitutional experts charge that these amendments are, "meant to neutralised the Union, if not kill it systematically."

Or is it? On this day 29-February-2012, who knows how these proposals if sanctioned will work out for all concerned? Whether the common man's dream of leading a secure life, with education and progress for his children will be fulfilled! Only time in the long run will shed the light on the future and the development of Pemba, Unguja, and Dar-es-Salaam!

Chapter 21

Nationalization

In 1970-1971 President Nyerere's government nationalized all private properties from which the owners were earning rent in excess of certain amounts. This was followed by the nationalization of all banks in Tanzania, as well as insurance companies, internal and external trade organizations, medical profession, communal educational institutions, hospitals and major industries, and commercial properties. These mass takeovers by the state changed the topography of the country, and more significantly, it radically altered the financial frameworks and mode of governance. Nationalization also resulted in untold misery for various segments of society for the loss of their personal properties and personal savings, their factories, certain businesses and educational institutions. Their hospitals were taken over and even the mode of running their small businesses was changed. Those were the days. People were shell shocked and overnight there was an exodus. Friends and even neighbors left without sharing a hint about when or where they were going. At that time there was a good presence of Ismaili community in the country. With the help of H.H. the Aga Khan, most of them were able to emigrate to Canada, U.S.A. Europe and Australia in search of a place in the Sun for themselves. Others tried to find their own way and migrated any where they could go. They left with their families, many never to come back.

All these sudden changes had taken a heavy toll on the economy, resulting in acute shortages of all kinds. This cast a suffocating shadow over people's life in the country. In Dar-es-Salaam the situation was so dire that even a few bars of Lux soap or a tin or two of cooking oil led people to being arrested for economic sabotage and hoarding. There was a pervasive atmosphere of fear throughout the country. We knew of cases where television sets were buried or abandoned in ditches in the middle of the night, and people began hiding their soap and toothpaste. Someone known to us was actually jailed for trying to hide his television set. We did not own any TV, and I did not mind standing in long queues waiting patiently for my turn to buy half a kilogram of salt, sugar or cooking oil etc. Shortages became 'normal', and endless waits in line for meager supplies was a part of the daily routine for the common man.

Our houses that we had just bought in partnership with Manmohan Shukla were also nationalized. And like innumerable other citizens we found ourselves deprived of our personal savings. Old timers like us still remember those days gone by when lists of buildings being nationalized were published in the newspapers each morning. For us of more serious concern and equally worrying was the fact that the remittance of foreign exchange, for educational purposes, was stopped, and all foreign travel was banned.

Our son and daughter, Atool and Abha had passed their Senior Cambridge exams earlier, and we had planned to send them to the U.K. for further education. The government regulations of those days required the headmaster of their school to issue a school-leaving certificate, only after all the other formalities were concluded. Permissions from the Principal Secretary of the Ministry of Education, the Principal Immigration Officer and the National Bank of Commerce were to be obtained step by step first, and the students had to put together all their documents including their passports, tickets and bank allowances for fees. Then and then only the student was permitted to receive his school leaving certificate and travel abroad. Jhaveriji had finalised all the formalities as required. Atool left for UK in 1967 and Abha joined him in 1969. For the first two years of our children's studies abroad their expenses were paid automatically from the National Bank to their college bank account. When the government stopped all remittances, Atool and Abha were left high and dry without any financial support in a foreign country. We had no foreign bank account or any trust fund through which we might have sent them money. It was disastrous and created a nightmare all round.

For both Atool and Abha it was a long and painful struggle. In order to cope with the financial emergency they changed their study courses and both joined Chartered Accountants' firms in London. Working in his basement 'office', as he called it, Atool wore all his sweaters, coat and overcoat against the freezing English winter without success. He and Abha had friends in similar circumstances, and these young people stood by one another and survived that treacherous phase, to become professionally qualified.

Suffering of the mind is more agonizing then suffering of the body. Mine was a cry of a mother, worrying about my children day and night and I did not know what to do! I was angry with Mwalimu and his advisors for what I felt were unjust policies that caused such suffering to children and affected their education; and I was furious with my husband for not making any provision, like others were doing, to support their kids in crisis. And I was angrier with my own self for being so helpless and I was hurting all over.

Further to add to my frustrations, due to monetary constraints prevailing in the country we could not even attend Atool's wedding on 14th July 1972 in London. Fortunately, during the time of Abha's marriage on 19th January 1976 financial conditions were improving in Tanzania and these restrictions were gradually being relaxed step by slow step. And through our friend Mark Bomana's kindly help we got the mandatory permission from The National Bank of Commerce, to buy our air ticket so that we could travel from Dar-es-Salaam to Delhi, with Rupees Two Thousand, 2000 /-, as traveler's checks for our expenses. I was relieved that at least we could attend our daughter's wedding and perform the traditional ceremonies.

Mercifully it is the law of nature that nothing goes on and on for ever and life always offers us a second chance called tomorrow. For our family all these upsets happened like a bad dream ages ago. Since then, we have moved a long way.

But if we take into account the over all conditions prevailing in the country, the bitter truth was that in spite of the fact that the nation's business and commerce was under central authority, the economy was in shambles. Thus after an initial phase of national euphoria and optimism ordinary Tanzanians were facing testing times with many setbacks. At the time of independence, people were expecting overnight progress and development which was not forth coming. Instead of that, came the days of Ujamaa—Socialism. The ideal behind Ujamaa was worthy and noble. It was based on establishment of socialist villages throughout the rural areas. Where people were expected to pool all their resources together and work on co-operative basis and achieve their own development and progress through self-help. Some villages progressed well under this scheme.

Mwalimu aptly explained time and again that, only people themselves can bring real development through their own efforts. But by and large, in practical terms Ujamaa resulted in uprooting villagers from their ancestral homes where even a baobab tree on the farmstead was considered ancestral habitat. Tanzanians have very strong emotional attachment to their land and cattle. But these new settlements belonged to everybody and to nobody in particular. Occasionally their cattle also belonged collectively to the villages. In this unfriendly environment people were feeling rootless and unwilling to begin tilling the land which did not belong to them. The farmers were just not ready for that kind of revolution. Moreover most of the cooperatives and other public institutions were incurring massive losses due to mismanagement and obvious corruption. And to cap it all, the war with Uganda took a heavy toll on the already crippled economy, with little or no funds or foreign exchange remaining in Tanzanian banks and no scope for private enterprise.

All this caused the many members of the society to lose confidence in Mwalimu's policies; and people for whom Mwalimu's word was gospel were now getting restless. They started grumbling and criticized his policies and some even tried quietly to put alternatives into place. President Nyerere then initiated modes of preventive detention to control and suppress the rising trend of protest in the country. It was being alleged that he was using it arbitrarily far too often without any regards to its legal ramifications. Being a lawyer and also the President of the Law Society people came home to see my husband to discuss these cases often lamenting that they did not know where their family members were detained. And I was a silent witness to these tales.

By and by, international organizations and legal fraternity noticed and commented frequently on this phenomenon taking place in the country. In September 1976, the International Commission of Jurists decided to organize a seminar on 'Human Rights in a One-Party State'

Amongst others they approached the government of Tanzania as well. President Nyerere supported them fully and the Forum was held in Dar-es-Salaam in September 1976. Of the 37 prominent Africans participating in the seminar from all over Africa, 14 were from Tanzania.

The proceedings of this conference were published in a book, in which Niall Mac Dermot, Secretary-General, of I.C.J, affirms Mwalimu's decision thus: "Approaches were made to governments, lawyers' organizations, universities and others within the region. The Tanzanian government kindly consented to allow the seminar to be held in Dar-es-Salaam, and President Nyerere gave his personal encouragement to it, while making it clear that the responsibility for the seminar lay entirely with the Commission of Jurists. The International Commission of Jurists would like to place on record its gratitude to President Nyerere and to the Tanzanian Government for the friendly encouragement and the assistance they gave . . ."

All the participants had considerable experience of various aspects of government, legal practice and the protection of human rights. They came from Sudan, Tanzania, Zambia, Botswana, Lesotho and Swaziland. Their meetings were held in private and they had agreed that the report of the discussions would not make personal attributions.

The list of the delegation from Tanzania who participated in the Seminar is like a list of, 'Who is who' of the then and even now eminent Lawyers, Academics, and Government and Party leaders: Mark Bomani who chaired the opening session, Daudi Mwakawago, Pius Musekwa, Telford Georges, K.L. Jhaveri, Nathan Shamuyarira, J.B. Mwenda and many other distinguished personalities presented various papers on different aspects of the subject under discussion. Jhaveri presented his paper on, "The Principles of administrative (or preventive) detention. [Note]

As noted by Niall Mac Dermot, Secretary-General, of I.CJ.

"Their discussions were frank and free, and all their papers were well received. Largely due to a very fine keynote speech by Mr. Pius Msekwa, Vice Chancellor of the University Of Dar-es-Salaam and a former Secretary of TANU, all the most important issues were raised from the beginning and were discussed throughout the seminar in a relaxed and open manner. The participants were able to agree upon a considerable body of practical conclusions."

Some seventy nine recommendations were made at the end of this seminar detailing legal prodders for the freedom of expression, association, worship, human rights, judiciary, legal profession and rule of law. President Nyerere and his government took all these recommendations positively, and took appropriate legal steps as recommended by various specialists on the subject. Consequently conditions in Tanzania improved visibly thereafter. For Jhaveri personally it was very satisfying to see the result of their joint-mission successfully accomplished. The entire proceedings of this seminar convened in Dar-es-Salaam from 23-28 September 1976 were published in a book form entitled, 'Human Rights in a One Party State' by International Commission of Jurist [1]

Being at the receiving end, bouquets and brickbats and more recently, footwear is inherent to any politician's public life. And Mwalimu was no exception. His popularity came at a price. His people had expected miracles and a government par excellence under his rule. Contrary to their expectations, the country was passing through difficult times and high corruption was raising its head constantly. Slowly his popularity was being eroded, and some leaders from his own party started to agitate for change. Eventually President Nyerere retired voluntarily from the government in 1985 and party politics in 1990.

The period following his retirement turned out to be watershed years of drastic changes in Tanzania. Soon many of Mwalimu's policies were reversed by the succeeding Governments. Now Liberalization and Ruksha, meaning License-permission Raj and any thing goes, became the buzz word. President Nyerere's ideals and goal posts were moved to suit selfish motives by some of his trusted cadres. His cherished Arusha Declaration, especially the leadership code was being completely ignored. After his retirement he commented often, on this trend and rightly warned his countrymen about the pitfalls facing them.

Quite a few of his socialist programs had failed, but weighed against those, his achievements are tremendous. His vision of the leadership code and the just distribution of wealth still remain relevant in contemporary Tanzania. That apart, his contribution towards African Liberation struggle was unique. In Tanzania, it is due to his courage and commitment that the Independence struggle in Tanganyika, by any yardstick like the fight between David and Goliath, came to fruition peacefully within comparatively short period without much violence. He introduced political stability in the country through putting into place the new constitution of Tanzania and reorganized the armed forces. In addition, he reinforced a sense of unity through mandating Swahili as the national language and introduced Universal Franchise. He practiced what he preached and through his inclusive personality and actions reminded us time and again that we are all Tanzanians first. Because of this foresight, Tanzania does not face tribal warfare like its neigbhours in Africa. Above all his integrity and simplicity is a shining example to leaders not only from Africa but world over.

In every age there are some leaders who possess the gift of foresight and vision and who lead their countrymen selflessly. Mwalimu was one such leader. He was born on 13 April 1922 and died on 14-October-1999. He had traversed a long and hard terrain since the time when he started attending school bare footed as a kid. He received the Colonial government scholarships specifically to be trained as a school master—a teacher, and to their char gain Mwalimu, the Teacher he became for the whole Nation! From the beginning up to his last moments he was 'bakabwela'—common men's voice spelling out their difficulties, aspirations and expectations to their government and to the world at large. The title of Mwalimu, the Father of the Nation remains with him for ever, now even after his death.

Mzee John Rupia, Julius Nyerere, Kanti
Jhaveri, Edward Heath, Bibi Titi

2. Huge crowd listening to Nyerere

Part of the huge crowd at the historical
Meeting on Mnazimoja grounds

Jhaveri, N.S. Patel and Haridas Sanghvi on
the car roof

Josheph Nyerere, Kanti Jhaveri, Julius
Nyerere, Rashidi Kawawa, Edward Heath

Law Society dinner, Urmila,
President Nyerere, K.Jhaveri, CJ P.T. Georges,
and Mrs. Indiraben Avatar Singh

With the President of India,
Dr. Radhakrishna

Minister Nisilio Swai, Urmila,
Mrs. Indira Gandhi, President Nyerere

Reminiscence with Mama Maria Nyerere.

Urmila in pensive mood

12 Urmila attending a U.W.T. Conference with topmost women
leaders of Tanganyika

Urmila attending UWT Conference with
woman leaders of Tanganyika.

10. Urmila welcoming Mrs. Nyerere at a musical concert (Mrs. Rao
Kamal Barot sitting next to Mrs. Nyerere)

"Urmila welcoming Mama Maria Nyerere at
Kamal Barot Musical Program"
Khatun Mawji, Urmila, Martha Bulengo,
Hilda Bomani, Mama Maria Nyerere,Indian
High Commissioner's wife Mrs. Rau, Kamal
Barot and Harji Bhai Arya

Participating in nation building program.

With Veenaben and friends on the Himalayas

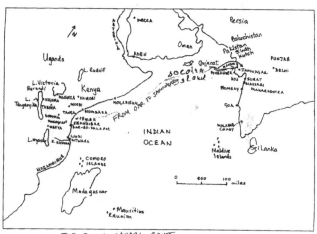

THE DHOW SAFARI ROUTE

Dhow safari from Dar-es-Salaam to
Jamnagar . . .

Part III

Chapter 22

Camaraderie Encounter with Wachawi, Mababu, Djini Witches, Village Ancestors, Genie And mad men

From early 1960s onwards the members of the Umoja WA Wanawake WA Tanzania-The National Women's Organization Central Committee, spent a lot of time being involved in grassroots work in different regions of the country.

Once we were having our regular Working Committee meeting in Shinyanga. After the meeting was over our group was visiting Mara and Nzega districts while other groups were visiting different areas as organized by the planning committee.

On this particular occasion after finishing our meeting in Shinyanga our group including Mama Sofia Kawawa, Sara Lusinde, Sara Nyerenda, Bi Hawa Maftah, Mama Mwasaburi Ali, and I proceeded to Mara and Nzega Districts

accompanied by local leaders. In Nzega, we were out in the
fields early in the morning as usual, clearing the ground,
digging, meeting different groups of people advising and
trying to find solutions for their problems. In most of these
villages women were facing lack of educational facilities for
their children, lack of water, medicines, poor health, and
problems with overbearing village elders and government
bureaucrats and very often with husbands as well. On this
particular day after spending the whole day out in he fields
we returned to the government guest house for an early
night. Suddenly we heard faint vigelegele, calling sound
made by women, mruzi, whistling sound made by men
and drums beating. It was a special type of calling and
drumming which became more eerie and insistent with each
beat. We could hear people rushing around in panic. There
was a slight knock on the door; quickly and quietly the
village elders came in, explaining that a group of wachawi—
witches were visiting and would be having ngoma, group
dance, that night under the mbuyu tree. All those who
heard the drums beat, must attend and take part in this
ngoma which was about sorcery and not very pleasant. After
this warning the chief advised us to switch off all the lights
and be very quiet, especially the muhindi mama—Indian
woman, "Because if the witches sensed her presence they
would definitely come to get her."

We were all at risk; I spent the night in a dark room
under a blanket with some of my colleagues. And to
preempt any problems, Mama Sofia Kawawa and a couple
of other senior members stayed in the front rooms in case
any unexpected visitors turned up to investigate! All the
lights were switched off save for a lantern, and Bi Hawa
went with another member from this village to attend the
witches' ngoma. Everybody assured me that I should not

worry and just go to sleep. But the reality was that all of us were awake till early in the morning listening to the drums beating loudly and dreading the knock on the door any time. The ngoma went on all night. Somebody asked me if I was scarred during the night. Yes, I was aware of the lurking danger and yet I felt safe with my friends: I had complete faith that whatever the consequences, we will stand together even in the most unusual and inhospitable situation. Next morning we left early in the morning before the villagers woke up from their stupor after witnessing the witches' ritual and playing ngoma all night.

Another equally memorable trip took place after our annual general meeting in Dodoma. After it concluded, we were taken on an official tour of the well-known Dodoma Hospital. At that time it was the main hospital for mentally disturbed patients who came from all over Tanzania. Our delegation had about ten-twelve members. We were being escorted by a team of senior doctors and officials. As I remember it, the hospital was housed in a fairly big building, with smaller units surrounding the compound area where the patients were allowed to move about. I had heard a lot about this hospital. Even as children if anybody acted up, we used to say that they needed to be sent to Dodoma Madhouse. So I was curious to actually see it. To my surprise my experience turned out to be completely unexpected.

The Senior Medical Officer had explained that a large number of patients in the hospital were violent and had to be locked up or restrained. Those who were not violent but simply ranting away without any logic were allowed to move about freely; some of them were said to be political prisoners. Some inmates were stark naked, often shouting for attention, and even discussing politics. Most of them were men. We were warned not to laugh at all. While we were being shown around a scantly dressed patient joined our group.

He followed me purposefully, held my hand firmly and began mumbling. He wouldn't let me go and kept walking in step and talking earnestly. Someone whispered in my ear, "Take it easy, Mama," and so I did. I kept on talking to him as we walked hand-in-hand, as if it was the most natural thing to do in the world. He went on for about half an hour before he lost interest and moved off. Now surprisingly after all these years when I think about it I find my experience surreal.

Amongst the inmates was a lone Polish woman who was said to have been there since World War II. She had reportedly lost her entire family in the war and had gone into shock, developing amnesia. I sat with her for a while, and her response to my gentle efforts to engage her was just a sweet smile.

Immediately after the Union of Tanzania was formed, we had organized another Annual General Meeting in Dodoma, at which Mwalimu was to be the chief guest and Vice President Karume from Zanzibar was scheduled to close our meeting. Mama Fatma Karume, a charming and ever-smiling lady, was leading a high-powered UWT delegation from Zanzibar, which included the wives of some of the very influential Revolutionary Council members from the Island. President Karume and his Revolutionary Council had absolute power in Zanzibar and their dictatorial conduct often reflected in some of their wives' behavior. We had heard that few of them were very demanding and fussy, with the result that many of us were looking forward to meet them rather tepidly.

Being the State guest Mama Fatma Karume was staying in the Government House, but the rest of the members of her delegation were sharing a school dormitory with us. It some how worked out that my bed was nearest in line of beds assigned to the Zanzibar attendees, as other members were playfully reluctant to occupy it. Next day early in the morning we were all busy getting ready as usual, our friend from Unguja Zanzibar in the bed next to mine called out and asked me to pull her bag out from under the bed, open it, lay out her clothes and things, hand her the toothbrush, and wait on her. I followed her instructions exactly, thinking she was unwell and needed help. The next morning began with the same routine. I noticed everybody watching me, and realized what was happening. Quietly I told her to get up, get ready chap chap and join us for breakfast. She was startled and gave me a sheepish smile. From then on our relationship became very cordial. This incident from a distant past lingers in my memory even after all these years because this was the only incidence when I was compelled to draw a line with one of the members for breaking the bond of sisterhood which prevailed in our organization.

One day Thekla Mchauru called. She told me that some of the central committee members were planning to travel by a small cargo ship to Mtwara. And from Mtwara catch the bus to Lindi to join the rest of the delegation and reach Lindi on time to attend our half-yearly General Meeting in Lindi. She invited me to join and I jumped at the chance. The other members travelling by boat were Mama Sofia Kawawa, Thekla Mchauru, Mama Sapi, Sara Lucinde, Sara Nyerenda, Lucy Lamek, Martha Bulengo and Lea Lupembe. We began the voyage in the morning, expecting to reach Mafia Island, our first halt by evening. It was a small cargo ship with upper deck, and apart from the Captain's quarters which he had kindly allowed us to use there were a couple of small cabins for us to share. The sea was calm, but as we sailed further out the June-July monsoon winds took over and the vessel began to roll with the winds. It was exciting, and held a hint of danger but not enough that we should become anxious. Our real worries began when we met another cargo ship slightly smaller then ours, stranded in the middle of no where in the ocean due to engine failure. Their captain requested our captain to help by towing the boat up to Mafia. They managed to tie both the vessels together with thick ropes. By this time it was already midnight, there was a gorgeous full moon shining overhead and the waves were getting high and tempestuous. There was lightning and thunder in the air and there was magic in the moments!

As we watched, suddenly the wind changed and some how the smaller boat became entangled in the connecting ropes. Consequently when our ship tried to move forward the smaller one would begin angling outwards in an arc ready to collide with our boat any time rather than trail us. The slightest move further made the length of the ropes between the ships shorter. We all started praying fervently. I was mesmerized by the spectacle and without being noticed quietly climbed the narrow stairs and reached the watchtower bridge on the uppermost deck. There on a small platform, holding flimsy support bars, under the radiant open sky I sat spellbound the whole night, watching the fierce struggle of our two cargo ships and the fantastic play of Mother Nature reminding us of our human fragility as well as our ingenuity. By now it had become too risky for me even to try and descend from my perch. Yet I felt completely at ease, watching all the actions that were going on for the whole night.

Both the ships were rolling and popping up and down like corks in the swelling seas in spite of being heavily laden with cargo. It was the deepest and darkest hour of the night when time stood still. I was aware that I could have been pitched overboard with the next surge, and nobody would have any clue about my disappearance. Below decks my friends were praying for the chance to stay alive and see their children once again. Staring at the heaving mass of dark waves, I too turned my mind to my children and my husband, now amidst skeptical thoughts about how long it might take me to drown. But Mother Nature was just teasing us. Soon the storm broke and as the pale moon watched the ember sun rose over the horizon ushering in the new Dawn. The winds and the waves subsided, the sea became completely calm as if nothing had gone amiss during the night and all was well. For me it was a sobering experience. I carefully descended and went below to our cabin. I told everybody that they had missed a grand show, and was told in no uncertain terms by my friends, greatly relieved to see me safe, that I was absolutely crazy to have taken such a risk!

Times are changing, gone are the days when women in Tanzania were satisfied with family planning and the pills. Now their limits, aspirations and goals have changed. Like the women world over they also want equal rights and equal opportunities for advancement in the society. UWT continues to Endeavour and help build this new world order. Mama Sofia Kawawa is no more, and many of my UWT friends and colleagues also either have departed from this world or like me are not keeping in good health. But our years spent together struggling and striving relentlessly for women's rights and progress in Tanzania linked us in powerful bonds of constant friendship and belonging. That bond was my mainstay all the time: whether I was sharing a meal, a song, a life time's story, holding hands with almost naked mad man, or listening to witches call!

My involvement with UWT helped me to become a better human being and enriched my life to a depth beyond description. Recalling my friends and experiences always brings about a concentrated, blessed fullness of heart that shines within me like a lighthouse beacon.

Chapter 23

Threats and Assault

Life is always uncertain. Sometimes when we forget our place in the scheme of things, unexplained and unexpected traumatic events circle around to punch us in the gut and jolt us back to reality.

During the administrations of President Ali Hassan Mwinyi who took over from President Nyerere from 1985-1995 and President Benjamin Mkapa who was the third President of the United Republic of Tanzania from 1995 to 2005, many private buildings earlier acquired by the government were returned to their original owners on humanitarian grounds. Ironically, our own property had been taken over and remained in state hands even while the Government had appointed Jhaveriji on the Commission which examined appeals made by individuals in distress against their buildings being nationalized. At the time the Commission had rescinded some of those orders on merit.

Pravin suggested that I should try to get our property back; he said that, Kaka—uncle, my husband, was now retired from Parliamentary and other official duties after a long service. Our own houses were nationalized while NHC, National Housing Corporation, which had inherited all the nationalized buildings, kept increasing rents, and the general cost of living was escalating all the time. He said I should at least try and do some thing about it.

Without consulting Jhaveriji, I gathered up my courage and quietly, on my own went through the bureaucratic maze and managed to get an appointment to see President Mkapa in his office at the State House. Even Pravin did not know about this development.

I arrived there at the appointed time with optimism and expectation that I was going to get a fair hearing from the President. In the State House office I was greeted by a gentleman who said he was the President Mkapa's personal secretary. He engaged me in a long conversation, during which he remarked that his last assignment had been at the Tanzanian High Commission in Delhi for three years, and that during his time there he had noted high level of corruption everywhere in India, and knew how corrupt the Indians are.

I agreed readily with him, replying that, yes there was indeed disgustingly colossal amount of corruption going on in India, but that I myself was not an Indian; I was born in Pemba and was Tanzanian. The fellow ignored my statement and then said openly right in the President's office in the State House that if I tried to meet the President without first dealing with him, I would regret it. It was obvious that, he was not only demanding a bribe if I wanted to see the President but he was also threatening me. And I was not prepared for that. On the contrary I was both angry and felt intimidated, reading his utterance as a direct threat. And for a moment was tempted to take up his challenge. But good sense prevailed. I realized that to antagonize that man by arguing with him was not worth it nor was it wise to meet him again.

The fact was that on many occasions Jhaveriji and I had been to the State House as honoured guests. Not only that I had also attended functions there in my own right and had been received by the President on many occasions. But this time around my visit to the State House turned out to be frightening for no reason or rhythm. Quietly I decided to close this chapter about regaining our house, turned over the last page of this pamphlet and moved on. Though, time and again it does remind me of my vulnerability and I thank my stars for my safe deliverance. There is a Cheroke Indian saying that we are never alone, even when we don't know it, God is watching over us, sitting on the stump beside us. When trouble comes, all we have to do is reach out to him. For we walk by faith, not by sight.

I have been a member of Chinmaya Mission since it was established in Dar. Each Wednesday our good friends Biharibhai Tanna and his wife Indiraben used to come home to pick me up. We regularly attended its study group meetings together at his Lohana Mahajanwadi flat. I was later appointed a trustee of Chinmaya Mision in Dar-es-Salaam. At one time, Swamini Vimlanandaji from the mission headquarters in Sidhabari India was visiting Dar-es-Salaam for a week-long programme of discourses and conducting classes on Indian philosophy and scriptures. I was attending these meetings every day. On one such morning I had just reached home after attending her morning exposition of the Gitaji, and was in an exalted mood. It was 8 a.m. Jhaveriji had his usual glass of milk and left for his office. I sat reading the newspapers while Amina, who worked in our house, was cleaning up. Suddenly I sensed movement near the front door and went to check. Those days' workers from the electric supply company that was installing meters for prepaid card systems were surveying our locality. So when I was confronted by three hefty men who were already inside the house. I assumed they were from the electricity company, and began rebuking them for not waiting at the door and instead walking right in.

In an instant two of them seized me, one gagging me with his hand and snarling that they were not fundi umeme—electrical engineers; "We have come to take your money, we have been watching you for the last few days, waiting for this opportunity. You had better listen to us quietly and remember no noise at all!" One man had a huge panga, hatchet, in his hand. He held it against my throat so that I could feel its sharp edge. The second man pinned my arms behind my back while the third flourished a smaller knife. I was helpless, and sheer shock left me so stunned and confused that it took me a few minutes to realize that I might well be harmed here and now. My deepest instincts flashed a warning to me to obey the thugs, follow their demands so that they would leave as soon as possible. This resolve steadied me though I was scarred. And as best as I could I said, "Sawa, all right, take whatever you want, here take my keys." They knew the exact location of my cupboard and commanded me to open it and told me to give them all the cash and dhahabu jewellery, with my own hands. I handed over the money, and also gave them my watch but I did not have any gold ornaments and, on instinct gave them some imitation jewellery that I had bought for Amina and Agnes.

They knew how to recognize real jewellery and threw imitation pieces back at me, demanding the authentic items.

"Look, you can see I am old, I do not wear any dhahabu, and apart from what I gave you I do not possess any dhahabu," I replied frantically. Infuriated, they began to ransack the cupboard. When my brother Mahen and Bhabhi went to London, Bhabhi had left a bundle containing her valuables with me for safe keeping. The bundle sat in full view on one side of the cupboard; by now I realized that if the thugs found it they will go crazy, and will finish me off for lying to them. But now it was too late for me to do any thing about it. I had already told them that I did not have any valuables with me; I was petrified, and with every second and every move it was becoming dangerous. Miraculously, my attackers ignored it altogether since my sister-in-law had tied her jewellery up in an old piece of cloth and I had kept it under an untidy pile of old clothes. I observed their oversight with a thumping heart and prayers on my lips I thought that it was just God's grace that had saved me.

Then they said, "Okay, let us now go to Baba's, my husband's, room, and give us all his money. Hurry up" I followed their instructions meekly and went with them to the next room which was our bedroom. There I opened the cupboard that was always kept unlocked any way, took the cash from a concealed place within it, and handed it over. The money was kept there for end-of-the-month expenses and bills. It was a fairly big envelope and they were happy. There was also a very sturdy steel cabinet in the room, which was made by our friend Mohinder Singh Parley Industries in Dar-es-Salaam. The thieves pushed me towards it, demanding that I open it. I was unable to; I handed over the key to them, they also tried and failed. This infuriated them all the more and I sensed their frustration being turned towards me. I was inwardly shaking. Quickly I asked them to please break the cabinet. They tied me up with a thick rope, and the man with the panga sat with me holding it to my throat. And thwack thha, thwack thaa, blow by violent blow, each seemingly to go right through me they managed finally to break the cabinet open, to find it full of files. They spied a brand new briefcase in there. So this panga person ordered me to open it. Well, I could not open that either! Again they had to break it but wait, what is all that, more papers!

The men were extremely enraged. By now they had spent over an hour and a half in the house with me as their captive. It was the longest hour of my life, and I had no idea how it would all end. I had realized that our neighbors were not likely to come by, despite all the noise the thieves were making. Fortunately my very old bogawala, vegetable vendor, came by on his usual morning round, calling out, "Mama Mboga, mama mboga!" All these years I used to habitually come out to greet him and have a chat, even if I didn't need to buy any vegetables that day. The old man fled in shock when one of the thugs suddenly emerged from the house and chased him off telling him that I was not well and the doctor was with me. Suspecting something was wrong, this brave bogawala returned and continued knocking on the door and calling to me 'Mama, mama.'Maa, maa. His action saved me, for the thugs swiftly began scooping up shoes, radios, tape recorders and whatever else came to hand, and left in a hurry after warning me that if I reported this to the police they would return and attack 'Mzee'—husband.

I managed to untie myself with difficulty, and ran into the garden shouting, "Mwizi, Mwizi!"—Thief, Thief! It was too late. They had already made their escape. Frantically, I phoned Arif in his office but there was no reply, nor was there any reply when I called Biharibhai. Fortunately I managed to reach Pravin who told me not to worry, and that he was coming to me immediately.

He picked up Jhaveriji from the office and took charge as soon as he entered the house. The moment I saw Pravin, I felt safe at last and allowed myself to let go and cried like a baby while he quietly held me. I smile now at the scene and still retain the relief of seeing him. We decided not to file a police report, and dismissed our house help Amina as we realized she was a drug addict and belonged to the gang of thugs. We heard of a similar incident elsewhere in our locality that same morning. The lady of the house whom I knew resisted the thieves. She was thrashed brutally and had to be flown out to London for emergency treatment.

All these years we always had an open house, never even locked our front door for the entire day. Jhaveriji being a Member of Parliament from Dar-es-Salaam Constituency, people from his constituency used to walk in and out of the house all the time, and they were always welcomed. My encounter with the thieves was shocking, frightening and extremely traumatic, but somewhere hidden inside me I had hope and trust which saw me through this ordeal. I feel that I came out of it as a more confident person and continued to attend morning lectures and evening discourses at the Chinmaya Mission, and carried on all my daily activities as usual.

The Gitaji reiterates that no power in the universe can hold back the situations that we have to face in our life, regardless of whether they unfold swiftly or slowly, transient or permanent, or whether they bring us joy or sorrow. And even if they defy our limited human understanding altogether, we have to strive and negotiate all circumstances and contexts with determination and equanimity and hope for the best.

Chapter 24

Travels; Moscow

I speak here of October 1970. It was the onset of winter in Europe and summer in Tanzania. I was one of three members from UWT Central Committee nominated to represent the women of Tanzania at the World Women's Conferences in Budapest and Moscow. Aeroflot, the Russian national carrier, sent an old aircraft to Dar-es-Salaam for us. Halting frequently like an Indian passenger train, we picked up delegates from other African countries on our way and reached Budapest after a seemingly endless flight.

Budapest, the capital of Hungary, is a beautiful city on the river Danube. It derives its name from the fact that one-third of it rests on hilly Buda and Obuda on the western bank of the river, and the remaining two-thirds rests on the flat terrain of Pest on the eastern bank. As state guests we were staying in a grand hotel on the Buda side, from where we had a panoramic view of the city. The two-day Conference, held in the Parliament building, was officially opened by the Hungarian President. This was the prelude to the Moscow conference and showcased the women's progress under the Communist regime. The delegates discussed how this progress can be shared by the women of the third world countries especially from Africa. After the conference we spent the rest of the week visiting museums, palaces, theatres and gardens. It was oblivious that the country was still struggling with the effects of World War Two and subsequent political and economical upheavals. But we were always greeted warmly by the Hungarian people.

The highlight of our trip was on the final night when we attended an official Banquet hosted by the Hungarian President. This was followed by a gala performance by the famous Hungarian Belle dance troupe at the grand State Opera House. After more then forty years one thing I remember most is the amazingly graceful way the artists, men and women danced. As if their bodies were made of soft rubber, they could dance, jump high and land beautifully on their toes without any effort! As it turned out this was just a glimpse of the full red carpet reception which awaited us in Moscow.

Upon arrival on 8th of October in Moscow we were welcomed by the Soviet Women's Committee and were escorted to the Hotel Moskwa. This grand hotel which entertained heads of state and official delegations was going to be our home for the duration of our stay. I shared a room with Lea Lupembe. From the moment we arrived in Moscow we were escorted day and night by an 'interpreter' ostensibly assigned to translate for us, but it was obvious her duty was also to keep a full-time watch over us. We were not allowed to go even for a short walk on our own. Our interpreter did not understand a word of Swahili language, in which Lea and I conversed. The next morning we were assigned a new interpreter who knew our language as well as English! The Tanzanian Ambassador's residence in Moscow was our second home. We spent some happy hours at the Ambassador's residence. One evening I offered to make the dinner chapattis. We could not find the rolling pin as his wife was away for a few days, so I improvised with a bottle and used it as a chapati rolling pin. It was fun and everyone enjoyed what I finally produced! During the first week we attended the Conference, and several meetings with the Soviet Women's delegation to discuss women's development programs to be launched during the coming years.

This was followed by official visits to view some of the rarest and most beautiful Russian art treasures. Our itinerary started with visits to the monument to Prince Yuri de Gorky, founder of Moscow, and the monument to Karl Marx build to commemorate the city's 100th anniversary. We visited the grand Kremlin Palace and Lenin Museum where we learnt all about the Russian Revolution and the entire history of the Communist Party. It was followed by a very pleasant leisurely walk around the St. Petersburg basilica and the beautiful Red Square, site for grand parades with ceremonial army band and drummers. Next on our itinerary were the visits to Hermitage Museum, St. Basil's Cathedral and the former Tsar's fabulous winter palaces housing valuable masterpieces by famous European painters. No words can describe the richness of the art displayed in the winter palaces. The guide explained that when the Russian Revolution occurred Comrade Lenin decreed that all wealth, including the palaces with their contents, now belonged to the state and the people, and would be preserved for posterity as a national asset. On 14-10-70 we travelled from Moscow to Kishiner, the capital of Moldavia, famous for its wine and hospitality. To my delight, we were heartily welcomed on the village boundary by exuberant village committee. They had brought bottles of their famous wine for the welcoming ceremony. It was a crisp morning; we stood in a circle and sipped from the same bottle that was passed from person to person till it came back to the first individual. We then joined in the villagers' folk dance. The welcome was followed by a sumptuous meal of specially prepared national dishes, delicate wines, luscious grapes and other fruits. Vegetarian dishes were specially prepared for me. The singing and dancing inherent to the welcome ritual was repeated at every village and vineyard cooperative where we were always treated to wine-tasting and 'breaking bread' ceremonies. The older village women teased me as if I was their daughter-in-law. I felt quite at home!

In Moldavia we visited hostels, hospitals, co-operatives, exhibitions, museums and a silk factory where silkworms were raised on mulberry trees as well as artificially. We were invited to visit the Parliament, followed by an official dinner. The simplicity and generosity of the people attracted me greatly. It was amazing to see the Moldavian women doing all kinds of heavy work side by side with men in harsh conditions, and it was indeed painful to see all aspects of the people's daily lives completely in the iron grip of state machinery. I did not see many children around and upon inquiry was told that under the prevailing system, all over the USSR, Russian children were considered national responsibility. The state started to take care of the child the moment he or she was born. They were enrolled in crèches, nurseries, children's hospitals, holiday camps, hostels, and educated. After qualification they were assigned jobs and placed into the system. Their careers were monitored and guided by the state agencies. This was an eye opener for many of us.

After our pleasant stay in Moldavia, soon it was time now to return to Leningrad, where we were scheduled to visit many interesting places and meet well-known personalities. We met the first-ever woman cosmonaut, Valentina Tereshkova. On June 16, 1963, she became the first women to fly solo into space at the young age of twenty six. Hers is a fantastic story. She grew up in a peasant family; became a Youth leader at her textile factory and had performed 90 parachute jumps by the time she was selected to fly out in a Vostok-6 spaceship. During her three day solo space flight Tereshkova circled the Earth 48 times. It was a rare opportunity and an honour to meet Valentina and hear about her experiences. Meeting her personally I also felt connected through her achievement with this historical moment in space travel.

That day ended with a fantastic performance by the famous Russian Circus. Last on the list, but interesting nevertheless we had our final meeting with the Soviet Women's' Committee to exchange gifts, bid farewell and thank them and for their marvelous hospitality. On 24-10-70 we were on our way back home.

Chapter 25

Varanasi

A blessing can manifest in many disguises. For me this time around it came as Veenaben Sharma's invitation to attend the official opening of the week-long 'Visit India Millennium Year' celebrations held in 2000 at Varanasi. It was organized under the joint collaboration of the Central and U.P. governments and some NGOs. Veenaben and her Prajya Foundation were also taking part in the conference as an NGO. One of the main themes of the week long conference was the environmental 'Save Ganga' scheme initiated by the late Rajiv Gandhi. At that time we were visiting our daughter Abha and her family in Delhi. I was thrilled with anticipation and promptly registered myself as an observer at the conference.

Call it by any name Banaras, Varanasi or Kashi, this historic city that promises salvation to orthodox Hindus is located on the banks of the great river Gangaji; mythical goddess, lifeline of the densely populated northern plains.

Its waters flow all the way from the Himalayan glaciers to the Bay of Bengal. In the higher mountains the river is still crystal clear, with powerful currents that attract adventurous people to go white-water rafting on its foaming rapids. Luckily in the past Veenaben and I had many occasions to visit ashrams on the banks of the Ganga, and watch its pristine waters while listening to its ancient mesmeric voice in serene solitude.

Sadly, near the cities, human presence and activity has profoundly changed the environment of the river. Descriptions of this environmental catastrophe and strategies to save the river were discussed for the duration of the conference. On paper it was an impressive scheme, but nothing much has changed over the years. Holy men and many others are still agitating and going on fast to save the Ganga while the holy river continues to be extremely polluted in all cities it passes through. But reportedly it is most contaminated on the waterfront of the Banaras Ghats where people perform their daily ablutions.

On this occasion, we travelled by Rajdhani overnight train from Delhi to Banaras where we were given accommodation at Banaras Hindu University, a venerated institution established over 150 years earlier. The "Visit India Millennium Year" celebrations officially began in the evening with speeches and ceremony. The entire Ganga ghat area was illuminated with multicolored necklaces of shimmering lights which reflected in the water; the temple bells started ringing and the famous Ganga Arti was performed with the collective chanting of mantras and hymns. Simultaneously, thousands of diyas and flowers were set afloat in the river. They bobbed on dispassionately, their beauty creating an aura of sacredness different from the surrounding energy of worship. It is true that a community ritual of this sort to honour and supplicate the wonders of creation and the cosmos is one of the oldest and most powerful expressions of human devotion to nature. As I stood there, rapt, I felt the combined call of the congregation rise in my heart as a prayer. Instinctively I also bent and floated my diya with a few flowers as my offering to the Mother of mothers, Gangaji.

The next day we were invited for a five-hour boat ride on the Ganges just before dawn. Sailing upstream gently on the water where the water was calm and clear, we watched the sunrise while Banaras woke to the sound of temple bells, conches and devotees performing early puja. Sound of bhajans-hymns wafted through the air as the first rays of the sun penetrated the morning mist, giving a wondrous and mysterious glow to the atmosphere; uplifting and precious. I was stirred to the depths of my being. At the end of the voyage we were treated to a sumptuous traditional breakfast and hot cups of masala chai in the boat.

Early next evening again we went for another boat ride to watch the sunset. Lights glimmered in the temples and faint sounds of the arti drifted over the dark water. When dusk falls the burning ghats of Banaras, where cremations have been taking place day and night without pause for centuries, become clearly visible. Those distant pyres, some blazing, some subsiding, some reduced to smoldering embers, others to heaps of cold ash, are a sobering reminder of our perishability and mortality, and of a core truth of our fragile and transient existence, that life and death are linked as eternally and seamlessly as day and night.

Latter on in the day we went first to visit the Kashi Vishwanath Temple, as usual it was full of pilgrims. For much of my adult life it had been one of my cherished hopes to visit Varanasi Banaras and have darshan at the

Kashi Vishwanath mandir, but even in my dreams I had never expected to have such an intense experience. I was awestruck to finally find myself in this ancient holy place. I was surrounded by multitude of people, and yet I felt all alone with myself and with over flowing happiness, I performed my puja in peace with a prayer in my heart.

We were circumambulating the temple complex when I observed a fairly big area cordoned off with an iron structure that protected a partly built mosque as well as symbols of a Shiva temple. On inquiry we were told that this enclosure was a relic from the era of Aurangzeb, the last Mughal emperor, who had begun to demolish the Shiva temple and build a mosque on that very site. According to the historian E.B. Havell, "The Afghans, who in 1194 A.D. burnt the Buddhist monasteries at Sarnath, probably laid waste Banaras also. Approximately in 1300 A.D. Alaudin Khilji is said to have destroyed a thousand temples. During the tolerant rule of Akber one of the earlier Mogul emperors, the city may have recovered some of the splendor which it had in the palmy days of the Hindu rule. But Aurangzeb in the seventeen century leveled the temples to the ground and caused several mosques to be built with the materials. The great mosques above Panchganga ghat, whose lofty minarets dominate the whole city, are one of the memorials of his intolerant zeal. [1]

To avoid dispute and inflaming of communal passions in a city with very large Hindu and Muslim populations, the site has been put under custodianship of the army and is being guarded by the army day and night.

During the weeklong conference, a full program of lunches and dinner serving different regional cuisine was organized for the delegates in five-star hotels. These were followed by corresponding cultural programs in the evenings. On the last day we had the rare treat of listening to a Shehnai recital, by the great Bismillah Khan in one of the ancient palaces on the Ganga Ghats. He had been a lifelong resident of Banaras, and at the time he was far advanced in age and not keeping in good health either. But the moment his lips touched the Shahnai all this was forgotten and he enthralled us with a virtuoso performance. It was followed by a typical Banarsi dinner served on banana leaves.

One evening Veenaben and I were privileged to have tea with the distinguished Chancellor of Banaras Hindu University, a deeply learned yet very simple man. After our meeting with him, his young son rowed us in his small boat back to our lodgings. While deftly handling the oars, for almost two hours he explained the scriptures, sang bhajans and spoke of his philosophy of life. This unusual voyage felt to me like a particle of the mythological narratives of the epics and Puranas.

After the conference I offered shraddh; I understood that this ritual is offered for the salvation of our dear departed ones. Not only that, but one can offer shraddh even for oneself. I found this interesting and was keen to learn more from the priest who had performed these ceremonies for me early in the morning. To my disappointment the priest was too busy and could not explain the meaning of the rituals which he had performed. I was feeling rather disappointed by the priest's lack of knowledge and indifference.

They say that if we want to meet real India we should travel by train in second or third class. That evening, while coming back from Banaras as usual Veenaben and I were in a crowded second-class train compartment, seated next to a newly wed young couple in all their finery sitting on the floor of our compartment sharing a meal completely absorbed in one another. There was hardly any space to move. Around

9 p.m. a dignified elderly person dressed in a simple white dhoti, banian and a blanket over his shoulders joined us. We made room for him to sit on our berth and started talking. I had a long philosophical discussion with him. He explained patiently all my mundane questions about the Shraddh ritual performed that morning, He added that life and death are synonymous, and similar to time have been flowing from eternity regardless of our needs. We should except it as natural process and not grieve for our dear departed ones but take it as continuation and celebration of life. Late that night I dozed off and suddenly woke up later to find that he was gone.

From Banaras we travelled to Sarnath and visited the Bodhi Tree. This tree came as a tiny sapling from the main tree in Bodh Gaya where Buddha Bhagwan gave his first sermon after he realized the truth and woke up from his long Samadhi. There were many pilgrims. Some were meditating and others offering flowers. The whole atmosphere was peaceful and tranquil, and the Buddhist monks were very friendly. From there we visited the attached library which is a rich source of information for the student of Buddhism, and contains more then hundred years old rare books hand written on parchment. Only the authorized monks are allowed to handle them.

Our visit ended at the famous Jain temple near by on the outskirts of Sarnath. Newly built, it was dedicated to the 11th Tirthankar. At that time it was being expanded and some construction work was still going on. We did not spend much time there, but all these places of worship and even museums have vibrant ambiance brimming with happiness and are always welcoming.

Chapter 26

Tryst with a Tantric and visiting Kumbh Mela

Exploring human environment in natural surroundings can be spiritually as well as emotionally elevating. Though once in a while these do turn unwittingly into challenging situations, as I discovered during my recent visit to Uttarakhand, India.

While on another journey with Veenaben, we were visiting villages by country buses and walking safaris on the high terrains of Himalayas in the Uttarakhand as part of a research project she was completing. Travelling in these areas is akin to travelling backwards through time viewing idyllic country scenes. Tiny hamlets with clusters of small houses, some built from red earth and cow dung and roofed with handmade tiles nestled on a hilly area amid lush, fertile green fields.

And yet the farmers looked improvised, and a lack of progress was evident all round. The Gram Panchayat, village leaders, in these villages invariably complained that after the crops were harvested, the farmers remained idle for almost six months of the year as there was no other work available for them. There were very few schools and clinics; the children had to walk on rough tracks for miles every day to attend school, and the sick had to manage some how to reach the nearest clinic to receive medical treatment. I found that as usual the women were most hard working and always welcomed us cheerfully.

In all these places it was marvellous to see the ingenuity of men in building their thatched huts and bricked little dwellings in their terraced fields. While the temples were built sitting pretty on tops of the hills and even hanging on the cliffs. Notwithstanding the beautiful surroundings, for me especially this was a tricky terrain to climb. And I was glad to accept help from our Guides as we climbed past these terraced fields and dwellings resourcefully built on the hillsides.

We always visited the temples which dotted the countryside. So when we reached the temple at Kharsadi we offered our prayers and met the people who had gathered there waiting to meet Veenaben. After the meeting, somebody casually invited us to go and sit on a nearby verandah. Soon a few others joined us there, eventually followed by a man who might have been in his fifties. This tantrik sat facing the crowd and one of his assistant arranged heaps of rice in front of him. I thought he was going to perform some puja. But he had other ideas on his mind! Soon he closed his eyes and went into a trance. His whole body started shaking violently, the contour of his face and even the voice changed and people began to ask him questions. They were searching for solutions to various problems mostly concerned with their health, family fights, petty quarrels and incidents of alleged injustices done to them. The man kept on throwing grains of rice at them, and started to reply argumentatively and angrily. Ultimately one of his questioners himself went into a trance, and started shaking furiously and babbling incomprehensibly. This carried on for almost an hour till the session ended. We too were invited to participate and ask our questions but we both declined his offer with alacrity and left quickly after paying our respects to him. This was my first experience of watching a 'possession by spirits' from close quarters. It reminded me eerily of my encounter with other members of the same fraternity in Nzega district near Shiniyanga in Tanzania when I was attending UWT Annual General meeting in Mtwara District.

Kumbh Mela

On another occasion I had the opportunity to visit the Kumbh Mela with Veenaben. Apart from being a spiritual experience our trip gave us a glimpse of history as it happened in this part of India.

That year the Kumbh Mela was being held in Triveni Sangam near Prayag in UP. Excavations have revealed that Prayag existed as a town as early as 600 B.C. Puranas as well record that Lord Rama, the main protagonist in the Ramayana spent some time in the Ashram of Sage Bharadwaj in Prayag before proceeding to nearby Chitrakoot. We visited both these Ashrams.

In 1575 Akbar built a fort on the bank of the holy Sangam and rechristened Prayag as Illahabad-Allahabad. The literal translation of Allahabad means 'Abode of God'. There are many temples and museums in the city including the Swaraj Bhavan and Anand Bhavan buildings which have been donated to the nation by the Nehru Gandhi family. These have been converted into musiums. We spent the whole day visiting all these historical sites.

Prayag is situated at the confluence of three rivers; Ganges, Yamuna and Saraswati where the largest gathering of up to twenty million pilgrims gather every twelve years and take a religious purification bath. In the snow peaks of Himalayas the sources of Ganga and Yamuna are only forty miles apart. They flow over four hundred miles before finally converging in Prayag. This place is referred to as Triveni Sangam.

We had reached Prayag-Allahabad in the evening. Early next morning we hired a taxi and went to the Triveni Sangam for a dip and a darshan. We were visiting the site purposely late, after the main congregation of pilgrims had left. The water was calm and inviting and Veenaben and I just walked in the river enjoying the soothing experience. I started to say my prayers but could not concentrate and some how felt agitated by the strong underwater current. A thought flashed through my mind that, we were standing at the Sangam where three rivers coming all the way from the Himalayas were meeting and realized that this fusion must be creating dynamic flow of energy at the meeting point, and the overspill of this energy was the mythical river Saraswati. It was amazing! Silently I offered my salutations to Mother Nature and continued with my journey onwards.

Life is full of these surprises. I remember, holding my mother's hand I had started visiting the temples in Dar-es-Salaam as a child. She had complete faith in Krishna, and Bhagwat, Ramayana, Mahabharata were her favourite books which she read every day. My parents loved nature and respected all life. They believed that there are divine aspects of gods every where in nature; we can worship a tree, a stone, a river, a mountain, the sea, the sun, moon, the stars, animals, any thing. In addition their religion taught them to work hard, do your best and move on. Ours was a simple life. I had imbibed these values from them and understood Krishna's Law of Karma with these guidelines. It continues to be my religion, my culture and my way of life whether in Africa, in India or any in other country.

With passage of time however, this was not enough. I wanted to find my own identity and purpose in life; understand the meaning of true religion and all pervasive nature of Brahmn, and felt a deep yearning to rest in Bhuma—the all-inclusive immanent Consciousness—Sat, Chit Anand. Over the years, I continued quietly to read and study scriptures, Veda Vedanta and philosophy of other religions as well. I visited holy places, attended lectures, discourses and was fortunate to meet learned men and women.

As time passed, on the strength of an unknown calling, I often stayed at the Divine Life Mission Sivanand Ashram in Rishikesh with Veenaben. Surrounded by green forest this Ashram is situated on the Himalayan foothills, facing holy river Ganges. The Ashram was established by renowned Saint Swami Siwananda. It was sheer bliss just to sit on the steps of Pujya Swamiji's kutir and watch the sparkling rippling waters of Ganges flow by and listen to the sweet sound of temple bells and hymns floating gently with the breeze from all directions. This abode of many learned Swmijis and mendicants turned out to be a sanctuary for me.

On one such pilgrimage after witnessing the famous Ganga Arti at Hardwar and visiting Rishikesh Veenaben and I reached the Siwanand Ashram early in the morning. After a quick bath and a hearty breakfast we paid our respects to the Senior Swamijis. In the evening we went fairly early to hear Swami Krishnanandaji's discourse. Before long the room filled up with an eager crowd, who came from East and West to hear the revered Swamiji. Soon he entered the room, set down on the dais and greeted his audience with joined palms. He seemed to know every one. I was sitting in the rear corner of the room, for some reason I could not understand, I was experiencing an invisible force of energy, mystical and yet real. I watched people sitting around me cross legged completely at ease. While even though, I was also sitting firmly on the ground, my legs were trembling and my whole being was shivering from deep within! This went on for days. I wanted very much to bow and pay my respects to him but I felt completely spell bound. Finally our visit was coming to an end. I was feeling strangely restless and one fine evening unknowingly and unprepared I took sudden courage and prayed to him for my mantra. By the grace of God difficult to describe, my wish was granted, he gave me my mantra and blessed me. I know that I have to travel a long distance before I reach my destination, but then I also know that my Guruji, Baba himself is guiding my steps.

Chapter 27

Mauritius

In 2005 we received several calls from my cousin Dr. Hansa and her husband, Dr. Mahesh Gunesee from Mauritius. They insisted that on our way from Tanzania to India that year, we must visit them. I had not seen Hansa for many years, nor had I met Maheshbhai, Both of them are Consultant Doctors who met and married in Jamnagar with Motiba and Faiba's blessings. While on our way to Delhi, I am glad we took the chance and broke our journey in Mauritius. Though meeting us for the first time, Maheshbhai put us at ease with his humorous comments from the moment we landed. He reminded me that I was his Patlasasu, wife's elder sister, and as such he was at our service! In spite of his busy schedule he kept his promise. He was very knowledgeable with a wonderful sense of humour, and said that he had started to write his memoirs. From him I learnt about the interesting history of Mauritius, which is similar to our own history in East Africa in many ways.

In February 2011 Maheshbhai died in Mauritius where his family has been based for the past four generations. He is no more, but he has left with us very pleasant memories of his wit and loving nature. In fact due to Hansa and Maheshbhai's gracious hospitality, Mauritius has been a lovely and memorable experience for us.

Hansa is born in Dar-es-Salaam in late 1930s while Maheshbhai was born in Mauritius. They qualified as doctors in Jamnagar-Gujarat. In 1967, after gaining some work experience in India both joined the government medical services in Mauritius; Hansa as the nation's first female gynecologist in the country while Maheshbhai joined as Orthopedic Surgeon. Since then for more then forty years, both of them have been doing path-breaking work in the medical field; often working for 24 hours a day without any off-duty in remote areas where they were the only medical personnel and surgery was an unknown phenomenon. One such example was their presence at the Hospital du Nord. Hansa remembers vividly, ". . . nothing was ready. No doctors were prepared to go there even for six months. There was lack of staff and it was far from easy to work there. But it was a great challenge for both of us and we did every first significant intervention there. The government took out a stamp depicting me performing surgery in the operation theater." Their life story reminds me of our forefathers in East Africa who worked with similar dedication.

In later years, both Hansa and Maheshbhai had to reduce their workload due to their own health problems. At the time of our visit they were continuing their consultancy work and acting in advisory capacity to various hospitals. Where ever we went, people rushed up to pay their respects to this much loved, pioneering couple.

Due to their deep professional involvement with all strata of the population, both of them were able to communicate in Creole, Bhojpuri, Hindi, French and English which is the official language in Mauritius. This linguistic diversity has its roots in Mauritius being an important link within the colonial slave trade. From 1815-35 the British East India Company shipped Indian convicts undergoing life imprisonment to Mauritius and other British colonies, including Australia and Kenya as 'coolies' i.e. indentured labour. These men were put to work building bridges, roads, railways, barracks, etc. In East Africa the majority of Indian coolies sent to build the railway system came from Gujarat, Kutch and some came from the North. These illiterate men were made to affix their thumb prints by way of signature on employment 'contracts' before being shipped out. Their contracts contained minute details of how many ounces of salt and chilli powder and how many cubic feet of air space by way of ventilation was permitted per coolie.[1] Mauritius officially commemorates this spectrum of their history through two public holidays each year; on 2 November for 'Arrival of Indentured Labourers' and 1 February for 'Abolition of Slavery.'

When we arrived in Mauritius Hansa was busy with her patients and Jhaveriji, preferred to stay at home. But I was eager to see as much of Mauritius as possible. And true to his word Maheshbhai took over as my guide happily. Mauritius is endowed with abundant natural bounty of lakes, rivers, forests, hills, pristine beaches with white sand, we visited them all. We started with the Botanical Gardens or Terres de 7 Colours-Chamarel, so named because the whole valley morphs permanently in all the colours of the rainbow. This unique phenomenon can be traced to volcanic activities in the area. It felt as if here the nature was in deep meditation. We visited the lotus pond, and made friends with an extended family of turtles over a century old, lazily basking in the sun. We also observed a rare type of huge tree on which it was said that only one flower blossoms once in every 100 years.

And we went to see the famous lake called Ganga Talav. Maheshbhai explained its historical background. About 125 years ago a simple man living in the north of the country had a vivid dream of a serene talav, lake, in the south from which 'Jhanvi' another name for the goddess Ganga, was emerging. He set off with some companions in search of this lake and when he found it, settled down on its shores. Over time the lake became a pilgrimage site. Some decades later, on his first overseas voyage the Sankaracharya of Hardwar carried a lota, small brass pot, of water from the Ganga and poured it into the lake. Thus establishing a link between it and the river Ganga, he named the lake, Ganga Talav. The Shiva Lingam there is considered to be the 13th Jyotir Lingam due to supernatural manifestations at the Lingam Sthapna. Many sanctified temples have been added around the 108-foot statue of Shivji. In spite of the crowds of devotees milling around, the whole environment is peaceful and tranquil. Maheshbhai had been a member of the temple committee all these years, I think since its installation and the priest was happy to perform a special puja for us.

In contrast to our orderly temple visit, the next day was quite startling. The occasion was the festival dedicated to Lord Murugan—Karthikeya, the brother of Ganapati. I saw a long procession of barefoot and open mouthed devotees' carrying kavdis, elaborately decorated wooden frames bearing idols, on their shoulders and climbing up to a hilltop temple step by slow step. Each devotee's tongue was pierced through with a long needle strung with lemons in such a manner that their mouths remained open with lemons dangling on both sides. Torso, stomach, back and thighs were similarly pierced with arrow-headed needles strung with lemons and arranged in a particular design. I was speechless, imagining the physical agony. Hansa had warned me that the spectacle could be disturbing, and I did find it so.

Mauritius is a cosmopolitan society with a robust economy based on tourism and sugar exports. All the religions co-exist peacefully, with churches, temples and mosques nestling side by side. Medical treatment including surgery and education up to the university level was completely free. One evening we attended an Indian wedding party with Hansa and Maheshbhai, where we met the PM of Mauritius, watched the Sege dance and listen to their traditional music. It was a treat to see those young men and women dance with gusto and listen to their music that is a blend of several different ethnic traditions and culture in Mauritius.

Our visit ended too soon! Following Sunday day over loaded with pleasant memories of Mauritius, we flew out to Delhi, our next destination.

Chapter 28

In the evening of my life

If you seek the grace of God with your whole heart, you may be assured that the grace of god is also seeking you.
Ramana Maharshi

A picture post natural harbour on the shores of the Indian Ocean, Dar-es-Salaam was endowed with a bounty from Mother Nature, scenic and serene! Early on a quiet Sunday morning it was sheer magic to hear all the church bells ringing as the town's people woke up leisurely.

This was the Dar where I played kho-kho, langdi, amli-pipdi, panchika and other childhood games, barefoot on the footpath near our house. And this city is where my own children played marbles, hockey, cricket and, carom. They swam in the Indian Ocean, enjoyed reading and took part in Boys Scouts and Girl Guides Activities.

Occasionally they tripped and stumbled and grazed their knees. And yes, this was the place where Jhaveriji started going on long walks with his friend Narotambhai Jani exploring old and new constructions in and around the town. It was the same Dar-es-Salaam visited by Motiba and Faiba where my parents spent a lifetime playing their innings with enthusiasm even when they confronted potholes and rough patches on their home front. And this is the home for which Jhaveriji and I still yearn.

Bapuji loved movies and music, and on Sundays he always went to the drive-in cinema. He had a fine collection of old stamps, coins, currency notes, records, and an ancient HMV gramophone player. He was an excellent swimmer, regularly swimming across the ferry creek up to his last days. He travelled by air for the first time at the age of 54, when we attended Mahen, my brother's wedding in Nairobi. And incidentally for me also it was a first time experience! Bapuji had his first stroke at a comparatively young age when he had just completed seventy years. He remained completely bedridden for some time. The young physiotherapist who came home to help him exercise was very keen to learn swimming, and my determined father used to tell her, "You teach me to walk and I promise to teach you how to swim." Self-reliance was his mantra. He did recover the use of his legs, made various plans including a trip to Bombay. He had his second stroke within six months on Monday 6th December 1971 while having lunch and feeding ras-rotli, fresh mango juice and chapatti, to my sister Neru's son Rajeevi.

We rushed him to the Agakhan hospital. Mahen my brother was consulting with the doctors, and I was sitting by his side, my mind blank and heart numb. I could feel Bapuji going and yet I felt helpless. I tried to understand life and the consequences of my loss while I could not even think straight. Before the day was out and we could fully realise what was happening, my father quietly departed at around 4 pm in the afternoon from this world. He was cremated on the same day. Ba was painfully shattered and upset with him for leaving so suddenly. We all tried in our own way to help her to get reconciled with the fact that he was no more with us and regain her composer.

I used to see Ba every evening so when I was visiting our grand children in UK and Germany, I had jokingly asked her to wait for me until I returned and not be in a hurry to leave. True to her word, Ba waited for me. When I returned from the trip, she was in her talking mood and would not stop talking about the days gone by. She died two days after my return back to Dar-es-Salaam. For years her heart had been missing a heart beat and finally gave up ticking altogether on 11 January 1983. But do parents really leave? As I look deep down within me I find their presence ingrained in my being.

After her death, those days gone by were filled with long drives in the evenings with my brother Mahen and Tarabhabhi, stopping on the way for Madafu and Zanzibar mix or a cold coffee regularly until the time when they joined their children in UK. Outgoing and friendly Mahen my brother was an enthusiastic volunteer at the T. B. Seth Library in his young age. He loved all sports and as a youngster, started playing Hututu, kho kho, gilidanda, marbles, at the Hanuman Vyayamshala and cricket, tennis, squash and many other games at the sports club. He was a Bridge Champion and taught many of his aspiring friends the intricacies of the game. In December 2009, at seventy seven, he lost his game plan against Cancer. He had called me only a few weeks earlier from UK and just out of the blue, said that it was time for him to say good bye. At that time I did not know he was battling with cancer, and scolded him for teasing me. He laughed at me and changed the subject. If only I could see him again and tell him, I miss him soo. He was younger than me, we were close and for me his passing away has left a deep sense of loss which refuses to be filled.

Asmani who was with us for almost twenty five years loved to listen to Swahili programs, especially news on the Radio. Every morning he gave me his graphic report with live comments, describing seriously on how he went the previous day and fought in any war that was going on some where or the other. Be it in China, India, Arabi meaning Middle East, or Africa. He was not much interested in goings on in Europe. He also insisted on getting an advance from me, regularly at intervals of about three-four years so that he could bring home a new model of a wife. And invariably he managed to do that by any which way. Even by exchanging his new bicycle in lieu of dowry! My children Atool and Abha grew up under his watchful eye. They had settled abroad after their respective marriages in the 1970s, and whenever they were visiting Dar, Asmani used to ask me to write and tell them to get him Sa-wristwatch, radio, and a bicycle, from 'Ulaya London', his generic name for all foreign places.

And Asmani used to tell our grandchildren that he was their 'Babu-Mdogo-Nanaji.' In fact I was able to travel abroad when all of them were born because of him; he looked after the house and Jhaveriji during my absence. Asmani had to give up working for us reluctantly, when his father died and he had to rush back to his village Manormango to look after his family farm. Otherwise it would have been taken over by village elders.

After him I remember Maria the home maker, who was working for us up to the time when we left Dar. Her daughter Sanaa was planning to become a lawyer like Baba-Jhaveriji; she used to come home to meet him and have a chat with him. It was wonderful to see Maria more determined to see that Sanaa's dreams were fulfilled.

Our neighbour Ruksmaniben and Umedbhai had four sons; Kanu doctor, Vipin Veterinary Surgeon, Jayant Accountant settled down in UK but the eldest Jay Kothari Civil Engineer stayed back with their parents as was the custom then. He married Pratibha from Zanzibar. For me Pratibha was always there with a helping hand whenever needed.

Pratibha' young daughters Puja, Preeti were my internet teachers and Rajesh Chohan was my computer guide. If by chance any pipes at home in Dar, got clogged or the light fittings needed attention, then Abdallah was the man to call. He used to arrive on his bicycle immediately and asked, 'Vipi Bibi?' What is the problem, Grandmaa?' Abdallah would give me full report about all that has been taking place in his life, since his previous visit over a cup of tea. Spend the whole day or two if need be and make sure that the problems were solved with out any Hassles for me. It is wonderful now to sit back and remember all these lovely people and convey my thanks to them from far away.

My basket of happy experiences keeps overflowing; we met Taiba, as a beautiful young bride just married to Arif. She loves reading. Like a daughter she shared her books with us, took me out regularly for morning coffee, visiting bookshops, and shopping. Now they call all the way from Dar-es-Salaam; Arif-Taiba-Rahmatben to enquire 'Ba kem cho? How are you Ba?'And the kids, Safwaan, Safiyah and

Rayaan, excitedly want to show off their Gujarati speaking skills right from across the Indian Ocean! It is amazing.

I well remember fondly my quiet evenings by the sea in Dar-es-Salaam, being greeted as Bibi, Grandmother by every one in our neighbourhood. The excitement of visiting the road side kiosk near our home on the Ocean Road Sea View, boisterously accompanied by Simon's kids for new School bags, pencils and exercise books, or just having a picnic of roast cassava, maize cob, Chips and an ice lolly, or an ice-cream cone on the sea front remain to be my idea of fun trips. Simon our gardener was the father of three children, Ashu, Ramazani and Mosi, all by three different women who followed different religions. So the children celebrated all the auspicious occasions including Christmas, Eid and Diwali.

Ashu's mother Justina had died when he was still a baby. He was very bright but disliked going to school. I used to tell him that if he did not study, how would be become a doctor and give me injections when I was ill? He used to laugh heartily, thrilled at the idea of injecting grimacing Bibi. Slowly he learnt to write the alphabet and hesabu, counting, and began attending school. He was very good in hesabu. The second one; Ramazani's mother had left him as a baby in his father's care when they parted ways. He was the quiet one and wanted to become a pilot. Mosi, the youngest, was so named because he was born on the 1st of May. The children would run to greet me, showing off their school uniforms and new cloths, home work and school reports pointing out the stars, and like all children expected their zawadi—presents on Eid, Xmas and Diwali.

We had a special ritual of measuring their increasing heights against mine, whenever they were wearing their new uniforms they claimed noisily to be catching up with me!

Mosi the youngest liked to follow me on my evening walks in the garden, make me laugh by dancing in the buff and making faces behind my back. By the time he was two he had started copying his older siblings and insisted on having his own pencil and notebook. Never mind if he held the pages upside down!

Abdu is another story. He had lot of hope, courage in abundance, and little else. He was a Standard Seven drop out, and started helping his father on the farm from a young age selling madafu, green coconuts. I was his regular customer. Abdu was very keen to continue his education and learn 'Kiingreza' English. I volunteered to teach him. From the outset he wanted me to talk to him only in English.

In the afternoon he arrived with his last batch of madafu. Sitting on our doorstep we tried to converse in English, copied the words, read picture books and laughed a lot. Steadily Abdu learnt to talk, read and write in simple English, and over time, through his own initiative and effort he became a wholesale vegetable seller in the big market at Kariakoo. I was family for Abdu, his Bibi-grandmaa. He informed me excitedly when he got married, had his first child and when he opened a post-office bank account. He had ambitions of becoming a truck driver, a far more profitable occupation he said, and came to me for advice as to whether he should pay 20,000 shillings as a bribe to a policeman in order to get a driving license. I told him to invest his money in taking driving lessons so that he could get a proper license legally. He went home to his village for some time and upon returning to Kariakoo, heard that we were planning to move to India. He rushed to our house in agitation, saying, "Bibi, how can you think of leaving without informing me and saying goodbye?" We set there on the doorsteps and had a long chat. These special relationships sharing love have left a deep indelible impression on my mind. As a young mother I was too preoccupied setting up our home base and now I was missing Atool and Abha and often felt deep yearning to share their childhood and growing up experiences with them. Abdu, Moshi, Ramazani, James and Sanaa helped to fill up that gap with hope and laughter.

There is a beautiful couplet in, 'The Wonder Years.'-" I remember a place . . . a town . . . a house like a lot of houses . . . a yard like a lot of other yards . . . on a street like a lot of other streets. And the thing is after all these years, I still look back . . . with wonder." Our home, a two bedroom house, was one such simple dwelling, filled with many moods. It was like a symphony of colors in contrast; some happy and playful while some were somber and sad.

When the Parliament was in session our house was a meeting place for upcountry MPs. N. K. Laxman-Babubhai to us, Dr. Krishna, Thankiji, Bhoke Munanka, Joseph Nyerere, Richard Wambura, Sophia Mustafa, Barbroo Johansson were regulars who came home to finish their discussions and arguments over their meals. Yet I never saw them loosing their cool. On the contrary together they laughed at themselves. I enjoyed watching Sophie out argue any of them if she disagreed with their points of view. And it was a pleasure to see Babubhai and his wife Shardaben together. I have yet to see Heaven, but if on this Earth, some couples are made for each other, they were! Being vegetarians and teetotalers ourselves I used to prepare only vegetarian food. Everybody enjoyed it. One day they were all having pan, betel nut, tambuu, after lunch. Bhoke, Josheph and Richard had declined the offer, but watching others enjoying the pan Barbroo was tempted to try it. She put the whole pan in her mouth like they were doing, and found the taste so foreign that she could not stomach it; neither would she spite it out. With her mouth full she protested, that it was too impolite! Ultimately she was coaxed to take it out amid laughter, tears and some coughing. She was such a gentle person! God bless her Soul. [1]

Jhaveriji's work as a lawyer continuously brought people from all walks of life to our house and table. We had wonderful friends in legal circles. He had joined the legal fraternity in Dar-es-Salaam on 5th April 1949, and was initiated into the affairs of the Tanganyika Law Society by the then President, the late K.A. Master. From 1964-75, he was President of the Tanganyika Law Society-TLC. In 1958 Jhaveriji was one of the lawyers involved in Mwalimu's trial for Sedition which was a nationally very significant case. Those were very busy years for him. Apart from his various commitments during his long career as a lawyer and as Member of Parliament, he was also a member of Civil Service Commission, Judicial Service Commission, Africanization Commission, and Legal Corporation for many years. Understandably, during the early period after the Independence, members of these commissions had a very heavy work load and met often. Their meetings always had long Agenda often 40-50 full pages, written in Swahili language. I used to translate these documents into English for my husband so that he could study them prior to the meetings and be fully prepared. This meant my racing with time to keep up with weekly translation deadlines, and the work also demanded that I be very careful, meticulous, and accurate as it affected people's careers and lives. I also needed to be especially conscientious and diligent and remain absolutely invisible at the same time. Nevertheless, I enjoyed the challenge. During those years Jhaveriji throve on work. He found it very satisfying and enjoyed it all the more when he was appointed a Judge of the High Court after he retired.

Besides that we were very much part of the Diplomatic circuits keeping in personal touch with diplomats from different countries including all the Indian High Commissioners starting from APA Pant, the first Indian High Commissioner to East Africa. I immediately after the Independence, Jhaveriji was appointed Honorary Personal Legal Advisor to the British High Commissioner Mr J.C. Strong who was a long standing friend. There after Jhaveriji continued in that capacity to all the succeeding British High Commissioners up to the time when he retired. Over the years, during this period many senior most members of the fraternity became our good friends.

I remember we had the honour of meeting Thurgood Marshall the famous American Supreme Court Justice who ended the racial segregation in public schools in USA. And we were meeting world leaders and figures like Britain's Princess Margaret, Prince Charles, the Duke of Edinburgh, Lord Denning, Dr. S. Radhakrishnan, and Mrs. Indira Gandhi.

During those years I was also very active with UWT activities and had many friends. Thus, we had the privilege of hosting and interacting with dynamic and learned personalities and important national and international leaders of the time. Being more emotional person then practical, my personal relationships with people throughout our public lives meant more to me then any thing else, and each encounter left its mark and helped me to grow.

Looking back through the passage of time, I am thankful that, from the beginning we have been blessed with many lovely friends through out our life. Their presences in our daily life remain to be my cherished memory, a bonus from the days gone by.

As I approach the end of this long long story of my life strangely, now my mind stands at ease. All the chattering demands of my past experiences for attention and resolution have been silenced. Nevertheless it has been a riveting exercise shifting and selecting through myriad of my experiences and write about it. At times the flow of my memory shifted course like the changing moods of a river. Some times it flowed like a gently gurgling brook, at another it came like a waterfall rushing with full force. And in yet another place it became just a meandering river, playing a game of hide and seeks. I am glad that however insignificant and limited it might be, I have tried to capture its mood, and penned it before it patters out completely in the mists of time.

It was my destiny to be born in that tiny little island called Pemba near Zanzibar. With faltering steps I have endeavoured to dance to the tune of my destiny. For me it has been a memorable journey.

Life goes on: The same surging waters embrace both the continents and the waves ceaselessly crash on the shores of Africa as on the shores of India. Followed by men and migration these tides continue to flow intertwined and merge again and again at some point on their seemingly endless journey!

Postscript

*P*resently we are settled in Noida just outside Delhi's eastern borders. Jhaveri and I have some health problems; the doctor comes home to attend to us when needed, and our children and grand children visit us often. Atool married his sweetheart Chandrika Mehta and Abha married Nitan Kapoor, her first love. We are blessed with four lovely grand children. I feel that having grandchildren take the happiness of having children, to a new height. They all address us as Ba and Bapuji, and we call them 'the gang of fabulous four', a name given to them by their Bapuji.

Following her successful assignment in Sudan with the UN, Ratna is now based in Afghanistan where she has been for the past five years also with the UN. And after gaining experience as a practicing solicitor for five years in London Meera is poised to start her course in MSc, Conflict and Development at SOAS, University of London. Rohaan a banker with Credit Suisse, now based in Zurich is looking forward to a brilliant career ahead, while Roohi who trained as a sociologist, is presently doing Graphic Designing course in Delhi. She is an artist who has several successful painting exhibitions to her credit and is already curetting major art exhibitions. I cherish and smile at

*the precious memories of happy times spent together with them
and get anxious when any of them face a problem. And I rejoice
in their achievements. They are my all in all, and more.*

*We have been blessed with a loving family who helped us
in every situation. Their loving and loyal presence ensured and
helped us to keep our feet firmly on the ground all the way, even
now at this age! Many members of our family and friends are no
longer in this inexplicable phenomenon we call 'the world'. As
for me, I am also waiting in the 'transit lounge' . . . Soon this
body-machine of mine however strong, is bound to stall, and
I will be on my way to the unknown destination that awaits
each of us! Whether we are ready or not, the busy Father Time
never waits. The sages point out that life and death, destruction
and creation are two sides of the same coin. It is the leaves that
have dried up in the summer and fallen in the autumn that
provide spring blossoms. There is always hope, glimmering in
the horizon, and a special glow to the sun rise for one and all
who care and dare to look!.*

*Indeed time has flown, even though it feels just like yesterday
that I was reading stories and sharing cookies with Atool and
Abha! The year now is 2013; there is a sea change in our lives.
Our children and grand children carry their worlds, through
their smart phones in their pockets! Internet has opened up the
whole wide world. A friend has rightly commented that internet
is equivalent of a magical brass lamp with an inbuilt know it
all genie at our command but we must learn to use it safely.
For me it is a boon. Now with the touch of my finger tips, I can
say Jambo, hello, to my family and friends far and apart, and
explore any subject to suit my fancy. But wonder of wonders,
without worrying about my shaky handwriting, be able to write
my memoirs which originated just as a floating wisp in the air
to fill up my time. As time passed, though encumbered with lack
of enough knowledge and insight, I dared to enhance the scope*

of my book and even ventured to step out of its boundary, and occasionally walked through the historical pages. But basically, all these writings remain to be my memoirs and I am glad that I have finished writing this small book.

Now I go for walks with my neighbour friend Rashidan. She says I could call her Rashida. Rashida grew up on a farm helping her parents to till the land and look after the dairy-cattle. She continued with her farming activities when she got married to her farmer husband. We enjoy going for walks in the evenings and have a good laugh comparing notes! She thinks I look poorly with my crop of grey hair, and for quite some time now has been trying to convince me to dye it red with mehndi. Once I asked her how old she was. She laughed and replied, "I have seen it all. I am older then you. I was already eleven years old and married during the harsh British Raj and the World War II. When my 'buddha' old man started dyeing his beard, he colored my hair as well . . . !" She added with a merry twinkle in her eyes.

As I continue looking back in the evening of my life with wonder, I understand perfectly well that not a single snowflake falls accidently in the wrong place: there is always a preordained trajectory and design which follow our steps!

No doubt, all my experiences, relationships, actions and reactions have molded my being. And today, I am what I am, yet for me the enigma 'Who am I?' remains . . . In her book Women Awakened, *Swati Chopra puts the question beautifully, I quote her to better express myself;*

A sari woven
From
The prickly yarn of
Roles and responsibilities
Mother, mother-in-law

Wife, sister, daughter
Aunt, grandmother
Who am I?
When not
Shrouded
In this sari?
A wind unbound
A wave of sound
A rhythm freed
A voice at ease
A keening call
Or nothing at all . . . !
When knots of I
Shrivel and dissolve
Who remains . . . ?
What dies . . . ?

And as I write these memoirs, I continue to wonder;

Who am I?
African,
Indian,
Gujarati
Or
Amalgam of
Many labels,
A cacophony
Of past and present,
Aspirations
Experiences,
Frailties,
Failures!
Tears and joy

Great moments,
And
Lessons learnt!
A tiny speck
Blessed to be
Just flowing, flowing
With the wind
Rejoicing
And
Dancing
In the rain!

References and Notes

Part 1, Chapter 1; Family Diary,

[Note-1] Pemba.

In Arabic, this beautiful Island Pemba where I was born is known as Al Zazeera-Al Khadra ('Green Island'). Its famous clove trees grow 10-15 metres high and can produce crops for over 50 years. According to official estimates Pemba has 3 million clove trees (karafu in Swahili / lavang in Gujarati), apart from other spices like cardamom (iliki / ilaichi), cinnamon (mdalasini / taj), nutmeg (kungu-manga / jaifal). It also produces rice, coconut, banana, cassava and maharagwe (red beans), and other cash crops like spices and copra for export,

The original inhabitants of these Islands are known as Waswahilis. Later on a large number of Omani Arab community settled down in Pemba and over centuries they intermarried and assimilated well with the Waswahilis. They are all identified as Wapemba and there is no distinction between different race-groups. However cultural differences remain within this community. The Arabs are fair skinned, their women lead a sheltered life, and men prefer to be self employed. Most of them are Muslims. They continue to be conservative in their outlook and tend to maintain their separate identity as Afro Shirazi even within the Isles.

The Waswahili men and women on the other hand do not mind working on their farms and doing other manual jobs. Few have embraced Christianity and by and large many of them are out going. Unfortunately the accumulation of antagonism and mistrust prevailing over the years had resulted in a sharp divide between the two main groups not only in Pemba but in Zanzibar as well. Thus up to now past elections have seen bloody political violence on the Islands. Presently the Tanzanian government is trying to alter this through putting into place educational facilities and development programs for the people in Pemba and Zanzibar Isles.

Chapter 2; Home,

[1] At the time of Independence, the Indian Primary school was renamed Matendeni Primary School, Indian Secondary School became Jangwani Girl's School where Mrs. Rahma Bomani took over successfully as its first Tanzanian School Mistress. And the Government Indian Boys School was renamed Azania Boys Secondary School. Amin Sir was one of the popular and very able teachers in Azania, who had groomed at least two generations of students including Atool and me. Later on he took over as Head Master of the school when Mr. Jones left.

Chapter 4, A Tale of Three Villages; Zanzibar,

[1] History of Zanzibar—Wikipedia

Chapter 6; Migrations,

[1] East African—15-21 dated 10-3-8, Nairobi-Kenya.

Chapter 7; World War II,

[1] [Tanganyika Rifles Mutiny January 1964, published by Dar-es-Salaam University Press page 15-16]

[2] World War Two Map,

[3] [Tanganyika Rifles Mutiny, January 1964 page 14-15]

[4] [Tanganyika Rifles Mutiny, January 1964 page 10]

Chapter 8; Our Dhow Safari,

[1] The fascinating exhibition about the sailors and sailing from Gujarat, compiled by the well known British reporter Sarah Bancroft with great care simultaneously records century's old rare maps, documents, articles, pictures paintings and hand written log books, recording those journeys by Indian pioneers to distant lands." Chitralekha dated 1st November 2010]

Chapter 10; Brick by Brick and Step by Step,

[1] Jangwani Girls School passed through several phases; it was first established as Lokmanya Tilak School and renamed Government Indian Secondary School, and once again as Government Central School where I also had my

secondary school education. Finally it became Jangwani Girl's School at the time of Independence; Mrs. Rahma Bomani took charge as its first Tanzanian Head Mistress. Abha our daughter still remembers her fondly.

When Atool joined Azania Secondary School for boys, Mr. Jones was the Head Master. After he retired, Amin Sir took over. Both these Headmasters were much loved by their students.

Chapter 12; Travel back in Time, Divisions:

[1] [Hatch, From Africa, 54, 44—page 27—as quoted by Susan Geiger in—TANU Women Gender and Culture in the Making of Tanganyikans Nationalism 1955-1965]

[2] [As reported by Zanzibar Samachar, from "Assorted History of Paro Family by Kassamali R. Paro}

[3] [Ibid.227, Provincial Commissioner to Chief Secretary, Dar-es-Salaam, November 19, 1931-Ned Bertz Dissertation, page 13 no.85]

[4] [TNA Secretariat File No.20496, Vol. 1, Acting Director of Education, December 30 1931, Pro. Ned Bertz Dissertation—page no 13-86]]

[5] [P. Saul, "Agricultural Education in Tanganyika: The Policy, Programs and Practices, 1925-1955," in S. Mbilinyi, ed., Agricultural Research for Development [Nairobi: East African Bureau 1973], cited in M. L. Mbilinyi, ""Teacher Training," 83. Ned Bertz Dissertation page 87, 66-103]

[6] [TNA, "Advisory Committee on Indian Education, Minutes of Meetings," Secretariat File No.12857, Vol.1 1928-1933. Ned Bertz Dissertation, page 64]

[7] Professor Ned Bertz Dissertation page 38-67]

[8] [TNA, "Advisory Committee on Indian Education, Minutes of Meetings," Secretariat File No. 12857, Vol. 1 1928-1933. Ned Bertz Dissertation, page 64]

[9] [W. Morris—Hale; British Administration from 1920-1954, PhD diss. University of Geneva, 1969, quoted in Mbilinyi, 79-80. Ned Bertz Dissertation, page no 66-no 45]

[10] [TNA, "Higher Education for Africans," Secretariat File No. 13658, Vol.1, 1942-7 Ned Bertz Dissertation page 66-68]

[11] [Cranford Pratt, 'the Critical Phase in Tanzania 1945-1968:' Nyerere and the Emergence of Socialist Strategy Cambridge University Press, 1976} Ned Bertz Dissertation page 70-90].

Part II

Chapter 13; Pre-Independence,

[1] Wikipedia, the free encyclopaedia; en.wikipedia.oro/ Wiki/Mau Mau uprising.

[2] [TANU Party's Annals

[3] Mr. H.R. Dharani's comments in Sunday News 18th January-1959-Dar-s-Salaam.

[4] Mr. K.L. Jhaveri's personal collection of Asian Association files: Most of the members who attended those meetings are no more with us. In fact their collective as well as individual contributions towards the Independence struggle in Tanganyika is forgotten and consigned to the lack of written history

Nevertheless, here is a list as compiled from these files; D. K. Patel, A. A. Adamji, Diwan Singh, M. A. Khimji, Tara Singh, Habibbhai Jamal all were respected as the wise old men of the group and everybody took their advice seriously. Others members of the core group who attended these meetings as and when required were Nurudin Sadikot—a close friend of my husband, M. Gopalan, Mahmud Ratansi, Avatar Singh S. Sonekhan, N.S. Patel, Edel Udwadia, H.R. Dharani, Shyam Sarda, Manubhai Dewani, Chandu Shah, D.M. Anjaria, and others. And of course K. L. Jhaveri was there.

The Annual General Meeting of Asian Association held at Bohora School Hall on Saturday 23-January-1954 at 5.15 p.m. under the Chairmanship of Mr. D. K. Patel elected Mr. M.A. Khimji as the new President. Members present at the meeting were: H.G. Hemani, K. L. Jhaveri, M.N. Ratansi, D. M. Anjaria, J. D. Shah, M. Gopalan, Habib Jamal, E. S. Udwadia, R. U. Patel, J. M. Fernandez, A. A. Adamji, S. Sohnekhan, C. D. Shah, K. G. Khanna, R.S. Patel, Ramji Velji, M.O. Abbasi, D. N. Shah, Ramji Kara, Mr. P. N. Kotak R. R. Jaffer, A. M. S. Versi, H.P. Shanghvi, H.M. Arab, C.H. Khanderia, M.R. Adhiya, Nizzamuddin,

Haridas Velji, B.V. Patel, Liladhar Vishram, M. Janmohmad, T.B. Sheth, Karsandas Muldas, N. D. Jhaveri, Juma Haji, M. C. Bhudhdeo, H.P. Shanghvi, Haridas Savji, M.M. Manji, Lavji Kara, Gulamali Mawji, J.K. Chande, Mr. Suleman, M. Mathuradas, B.V. Patel, K. Jasraj, M. Janmohamad, Karmali M, S.C Patel, Fakru Bharmal, N.S. Patel, and Alibhai Bhatia. For obvious reasons this list cannot be a full list of all the members of the Association.

The Indian Association owned three properties in Dar-es-Salaam which were transferred to Asian Association. Subsequently when TANU opened its doors to other races Asian Association was wound up. They formed the Dar-es-Salaam Secondary School Society (DSSES) and decided to handover the three properties inherited by them to the DSSES and established Shaban Robert Secondary School on 26th January 1963.

Its original building was built by G. A. K. Patel & Co LTD, and Jivrajbhai Patel was named the secretary to the Society. Mr. Gopalan spent day and night selflessly to get the school functioning as a Secondary school.

Apart from this report, Robert G. Gregory in his book South Asians in E.A; An Economies & Social history 1890-1980, chapters 7-8-9 Law Medicine and Teaching, has also recorded that one of the founding members of the Asian Association N.S. Patel was at one time its secretary and Vice-President. With K.L. Jhaveri he helped start the multi-racial, 'Shaban Robert School.'

[6] K. L. Jhaveri, Marching with Nyerere page 30 and pp4, 1999, B. R. Publishing Corporation New Delhi

[7] Kesi ya Julius Nyerere 1958, page 2 introduction, 1990 by Tanzania Publishing House, Dar-es-Salaam

[8] 'Marching with Nyerere', pp 54-55-56 1999. BRPC India Ltd, K. L. Jhaveri]

Chapter 14: Travails and Triumph,

Notes—1; A Bhatia born in Dar-es-Salaam in 1912 where his father was a Customs Official in the German Government, H.R. Dharani was late in studying law as he had volunteered for service in World War II. He started his practice in Dar at the age forty four in 1956 after the War was over. Catering to clients of all races, he developed an extensive legal practice. He wrote for the press and acquired agricultural property and became the largest milk producer in Dar.

[1], Marching with Nyerere, p 90 K.L. Jhaveri B. R. Publishing Corporations, New Delhi-110035]

[2] Cited in Sophia Mustafa, 'The Tanganyika Way, A Personal Story of Tanganyika's Growth to Independence' [London: Oxford University Press, 1962

[Note-2; At that time it was considered unpatriotic to have these divided loyalties, but currently in Tanzania, constitutional changes are being considered that would permit dual citizenship for Tanzanians supposedly to encourage entrepreneurs and investors.

[3] K. L. Jhaveri Personal Files

Chapter 15; Uhuru-Independence

[1] I have tried to paint a word—picture of this period from our personal records and diary and my own impressions as they come alive.

Chapter 16; Where are the Women?

[1] Hatch, New from Africa-London1956, as quoted by Susan Geiger in 'TANU Women-printed in USA page 55-58-57

[2] Translation by Madaraka Nyerere TRANSLATION: Congratulations my child Congratulations to you, and to me also. Congratulations, congratulations my child . . . .

Chapter 18; Zanzibar Revolution,

[1] Two brave young Italian reporters Jacopetti and Prosperi did manage to make full 1964 documentary," Adios Africa"

Note; this evidence is available in CD form on line.]

[2] Gaby Magaya, Daily News dated 12th January 2008]

Chapter 19; The Tanganyika Rifles Mutiny,

[1] Tanganyika Rifles Mutiny January 1964, page 125-135. Published by Dar-es-Salaam University Press 1993.

[1] Rashidi Kawawa interview, 29 Jan. 1988Tanganyika Rifles Mutiny page 90 Dar es Salaam University Press]].

[2] [Tanganyika Rifles Mutiny January 1964, published by Dar-es-Salaam University Press. page 94-95,

[3] [Tanganyika Rifles Mutiny January 1964 page 89, published by Dar-es-Salaam University Press.]

Part III

Chapter 20; The Birth pangs of a New Nation,

[1] 'Nyerere of Tanzania' by William Edget Smith-page 152-published by Zimbabwe Publishing House.

Chapter 21; Nationalization,

Note; Mark Bomani who was former Deputy Director, U.N. Institute for Namibia and former A.G, and MP of Tanzania and former Member of TANU National Executive Committee 1965-75.

O.E.C. Chirwa; Advocate, Queen's Counsel, Vice President of Tanzania Law Society; former Minister for Justice Malawi(1961 to 1964) Asst. Commissioner for Lands Tanzania,

Gamaliel M. Fimbo: Law Lecturer University of Dar-es-Salaam.

Philip Telford Georges—Barbados Professor of Law, University of West Indies; former Chief Justice Tanzania and former High Court Judge, Trinidad and Tobago.

K.L. Jhaveri;Advocate, Member Judicial Service Commission; Director, Tanzania Legal Corporation; former elected Member Tanzania Legislative Council 1959-60 and

Parliament 1960-65; President Tanzania Law Society 1964, 1967-75.

Horace Kolimba, Principal Secretary, Ministry of Manpower Development.

M.H.A. Kwikima, Advocate Administer General; Former Resident Magistrate and Acting Judge.

Damian Z. Lubuwa: Deputy AG Tanzania, Former Chief Corporation Council of Tanzania Legal Corporation.

Mrs. Thekla G. Mchauru Member of Permanent Commission of Enquiry; formerly teacher 1938-40 Staff Nurse, Community Development (1954-1968) Sectary General of Umoja Wa Wanawake wa Tanganyika U.W.T. Women's Organization 1968-76.

Lamek Mfalila High Court Judge, former Resident Magistrate 1965-69; Secretary and Legal Council to Tanzania-Zambia Railway Authority, Registrar of High Court of Tanzania (1970-72.

T.L. Mkude. Corporation Council Tanzania Legal Corporation, former Law Lecturer Dar-es-Salaam.

Pius Musekwa: First Vice-Chancellor of the University of Dar-es-Salaam University; Chairman, Vice-Chairman or member of various governmental boards and committees, former Executive Secretary of TANU.

John B. Mwenda, Member of Permanent Commission of Enquiry, Assistant Labour Commissioner, Director of

Revenue and later Financial Operations Controller at the Treasury; and

J. S. Warioba Attorney—General of Tanzania.

The list is derived from, the introduction by Mr. Niall McDermott—Secretary General, International Commission of Jurists.

[1] Human Rights In A One Party State—International Commission of Jurists, First Published in Great Britain and associated Territories in 1978 by Search Press Limited, 2-10 Jerdan Place, London SW6 5PT in conjunction with the International Commission of Jurists, Geneva, Switzerland.

Chapter 25; Varanasi,

Benares, 'The Sacred City, Sketches of Hindu Life and Religion' Chapter 25; Varanasi,

Benares, 'The Sacred City, Sketches of Hindu Life and Religion' by E.B. Havell, A.R.C.A. Pages 45-46

Published by Book Faith India, 414-416 Express Tower,

Azadpur, Commercial Complex, Distributed by Pilgrims Book House: First printed by Thacker Spink &Co. in 1905.

Notes;

E.B. Havell (1905), Banaras: The Sacred City (New Delhi: Book Faith India), In his preface the author writes, "These sketches are not offered as a contribution to oriental scholarship or to religious controversy, but as an attempt to give an intelligible outline of Hindu ideas and religious practices, and especially as a presentation of the imaginative and artistic side of Indian religion . . ." The book is lucidly presented, describing history of Banaras or Kashi of the ancients through the ages. Originally published in 1905, the 124 pages book contains many illustrations, descriptions of all the bathing Ghats, palaces monuments and even tries to explain the Indian philosophy.

Chapter 27; Mauritius,

[1] Introduction by Leela Gujadhur Sarup, "Colonial Emigration 19th-20th Century, Indentured Labour-Slavery to Salvation; part 1 of 3, Colonial Emigration Acts 1837-1932.

Chapter 28; In the evening of my life,

[1] Barbroo Johansson had arrived in Tanganyika in 1946 as a Swedish missionary. She founded the very first girl's middle school in Bukoba region, and later joined Tabora Girl's school as Head Mistress. She joined the Independence struggle and was elected Parliamentarian from Bukoba. She also played a leading role in Adult Education literacy campaign. Barbroo retired from service in 1985 and moved back to Sweden for health reasons, where she died in 1999. Completely unassuming, she was a very kind and gentle person.